Teaching School Jazz

# Teaching School Jazz

*Perspectives, Principles, and Strategies*

EDITED BY

## Chad West

AND

## Mike Titlebaum

OXFORD
UNIVERSITY PRESS

Oxford University Press is a department of the University of Oxford. It furthers the University's objective of excellence in research, scholarship, and education by publishing worldwide. Oxford is a registered trade mark of Oxford University Press in the UK and certain other countries.

Published in the United States of America by Oxford University Press
198 Madison Avenue, New York, NY 10016, United States of America.

Library of Congress Cataloging-in-Publication Data
Names: West, Chad. | Titlebaum, Michael, 1968-
Title: Teaching school jazz : perspectives, principles, and strategies /
edited by Chad West and Mike Titlebaum.
Description: New York, NY : Oxford University Press, [2019] |
Includes bibliographical references and index.
Identifiers: LCCN 2018021598 | ISBN 9780190462574 (cloth) |
ISBN 9780190462581 (pbk.) | ISBN 9780190462611 (companion website)
Subjects: LCSH: Jazz—Instruction and study.
Classification: LCC MT733.7 .T43 2019 | DDC 781.65071—dc23
LC record available at https://lccn.loc.gov/2018021598

Hardback printed by Bridgeport National Bindery, Inc., United States of America

# Contents

# Preface

"It just goes like this, 'doo ba doo bop'. You dig?" Historically, this was the way jazz was learned, informally, and for many early aspiring jazz musicians—*they dug*. Many still learn this way today, and in fact this may still be the best way of learning jazz. Think about it: you are a professional jazz musician who has a self-motivated, highly curious protégé who listens to you, copies you, transcribes your solos, and hangs on your every piece of advice. You don't have to be a great jazz *teacher* for this student to learn jazz. However, those of us who are not professional jazz musicians and/or who teach music in schools *do* need to be great jazz teachers for students to learn jazz.

First, even if we are professional-level jazz musicians, we cannot rely on the time-tested, master-apprentice–based pedagogy that works beautifully for the highly self-motivated few but virtually not at all for the rest of the students who could potentially experience this great American art form. Second, our job as school music teachers is not to prepare professional musicians (although we are always thrilled and sometimes a bit scared when this happens), but rather to bring music to as many students as possible. Jazz is but one more tool for reaching as many students, with all their diverse musical interests, as we can.

So, how do we acquire the skills to effectively teach jazz? More often than not, our college teacher education programs have prepared us to teach concert band, orchestra, and chorus. We know from previous research what school jazz educators spend their time teaching, but we do not know how they teach those things or why. We also know instructional strategies that are correlated with high student achievement in jazz, but we do not know whether school jazz teachers are utilizing them or what they look like when they do. What do those who perceive themselves as effective school jazz educators do, how do they do it, and why? My doctoral dissertation research, completed in 2011, sought to answer those questions.

Since data from my dissertation suggested that taking a college jazz pedagogy course significantly correlates with one's perceived ability to teach school jazz, in 2012 I decided to write a jazz pedagogy book to be used as a primary text for a collegiate-level jazz pedagogy course, a supplementary text for a general instrumental methods/pedagogy course, an introduction for novice jazz teachers, and a resource for veteran school jazz teachers looking to deepen and expand their practice.

In addition to having previously been a commercial jazz trumpet player and school jazz educator, I was also now an experienced writer and college music teacher educator, thus possessing all the ingredients required to write, well, a mediocre chapter or two. Enter my friend and colleague Mike Titlebaum, director of jazz studies at Ithaca College. Mike had spent a decade teaching jazz at the college level after many years as a successful jazz saxophone player in New York City. Surely, we thought, together we would be able to write a comprehensive and compelling text, but we soon realized we were going to need a team of specialists to fill the many holes of which we were becoming increasingly aware. So we first determined the topics that should comprise a comprehensive text for teaching school jazz and then went about finding those specialists. The many contributors to this book make up our team of experts who helped us turn what was a fuzzy, incomplete picture into a comprehensive, high-resolution digital image. For those who have never played or taught jazz, it is our hope that this book provides you with the resources to begin developing these skills; for those who are seasoned school jazz teaching veterans, we hope this book will not only affirm what you already know and do, but will also provide you with fresh perspectives, principles, and strategies for teaching school jazz not just to the self-motivated, highly curious protégé, but more important, to the many school music students whom we are fortunate to teach every day. You dig?

# Acknowledgments

We wish to acknowledge the many colleagues who assisted in this project. Each chapter in the book was reviewed by either a contributing author of this book or an outside reviewer. These reviewers included the following individuals:

Christopher Buckholz, associate professor of trombone, University of New Mexico

Frank Gabriel Campos, professor, performance studies, Ithaca College

Michael Caporizzo, assistant professor, performance studies, Ithaca College

Matthew Clauhs, assistant professor of music education, Ithaca College

Bruce Dalby, emeritus professor of music, University of New Mexico

Chase Ellison, doctoral candidate, Eastman School of Music

Daniel Fabricius, lecturer, music education, Ithaca College

Andrew Goodrich, assistant professor of music, music education, Boston University

Christopher M. Marra, assistant professor and director of instrumental activities, Seton Hill University

Jessica Vaughan-Marra, assistant professor and coordinator of music education, Seton Hill University

Josh McDonald, teaching assistant, music education, Boston University

C. Michael Palmer, assistant professor of music education, Ball State University

Gary Prince, jazz program chair, Levine Music

Russell A. Schmidt, Valley Jazz Cooperative, director

Michael Treat, band director, DeWitt Middle School, Ithaca, NY

Nick Weiser, assistant professor, head of jazz studies, State University of New York at Fredonia

Thank you to Matt Gorney, Ithaca College digital media coordinator, for the recording and production of all Ithaca College videos found on the companion website. Finally, a big acknowledgment to Norm Hirschy at Oxford University Press for his invaluable guidance and patience from submission to publication.

# Contributors

**Christopher Buckholz**, associate professor of Trombone, University of New Mexico

**Frank Gabriel Campos**, professor, performance studies, Ithaca College

**Matthew Clauhs**, assistant professor of music education, Ithaca College

**Bruce Dalby**, emeritus professor of music, University of New Mexico

**Gregory Evans**, lecturer, Ithaca College; visiting lecturer, Cornell University

**Daniel Fabricius**, lecturer, music education, Ithaca College

**Catherine Gale**, freelance vocalist and instructor of music, Opus Ithaca

**Andrew Goodrich**, assistant professor of music, music education, Boston University

**Michael Grace**, music teacher, Ann Arbor Public Schools (ret.)

**C. Michael Palmer**, assistant professor of music education, Ball State University

**Russell A. Schmidt**, Valley Jazz Cooperative, director

**Bob Sneider**, associate professor of jazz and contemporary media, Eastman School of Music

**Mike Titlebaum**, associate professor and director of jazz studies, Ithaca College

**Michael Treat**, band director, DeWitt Middle School, Ithaca, NY

**Nicholas Walker**, professor, performance studies, Ithaca College

**Nick Weiser**, assistant professor, head of jazz studies, State University of New York at Fredonia

**Chad West**, associate professor and chair, music education, Ithaca College

# About the Companion Website

Since jazz is an aural art form, the text would be woefully incomplete if it did not provide numerous video, audio, and visual examples demonstrating the principles, perspectives, and strategies presented in the narrative. Therefore, Oxford has created a password-protected website to accompany *Teaching School Jazz: Perspectives, Principles, and Strategies*. Readers are encouraged to consult this resource in conjunction with each chapter of the book. Examples available online are indicated in the text with Oxford's symbol ⊚.

# Introduction

My research found that, in addition to taking a college jazz pedagogy course, the preparatory experiences most strongly correlated with one's perceived ability to teach jazz were listening to jazz and playing as a professional jazz musician. However, non-jazzers should not be discouraged, as my findings also suggest that being a competent school jazz educator is more dependent on one's overall musicianship than on one's ability to play jazz. Further, while not every reader of this book will play jazz, everyone can be a jazz *listener*; therefore, numerous musical demonstrations are provided at the companion website, and albums, artists, and musicians are recommended for further listening.

The first two chapters of this book are especially aimed toward the novice jazz educator. The first chapter, "Broad Landscape of School Jazz Education," explores what school jazz education *looks* like, who is teaching it, their experiences, what they think about jazz, and why they teach it. The second chapter, "Jazz for Non-Jazzers," provides a basic overview of (a) styles such as swing, Latin, bop, and blues; (b) rhythmic solfège; (c) articulation; (d) ornamentation; (e) improvisation; (f) intricacies of the rhythm section; and (g) rehearsal and stage setup of the beginning jazz band. The remaining chapters of the book presume some basic and foundational knowledge about jazz as points of departure, so chapter 2 serves as that starting point.

## Thoughts about Teaching School Jazz

My research suggested that the most valuable reasons for having a school jazz ensemble were that jazz is fun, is motivational, keeps students interested in music, teaches students a new skill set, is closer to the kind of "outside-of-school" music that students might engage with, and provides students with experience playing one to a part. Given these values, the rapidly changing landscape of public school education, and the ever-changing student learner, Russell Schmidt's chapter "Pedagogical Language of Jazz" outlines practical, effective teaching techniques applied to jazz ensemble instruction, such as efficient rehearsal technique, the value of role modeling, maintaining student engagement, and accommodating individuals with vastly different skill levels in the same ensemble.

# Actions of Teaching School Jazz

Years of cognitive research tell us that humans construct meaning through interacting with more knowledgeable peers and mentors. While my research confirmed previous findings that school jazz educators value peer mentoring, the data showed very little evidence that school jazz teachers use peer mentoring, cooperative learning strategies, or student-centered instruction in their ensembles. Andrew Goodrich's chapter "Social Language of Jazz" explores the various facets of social interactions in jazz via mentoring. His chapter draws connections between historical jazz mentoring practices and how directors can incorporate them into the school jazz ensemble, including (a) adult mentoring, in which teachers receive mentoring from jazz musicians and jazz educators; (b) how teachers can provide mentoring to students; and, (c) peer mentoring, in which teachers guide and instruct their students how to mentor each other in the areas of teaching, learning, leadership, and social connections.

# Teaching the Rhythm Section

My research found that in addition to mentoring, one of the most important elements for successfully teaching school jazz is the ability to competently teach the rhythm section. Considering that many teachers' primary instruments are something other than a rhythm section instrument, and that most band directors do not teach piano, bass, drum set, or guitar in their concert bands, the idea of teaching the rhythm section can be frightening. The West, Palmer, Grace, and Fabricius chapter, "Beginning Rhythm Section," explores ways to take a concert band snare drummer, classically trained pianist, orchestral bass player, and self-taught guitar player and turn them into a functioning jazz rhythm section. Daniel Fabricius's chapter "High School Rhythm Section" provides a basic overview of teaching various styles (such as swing, shuffle, Latin, rock, and funk) as well as specifics about each of the rhythm section instruments (piano, guitar, bass, drums, percussion, and vibes) in relation to those styles as students develop into jazz musicians who can competently play from charts with minimal notation.

*Delving deeper.* For readers looking to delve deeper into the teaching of specific rhythm section instruments, Bob Sneider's chapter "Jazz Guitar" explores the intricacies of teaching jazz guitar, with emphasis on comping, Freddie Green and the rhythm guitar school, improvisation, the key center approach/blues scales, the language-based approach/transcription/loop exercises, the theoretical-based approach, bebop scales, and modal approaches. Russ Schmidt's chapter "Jazz Piano" examines the role of the instrument in jazz ensembles, providing various harmonic exercises and an overview of basic, flexible voicings that are useful in many different jazz styles. Nicholas Walker's chapter "Jazz Bass" provides practical advice on left- and right-hand technique, bodily comportment, equipment regulation and setup, progressive musical exercises geared toward understanding root movement, and connecting chords with walking iconic bass lines. Finally, Greg Evans's chapter "Jazz Drums" provides information on the ergonomics of setup, the functions of the sound sources, the "bottom-up" approach to keeping time, turning a nondrummer into a *functioning* member of the rhythm section, a comprehensive approach to transitioning from timekeeping to improvising, and South American and West African rhythms and various other grooves.

## Teaching Woodwinds, Brass, and Vocalists

While many readers will be familiar with teaching brass players, woodwind players, and vocalists, a seasoned lineup of authors in this book provides practical perspectives, principles, and strategies for teaching these students in jazz ensemble. Bruce Dalby's chapter "Beginning Woodwinds and Brass" covers concepts and skills such as teaching style and articulation, jazz rhythmic and harmonic characteristics, and fundamental jazz riffs. Andrew Goodrich's chapter "High School Woodwinds and Brass" provides the jazz ensemble director with musical exercises and teaching strategies to teach, improve, and maintain intonation, groove, balance, blend, articulations, and interaction with the rhythm section.

*Delving deeper.* For readers looking to delve deeper into the teaching of specific woodwind instruments, brass instruments, and vocalists, Mike Titlebaum's chapter "Jazz Saxophone" introduces techniques and articulations specific to jazz saxophone style, such as subtone, tongue stopping, and half-tonguing. Frank Campos's chapter "Jazz Trumpet" provides an overview of the physical and musical challenges that jazz trumpeters face and offers solutions to the most common problems encountered with young trumpet players, providing specific exercises to develop and improve range, endurance, pitch, time feel, jazz trumpet sound, jazz articulation and phrasing, lead playing, and section playing. Chris Buckholz's chapter "Jazz Trombone" discusses stylistic sound quality, technical solidity, accurate, flexible intonation, big band section playing, equipment, and practice strategies unique to the aspiring jazz trombonist. Finally, Catherine Gale's chapter "Jazz Vocal" aims to dispel the myth that jazz singing is completely different from classical singing while pointing out the subtle differences between them. She covers (a) teaching the differences in timbre and vibrato that create the unique jazz vocal sound; (b) centering jazz vocal intonation; (c) avoiding some of the most common pitfalls of jazz diction; and (d) a progressive discussion of types of vocal improvisation, from strategic variation in rhythms and melodies to scat singing.

## Teaching Improvisation

My study also found that along with competently teaching the rhythm section, one of the most important elements for successfully teaching school jazz is the ability to competently teach improvisation. Those who perceived themselves to be highly capable school jazz educators focused on scales, modeling, listening to and watching recordings of seasoned improvisors, using group improvisation, and aural techniques. Specifically, two themes emerged: confidence and competence. Therefore, chapters in this book address the topic on both fronts: helping students want to improvise and helping students improvise well. Michael Treat's chapter "Beginning Improvisation," begins with a mindset for introducing young students to improvisation and suggests activities for doing so, including communication;

phrasing; tension and release; and the ability to simultaneously create, perform, and respond to music.

*Delving deeper.* Michael Grace's chapter "High School Improvisation" presents detailed exercises for helping students express the tonality of the piece, which includes the basic key and associated tonicizations. The chapter outlines a sequential process whereby jazz teachers can provide students with the tools to successfully negotiate the blues progression as well as $II^7$-$V^7$-I changes and their alterations with major, minor, dominant, and bebop scales, triads, and permutations with increasing levels of sophistication. Finally, Mike Titlebaum's chapter "Internal Language of Jazz" presents exercises for developing beginning through advanced students' rhythmic and tonal audiation skills in jazz. The chapter provides a progression of rhythmic groove exercises that jazz teachers can use to improve the rhythmic feel of ensembles of any age. Methods are presented for getting students' heads out from behind their music stands and on their way to becoming more active listeners as well as more tonally and rhythmically independent performers.

# Jazz Literature

Findings from my research suggest that choosing, teaching, and rewriting jazz literature are topics that are as important as they are often misunderstood. Dan Fabricius's chapter "Choosing Jazz Literature" discusses the selection of appropriate literature for jazz ensemble study and performance, including the various aspects of matching the literature to the group, considering the type of performance, literature difficulty, instrumentation, and the presentation of various styles of jazz through the literature. Nick Weiser's chapter "Teaching Jazz Standards" provides strategies for learning and internalizing the core jazz repertoire. The chapter gives historical context to the development and evolution of the jazz standard canon, looking to the songbook folios of the great American tunesmiths and to original and seminal recordings as sources for the study of this music. Emphasis is given to the practical issues of selecting age- and skill-level-appropriate tunes; memorizing melodies, chord progressions, and lyrics in multiple keys; and devising improvisational exercises specific to individual compositions. Finally, Matthew Clauhs's chapter "Arranging for School Jazz Ensembles" demystifies the process of writing for a school jazz ensemble so that arranging becomes a part of the culture in a school music program. His chapter explores (a) considerations before arranging, (b) writing for the rhythm section, (c) writing for winds, and (d) basic harmonization techniques.

# Final Thoughts and Future Questions

Interestingly, the majority of survey respondents in my research indicated that their school jazz ensembles are co-curricular; meet outside of the normal school day; and rehearse, on average, eight times per month. Why do we devote relatively little time to jazz in relation to other musical offerings? My guess is that many would say it is because there is only so much time in the school day, and music teachers have to make decisions about how to spend that time. Understood. My question then becomes: Why do music teachers choose to dedicate more time to teaching concert band than jazz band? Certainly some music teachers see a music hierarchy in which concert band is elevated above jazz. The editors of this book reject the notion of musical hierarchies altogether, in particular those that would espouse value-laden qualifications between "high-brow" and "low-brow" music, between opera halls and Broadway stages, between orchestras and garage bands, and between school music and music in society. Imagine what a powerful experience school music could be if we facilitated experiences in which students were free to explore their musical interests rather than to learn ours. For students who want to explore jazz, we hope this book contributes to that end and does so in a way that honors the countless dedicated teachers who teach music every day in our schools.

# PART I

# School Jazz Education

# Broad Landscape of School Jazz Education

## Chad West

When considering the broad landscape of school jazz education, I interviewed two highly respected school jazz educators. From those interviews, I developed questionnaire items that I used to survey a large-scale, national sampling of school jazz educators. In particular, I wanted to know the thoughts and actions of those who perceived themselves to be highly capable of teaching school jazz. The two interview participants from my study on jazz education, Bruce and Emily, are both highly respected, expert music teachers who have taught middle school jazz ensemble from very different perspectives and with very different approaches. Bruce considers himself an experienced music teacher who happens to also teach jazz, rather than a professional jazz musician. Emily, on the other hand, considers herself both an experienced music teacher and a professional jazz musician. Both participants have served as officers in the Michigan School Band and Orchestra Association (MSBOA), have been selected by MSBOA as "Band Director of the Year" within their districts, and have mentored numerous student teachers.

While not recognized specifically as an expert *jazz* educator, Bruce has a reputation among his colleagues for being an excellent music educator, as evidenced by his numerous appearances throughout the state as an adjudicator and clinician. Emily's expertise as a jazz educator is evident in the success her jazz bands have achieved. Her jazz ensembles have received straight superior ratings for 26 years in the state jazz festival and have consistently earned top awards at competitive out-of-state events. No Michigan middle school jazz ensemble has achieved such a record of success during the same period. Case studies of Bruce and Emily open each chapter in this book. This chapter introduces readers to Bruce and Emily by describing their differing thoughts about and approaches to teaching school jazz and contextualizes these thoughts and approaches within the findings from the survey data.[1]

# Value of School Jazz

In interviews, Bruce clearly described a hierarchy within his music program, in which the concert band classes hold a place of much more prominence than the jazz band classes: "I always tell the kids 'it's dessert' because every now and then someone will say 'can I be in jazz band and not be in concert band?' and I say, 'no, you can't have dessert if you don't eat your dinner.' You gotta have your nutrition first."

Whereas Bruce takes a very serious approach to students' learning and performance quality within the *concert* bands, he feels that there is less expectation for the students to learn as much or perform as well in *jazz* band. Furthermore, jazz band affords students of different ages a place to socialize. "I want it to be enjoyable. It is more important to me that it is enjoyable at that level than having them be really good. Because it's not—it never will be."

On the other hand, Emily, being a trombone player in both a professional orchestra and numerous professional jazz ensembles, values both concert band and jazz ensemble and views them as equally important musical activities with slightly different aesthetics. Rather than conceiving of a hierarchy between different ensembles within the overall music program, Emily compares the ensembles in a music program to spokes on a wheel, of which the concert band is the hub. Emily focuses on helping students play their instruments well regardless of the ensemble in which they are playing at the moment. "The number one thing is how do you play your horn, because that is not going to change; whether you are playing weddings or funerals or circuses, you play your horn." Findings from the survey data suggest that the higher the level of one's perceived ability to teach jazz, the more likely one is to feel that concert band and jazz band are equally valuable.

Bruce and Emily both talked at length about the reasons they value having a middle school jazz ensemble. Among their most valued reasons were that jazz is fun and motivational, it keeps students interested in music, it teaches students a new skill set, it is closer to the kind of "outside-of-school" music that students might engage with, and students get experience playing one to a part.

# Less Pressure to Perform Well in Jazz

Bruce's middle school jazz ensemble meets once a week in the morning for 25 minutes and rehearses with "whoever shows up." Consequently, he does not have a curriculum and does not have any performance expectations of the students other than to "understand what it means to take a solo" and to "put a few tunes together for the concert." Whereas he takes a very serious approach to students' learning and performance quality within the concert bands, as noted previously, he feels that there is less expectation for the students to learn as much or perform as well in jazz band:

> In concert band, I've got a curriculum, I've got expectations, I've got "fill out your
> practice record and have this learned by such and such a time." "We're going to festival

in two weeks and it has to get better and better." In jazz band, it's just like, "I'm so happy you're here and let's play Spiderman" or whatever it is we're playing. We'll have three tunes we play through and it's fun, but there is not the level of performance expectation. And there is not the performance pressure. We'll perform, but mom and dad are going to clap. If the kid walks out with his underwear on his head, mom and dad are going to clap, you know. And that's good enough for me. That's what we're there for.

## Adjudicated Events

Bruce has never taken his middle school jazz ensemble to an adjudicated event, and not until three years ago did he take his high school jazz ensemble. Even though he takes his middle school and high school concert bands to adjudicated events (festival) every year and receives ratings, several years ago he was amazed to learn that jazz ensembles also perform for and receive ratings. When he finally did take his high school jazz ensemble to festival for ratings after 30 years, they received straight IIs. "It was like 'OK, you know,' if my symphony band got straight II's I'd be slitting my wrist, but it was like, great, fine." Bruce recalls that a jazz ensemble at that event got straight IIIs, and he was shocked that adjudicators would give a jazz ensemble such poor ratings. "You know, these kids are just doing this for fun. You know, this is dessert. That's like saying, 'your chocolate cake is terrible.'"

Emily, on the other hand, takes her jazz ensemble to adjudication because she feels that it is one more opportunity for the students to play and to improve based on feedback from the adjudicators. She values the experience the students get performing at different venues because they are "all the things that happen in the real world, all the variations that you don't have if you only play at home." To emphasize the motivational factor and educational experience, Emily always reminds the students that adjudicated events should be motivational. Music is not and should not be competition: "I tell the kids, 'well, what if every time one of your parents cooked something at home it was graded?' You do it because you love it. You cook because you love it. You read because you love it. You write because you love it. You should play because you love it; not because someone says you're the best. That is pretty dangerous stuff because there is always a better group out there. Who would want to cook if every time you did, a number popped up—8 or 8.5?"

## "Teaching" Happens in Concert Band

While it would be inaccurate to say that Bruce does not "teach" in jazz ensemble and that students do not "learn" while they are there, it would be accurate to say that the impetus behind Bruce's middle school jazz ensemble is not as much teaching and learning as it is student motivation and enjoyment of playing. "I don't do a lot of teaching at the middle school— not in jazz band. We're there to play the music and to have a good time and maybe have a donut afterwards." Bruce feels that instrumental pedagogy instruction is best delivered in the concert band setting. That is where students learn the fundamentals of tone production, embouchure, hand position, etc., and is the setting in which students' internal musicianship is *intentionally* developed: "The teaching part of it happens during [concert] band. I'm not delivering a lot of curricular instruction during jazz club. I'm always telling the kids in [concert] band when it is time to get serious, 'this isn't a club, this is a class—get serious.' Jazz is a club—they're there for fun. I'm not delivering a lot of 'do it this way' kind of instruction."

Emily's feelings about this topic are similar to Bruce's. While students do get better at their instruments in jazz ensemble, and Emily does teach some instrumental technique when needed, it is not the focus in her jazz ensemble. Technique instruction primarily happens in concert band, and in jazz ensemble the focus is on style:

> In concert band, it's about how to play your instrument. It's about techniques and you learn all the tricks of how your instrument works. Then in jazz band you can take all of that knowledge that you developed in concert band. You don't get that much of it in jazz band. You get it when you need it. But, in concert band it is a never ending how do you sit, how do you hold your horn, how do you tune it, and then in jazz band you can say, "well, 'let's talk about style; let's talk about theory.'"

## General Musicianship versus Jazz-Specific Expertise

Bruce believes that along with strong teaching abilities and a basic understanding of jazz styles, the teaching of middle school jazz ensemble is dependent on one's overall musicianship. He compares the teaching of middle school jazz ensemble to the teaching of any other genre of music with which one is not specifically familiar. While music teachers might not play the violin, those music teachers could still teach orchestra as long as they were good music teachers, familiar with orchestral styles, and sensitive musicians in general. "I suppose it would be like if I had to teach orchestra but I had never played violin. I would just have to learn about violin. The difference being that I have played the literature. I just didn't play it on violin." Bruce feels that a good musician/teacher with a basic understanding of the stylistic nuances of the genre can be effective at teaching that genre at the middle school level, since individual genres are simply an outgrowth of the larger musical discipline:

> All of this stuff has to do with just your basic musicianship. I have never played in a woodwind quintet, but I can teach woodwind quintets how to interpret whatever they play. There was a wonderful quote [from a conversation] between Bobby McFerrin and Leonard Bernstein. Bobby had to conduct some orchestra and was trying to get a conducting lesson with Bernstein and he said, "I don't know how to do this—I just do jazz." And Bernstein said, "It's all jazz." It's all music in one way or another. It is like dialects. It is all the same language; you are just learning nuances and dialects.

Similarly, Emily feels that successful jazz teaching at the middle school level has more to do with one's ability to motivate and relate to middle school students; however, she notes that music teachers should continually strive to increase their expertise in all genres of music, and that is best achieved through playing in ensembles:

Play in a quintet. Play in an orchestra. Play in a campus orchestra and play your secondary instrument and have that experience. You are going to have to teach all of those things. What downside is there for you to have to do it? I think early on you can be a snake oil salesman and play tunes that aren't real solid traditional jazz tunes. I mean you can play light easy swing stuff. You can play pop stuff and that's all good. It gets kids thinking about jazz. But down the line you are going to wish that you had those jazz experiences.

## Jazz Teachers Should Play Jazz

Bruce considers himself more of an *expert music teacher* who teaches jazz with a reasonable amount of competence, rather than a *jazz education expert*, specifically. He believes that the truly expert jazz educators are "immersed in the jazz idiom," but that good middle school jazz teaching is similar to good teaching in general: "The same thing that makes any teacher good—the ability to communicate and then insistence and persistence and you just don't give up. I'm living proof that you can get away with a rudimentary jazz education by just being a good teacher, but if you really want to be something more than that and offer something more than 25 or 30 minutes a week before school, then you had better be conversant in the idiom."

Conversely, Emily values being a player as much as she values being a teacher, because she feels that continuing to play your instrument positively impacts your teaching. There will always be better players than you, but by continuing to play your instrument, you stay engaged in the art form that you are teaching. Also, when students see you as a player as well as a teacher, it elevates your credibility with them and serves to blur the distinction between theory and practice or teaching and playing:

I always have this argument with my husband; he says, "you're a teacher that plays trombone." I say, "no, I'm a trombone player that happens to be teaching today." I really think that it is important that you get in front of the kids and you say, "look, today I am the one in front. In band, I've got the baton and in jazz band I'm leading the group, but tonight you can see me—I'm playing tonight here, I'm playing next week there. We're playing at this jazz festival, or I'm playing this symphony gig, or I've got this brass gig. Come hear me play and critique me. It's fine." I'm not an exalted teacher; I'm a trombone player. We're all doing the same thing. We're all musicians.

## Improvisation

Bruce's approach to the teaching and learning of improvisation is rooted in and is consistent with his overall philosophy of middle school jazz ensemble. In jazz ensemble, Bruce is more focused on his students having fun and enjoying playing their instruments than on the students becoming solid *jazz* musicians. The same is true of his beliefs about middle school jazz improvisation. He would rather the students developed confidence and comfort improvising than necessarily a high level of proficiency: "Just doing it and not worrying about whether it is right or wrong. What I want to hear from them is a lack of self-consciousness. I don't want them to feel nervous about it. I want them to be free to make all the mistakes they feel like making. There are no mistakes; there are just unfortunate choices. For me, that is the most important thing, that they just feel like they can do it without fear. I'll never tell anybody, 'wow, that was a terrible solo.' "

Emily also wants her students to develop confidence and comfort when improvising and feels this is best achieved through helping them to achieve early success. Her main goal is for students to play stylistically correct:

> I always tell the kids, "it's like anything—it's not as much what you say as how you say it." So, [I want them to play characteristic of the style]. If we're playing a Latin tune and they're playing even 8th notes, that makes sense. If we're in a swing tune and they're playing even 8th notes, that doesn't make any sense. So, just play stylistically and you'll start to find the notes that you like to play, the notes that fit. So, initially, you get the kids playing the right style so that even if they just pay a few notes within a scale or a chord, they're in the right style and they sound pretty good—it's all about success.

## Preparation for High School Jazz Band

Much of what Bruce thinks about middle school jazz ensemble (and middle school music in general) is influenced by the fact that he is also the high school band director. Bruce believes that middle school band, in general, serves primarily as preparation for high school band. Therefore, middle school band is necessary to prepare students with the skills they will need to have a truly meaningful musical experience once they are in high school:

> One of the things that is almost liberating about doing 6–12 is that my own personal investment is in the kids [at the high school]. So, if by the time they get out of 8th grade we have not had a great experience, it's OK because I know they will [at the high school]. If I was only teaching the middle school level, I would say, "I want this to be really good by such and such a time. I want them to be able to do this, and this, and this." But if they don't get it [at the middle school] because they don't have the time on task necessary to do it, I know they'll get it at the high school. We'll get it eventually because I've got them for 7 years. I don't just have them for three years, so that helps. It makes me a little bit more relaxed with things like middle school jazz band.

Similar to Bruce, Emily wants her middle school students to learn the stylistic elements of jazz so that they can continue playing in the future: "I don't feel the need to be the baby Ellington band at this age. I think that's great, but there's time for that. I'm hoping that the kids aren't going to fall off the banana boat here and never play in another jazz band. I would rather have a tune that's motivational and fun and teaches all those skills, and down the line they can play the real thing. If they're still playing jazz in three years, as a horn player, they can probably play almost any tune that's out there."

## Questions for Discussion

1. Bruce describes the concert band as "nutrition" and the jazz band as "dessert." In what ways do you agree or disagree with this metaphor?
2. Bruce describes not worrying about whether his students learn much about jazz in middle school because their "truly meaningful musical experience" begins in high school. Thus, his focus is just on getting them to have fun in middle school jazz band so they will choose to take jazz band in high school, where they can really develop musically. Should this be the focus for middle school jazz bands, or should directors focus on making middle school jazz band an authentic jazz learning experience?
3. Both Bruce and Emily talk about how the instrumental pedagogy happens in concert band rather than jazz band. Is jazz band not suited to teaching instrumental pedagogy?
4. If jazz band is more of a performance class than a "nuts-and-bolts" instrumental development class, how might this affect student perceptions of jazz band? Students' motivation for being in jazz band?
5. Both Bruce and Emily feel that being a good school jazz educator is more dependent on one's ability to teach and one's general musicianship than on one's specific ability as a "jazzer." How do you feel about this?
6. Emily talks about playing in jazz bands to help the teacher develop as a jazz educator. Have such experiences helped you in that pursuit? Were they as valuable as or more valuable than taking jazz-related pedagogy courses? Do band directors need to continue playing their instruments to be great music teachers?
7. How might taking your bands to adjudication influence students' approach to making music—both positively and negatively?
8. At the middle school level, Bruce values participation more than instrumentation and thus allows students with all instruments to join. Where do you stand on this issue?

## Note

1. For the complete study see C. West, "Teaching Middle School Jazz: An Exploratory Sequential Mixed Methods Study" (PhD diss., University of Michigan, 2011). *Dissertation Abstracts International* 72(8).

# Jazz for Non-Jazzers

Chad West

## Bruce's and Emily's First Experiences Teaching Jazz

When Bruce first started teaching, there was no jazz band at his school, and he was not interested in starting one. Bruce decided to start a jazz club because he thought that he could "get more students enthusiastic about getting up at 7:30 in the morning for a jazz group" than he could for other types of musical groups. Bruce recalls his first middle school jazz band:

> There were some charts in the drawer and I pulled them out and we went
> through them. It was not too terribly different than what I do now, except
> I didn't really have a sense for what kids in 6th, 7th, and 8th grade were capable
> of doing. I'm quite sure that I asked them to do music that was too hard for
> them. As I think about it, I am quite sure that I did that.

Similarly, Emily began her public school teaching career in the late 1970s with Detroit Public Schools. Students did not have their own instruments, there was no money in the budget for music or supplies, and students were placed in classes with high student to teacher ratios. Emily notes that her job back then was more about teaching extramusical things having to do more with life in general than with music. Nevertheless, she remembers fondly the students at her first school and recalls how her first jazz band met during lunch and was very unstructured:

> One of the kids brought in the drum set that he had bought for 25 bucks at
> the pawnshop and we rigged up some cymbals on a Manhasset music stand.
> That was our cymbal stand—a Manhasset without the top stand and a cymbal
> somehow affixed to it with some nasty bolt. It had to be something that you

> could only imagine on the *Simpsons*' to see this drum set, but by God, we did it and we played some little head chart. We played the Little Sunflowers of the world and the kids dug it and that's where it started. So, at that point we had a jazz band and we played whatever I could write out for them. Never full instrumentation, but some improvisation. Everyone would do all that they could. That was the beginning of teaching jazz band for me.

In my experience, many music teachers do not teach jazz ensemble, not because they do not have the musical ability to do so, but because they *believe* that they do not have the musical ability to do so. Since jazz participation is often not a required part of teacher preparation programs, and since many band directors play instruments such as horn, oboe, or bassoon that have precluded their participation in traditional jazz ensembles, many feel unprepared to incorporate jazz into their programs. Of all the presentations I give on various topics at music education conferences, the one that is in most demand is that on jazz for "non-jazzers." That session is intended to relay some basic information about jazz and teaching jazz to those who perceive themselves to be "non-jazzers." After I give this presentation, members from the audience often come up afterward and tell me things such as, "I never realized that I already knew this stuff" and "this is not all that different from the musicianship skills I already have."

While there *are* differences between concert band and jazz band, statements such as these let me know that I have accomplished my mission: taking the fear, and subsequent inaction, out of teaching jazz through affirming the natural musical instincts music teachers already possess. Once they *believe* this, the rest is mere details, which jazzers understand innately and non-jazzers can learn. The remainder of the chapters in this book presume some basic and foundational knowledge about jazz and experience teaching jazz as points of departure for the more detailed and sophisticated topics they explore. This chapter serves as a starting point by providing an introduction to some basics of teaching jazz—(a) swing style, (b) rhythmic solfège, (c) articulation, (d) Latin and rock style, (e) rhythm section, (f) improvisation, and (g) rehearsal and performance stage setup—as these are the elements that most contrast with what many of us are already familiar with: teaching concert band.

## Swing Style

One of the most apparent differences between concert band playing and jazz band playing is the treatment of rhythm; concert band rhythms are generally played straight, whereas jazz rhythms are generally swung. To describe this from a theoretical perspective, we might say that swing eighth notes are treated like triplet figures (see figure 2.1). But this example is only an approximation of what is actually happening when professional jazz musicians play swing patterns. Tempo has a lot to do with how eighth notes are swung; the faster the tempo, the straighter the eighth notes usually become, and vice versa. The style of the piece also has a lot to do with the swing feel; sometimes the patterns are closer to straight eighths and at other times they are played like a dotted eighth-sixteenth figure (or almost even a double-dotted

**FIGURE 2.1** Written vs. Performed Swung Eighth Notes

**FIGURE 2.2** Swing Continuum

eighth-thirty-second pattern, such as Roy Harnes's cymbal pattern over Oliver Nelson's "Yearnin'"). Listening to a variety of professional jazz musicians playing in a variety of styles will reveal just how wide this continuum can be (see figure 2.2).

While it may be helpful to conceive of swing rhythms as falling on a continuum somewhere between straight eighths and dotted eighth-sixteenth figures depending on style and tempo, I do not suggest *explaining* this to students. The most effective (and authentic) way to learn swing style is to listen to professional jazz musicians. As has been said, a picture is worth a thousand words. In this case, a musical sound is worth a thousand verbal explanations. By listening, students will absorb stylistic nuances that they may not otherwise be able to put into words—this is good! Think of the way people learn language: before humans learn to read and write, they learn to speak. But even prior to learning to speak, they listen. If we compare the development of language skills to the development of musicianship skills, we can see how important it is that students listen to jazz from the very beginning. By far the easiest and most effective (and authentic) way of learning jazz style is to listen to great jazz musicians performing jazz.

## Rhythmic Solfège

Listening to a jazzer verbally describe a certain rhythm or style, we will often hear something that sounds like a foreign language—and it *is* a language of sorts. In academic terms, we might refer to this as *rhythmic solfège*. Just as we use traditional melodic solfège to attach names to pitches, jazzers often use a system of attaching names to rhythms and articulations. While this practice is common, it is not universal. At least one beginning jazz method book, *Essential Elements for Jazz Ensemble* by Mike Steinel, has codified a system of jazz rhythmic solfège (see figure 2.3).

Since the upbeats of swing eighth notes are generally accented and quarter notes are generally played short, using words such as *doo, bah*, and *dot* can help convey style and articulation. Of course, the best way of teaching style and articulation is through modeling on an instrument, but a vocal model using rhythmic solfège can also convey large amounts of information quickly and is just one more way of demonstrating for students. It is also a convenient way of talking about jazz rhythms. For instance, look at figure 2.4 and compare the way it is written with the way it would be chanted and subsequently played using rhythmic solfège.

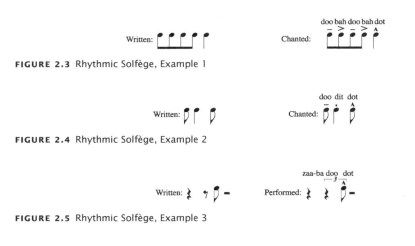

FIGURE 2.3 Rhythmic Solfège, Example 1

FIGURE 2.4 Rhythmic Solfège, Example 2

FIGURE 2.5 Rhythmic Solfège, Example 3

FIGURE 2.6 Treatment of 8th Notes Followed by a Rest vs. by a Note

From this, we can see the difference between how this rhythm would be interpreted in concert band and how it would be played in a jazz ensemble. In this case, rhythmic solfège conveys both the length of the notes and the articulation type. Thinking back to how the first eighth note is performed in swing style, recall that it is really equal to the first two eighths of a quarter note triplet, rather than a straight eighth note in concert band style. You could explain this to students in theoretical terms as I have just attempted to do (not recommended), or you could use rhythmic solfège to model it, which would be much more effective.

Another instance in which using jazz rhythmic solfège helps solidify time is when students enter on the upbeat. Take for instance the entrance on the & of 2 in a concert band setting, the performer would play exactly when the foot comes up. But in swing style, where we are handling eighth note patterns as triplets, such an entrance would be early since the upbeat should occur as the third note of a quarter note triplet rather than the second note of a quarter note duplet. Instead of playing directly on the & of 2, I encourage students to count *zaa-ba-doo-dot* and play on the *dot*. This ensures that they wait until the last eighth note of the quarter note triplet rather than entering early on the & of 2 (see figure 2.5). Another rule of thumb with eighth notes that occur on the upbeat is to play them as a *dot* when followed by a rest and play them as a *bah* when followed by a note (see figure 2.6).

As can be seen in many of the examples, swing quarter notes are generally played short and swing eighth notes are generally played long, which runs counter to concert band notation. In addition, the accents fall on 2 and 4 in swing, whereas the accents in concert band are played on 1 and 3 (see figure 2.7). Swing quarters are often presumed short even when

FIGURE 2.7 Written vs. Swung Quarter Notes

FIGURE 2.8 Written vs. Performed Swing Line Using Jazz Articulation and Rhythmic Solfège

they are written as an eighth tied to another eighth and/or cross over a bar line (such as in the intro to "In the Mood") (See ⊙ video 2.1, Jazz Notation Using Rhythmic Solfège.)

# Articulation

Following is a checklist of general rules of thumb for jazz articulation:

- Articulate swing eighth notes with a *doo* syllable rather than a *tah*.
- Notes followed by a rest are released using the tongue to stop the air (something that is not encouraged in concert band playing).
- Eighth notes are generally played long except when followed by a rest.
- Quarter notes are generally played short.
- Accents occur on 2 and 4 for quarter note patterns and on upbeats for eighth note patterns.

Figure 2.8 is an example of how a typical swing line might be notated versus how it would be performed, illustrating all of the various ways of handling swing patterns previously described.

# Latin and Rock Style

First, a word about words: I am using the term *Latin* here to refer to what is generally known as Afro-Cuban. Certainly there are many genres within "Latin" music, many of which, such as the bossa nova, are not at all similar to Afro-Cuban music. The term *Latin* is far too general to have much meaning to serious jazzers, but for convenience, and for our purposes here, I refer to music from the Afro-Cuban genre as simply Latin. As we can see from all of the preceding examples, swing rhythms and articulations are performed differently than they are notated. Latin charts, however, are performed more like they are notated. In Latin styles, the eighth notes are played straight rather than swung, eighth notes are played short, and quarter notes are played long, just as one would expect in concert band. The main difference between the treatment of notation is not in note value, but in articulation (see figure 2.9).

**FIGURE 2.9** Latin vs. Swing Articulation

**FIGURE 2.10** Jazz Ornamentation

As we see from the example, Latin style requires a longer and smoother quarter note and a shorter and harder eighth note articulation than one would play in concert band. In other words, the note lengths are exaggerated. Similar to swing articulation, eighth notes occurring on the upbeat are articulated with a *dot* when followed by a rest. Last, another thing that differentiates jazz style (Latin/rock or swing) from concert band style is the unique use of ornamentation (see figure 2.10). (See ⏵ video 2.2, Jazz Ornamentation.)

## Rhythm Section

The rhythm section as a whole has two responsibilities: to complement the horn section and to play together as a cohesive unit. In order to complement the horn section, individual players need to know their roles within the jazz ensemble. At a beginning level, I suggest helping the bass players understand their role primarily as timekeeper. A walking bass line provides a consistent rhythmic and harmonic line for the band to listen to. The drummer also provides the time, but the drummer's main job is to control the style and dynamics of each piece. Last, the roles of the piano player and guitar player could best be described as witty conversationalists. Their main job is to fill in the rhythmic and harmonic gaps by comping, or *complementing*. To help beginning rhythm section players understand their roles in playing together as a cohesive unit, I teach something that I learned from Mike Grace called the *magic triangle*, whereby I teach the bass players to let their 2 and 4 be dictated by the drummers' hi-hat and teach the drummers to let their ride cymbal be dictated by the bass players' walking bass line (see figure 2.11). The last leg of the triangle involves the drummer making sure that the 2 and 4 on the hi-hat aligns with the same beats on the ride cymbal. The benefit of teaching students to think this way is that it helps them lock into each other while avoiding situations in which either player is solely charged with dictating the time (see ⏵ video 2.3, Magic Triangle).

## Improvisation

Many of us are familiar with the look of terror in our students' eyes when they are asked to improvise. In fact, even many of us, as professional music educators, would be reticent to bear our souls and reveal our musical weaknesses to listeners by making something up that is not

**Bass**
Takes 2 & 4 from hi-hat

**Ride Cymbal**
Takes 1,2,3,4 from bass line

**FIGURE 2.11** The Magic Triangle

notated, yet improvisation is at the very heart of jazz, and ignoring it in our jazz ensembles ignores the authenticity of the genre and deprives our students of the opportunity to develop this critical element of basic musicianship: creativity. I have heard many school jazz bands that play their arrangements beautifully but do not include improvised solos in the performance. I argue that this is not an authentic representation of the genre and the art of jazz, but simply a smaller concert band that plays different literature in different styles. To teach jazz is to teach improvisation.

But let us back up for just a moment: *improvisation* is a scary word. *Creativity* is less scary. Human beings are naturally creative; anyone who has watched a small child at play can attest that we come hardwired as creative beings. It is only after years of societal enculturation that we become increasingly inhibited and less likely to creatively explore for fear of ridicule. Regrettably, school music teachers often inadvertently reinforce these inhibitions every time we help students correct a notated musical passage in rehearsal. This is not to say that we should not help students to accurately read printed notation, but when this is the majority of what we do, we are sending a very powerful message to students that there is a right way and a wrong way and that deviation is a problem in need of correction; therefore, it is no wonder that students who have been taught this way are hesitant to venture creatively when asked to improvise.

While all would agree that improvisation, or musical creativity, is inherent to the art of jazz, I go further, arguing that it is a basic element of musicianship that can and should be developed regardless of the genre. Often, as students gain proficiency reading notation and manipulating their instruments, they become less willing to improvise; therefore, it is usually best to get students to be creative as early as possible.

I find it helpful to think of musical creativity simply as the students' ability to generate musical ideas apart from that which is externally dictated to them by written notation. Learning by ear is an important first step in developing creativity. When students learn to rely on their ears to recreate a tune or a musical passage, they not only develop the ear-to-hand coordination required when improvising, but they also, perhaps more importantly, begin to associate music with sound rather than with site. From the first day of musical instruction, I have students "improvise." If they have learned only one note, I ask them to make up some rhythms on that note. If they cannot yet make a sound on the instrument, I ask them to make up some rhythmic and tonal patterns vocally. If they cannot or are hesitant to use their voices, I ask them to make up some rhythms using body percussion. The point is that incorporating opportunities for students to be creative from the first day of musical instruction, as rudimentary as those opportunities may be, signals to students that musical creativity is a basic element of musicianship, rather than an advanced skill to be developed later in jazz band. Before our students become sophisticated jazz improvisers, they must become *comfortable music creators*.

When students are comfortable making things up from day one, getting them comfortable to improvise in jazz band down the road is a relatively easy thing to do—especially if we start with group improvisation, in which everyone improvises at once. I like to use a method adopted from Chris Azzara's *Developing Musicianship Through Improvisation* (Azzara and Grunow 2006). First I model the tune and have students learn it by ear. Second, I model the bass line (roots of each chord) and have the students learn it by ear. Third, I have students make up rhythmic improvisations on the root notes. Fourth, I model the first five notes of each scale of the chord changes and have the students learn them by ear. Finally, I have the students improvise using rhythmic and melodic patterns over the first five notes of each chord change (see ⏵ video 2.4, Teaching Beginning Improvisation).

## Rehearsal and Performance Stage Setup

When rehearsing the beginning jazz ensemble, I suggest arranging the players in a box facing inward (see figure 2.12). This allows the students to hear and see one another and helps with balance and time. Performances require a different setup than rehearsals. In performance situations, the rhythm section is placed to the left of the horns, and the horns make three rows with saxes in front, followed by trombones, and trumpets in the back (see figure 2.13). Following are suggestions for arranging an ensemble in a traditional big band performance setup:

- Place lead players in the middle of the section so that the other section members can hear them more easily.
- Align players so that the lead player in each section is vertically aligned with the lead players in the other sections. This sets the tenor I apart, but since tenor I is often the primary soloist, it makes sense to have that player in front of the rhythm section.

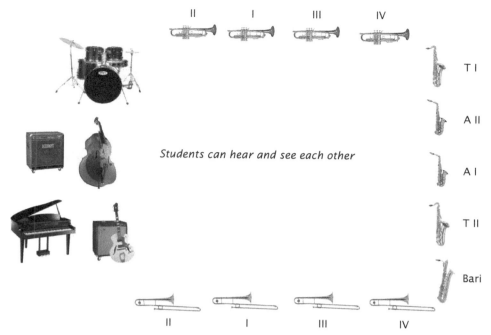

**FIGURE 2.12** Rehearsal Setup

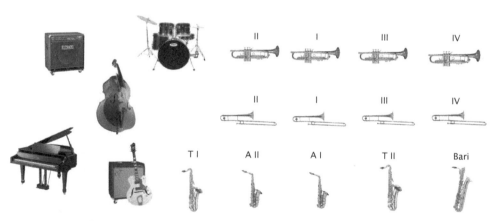

**FIGURE 2.13** Performance Setup

- Place the bass player to the left of the ensemble and the bari sax and bass trombone players on the right side of the ensemble.
- The drummer should be placed right next to the trombones so that the lead trumpet player can hear and *see* the hi-hat.
- The bass player should stand close to the ride cymbal and where the drummer can easily see the bass player's hands.
- The bass player and the guitar player should stand in front, but not directly in front, of their amps so they can hear themselves.

- The guitar player and piano player should sit where they can see each other, and the piano should be angled where the open lid is open facing the ensemble.
- Have the trumpet section stand on risers, the trombone section stand or sit on stools, and the sax section sit in chairs. This will produce a tiered effect in which all three sections can be easily heard.

## Conclusion

As you can see from this chapter, there are many differences between teaching concert band and teaching jazz ensemble, but there are also many similarities. Good tone is good tone. Good technique is good technique. Good musicianship is good musicianship. We teach good rhythm and intonation in our concert bands, and we also teach these things in our jazz ensembles. We teach students to balance and blend within the concert band, and this is no different in jazz ensemble. Improvisation is inherent to the jazz tradition, but it is not exclusive to it. The fact is, many of our musical instincts and musicianship skills transfer regardless of the genre of music we are teaching. Of course there are some differences, and hopefully this chapter has illuminated some of them. The would-be jazz educator who wishes to go no further than to absorb the information and implement the suggestions put forth in this chapter would be well on the way to competently teaching a middle school or even high school jazz ensemble. For those who wish to delve further, I hope you enjoy the subsequent chapters in this book.

## Questions for Discussion

1. Bruce recalls that when he first started teaching, there was no jazz band at his school, and he was not interested in starting one. What are some of the reasons for starting a school jazz band? What are some of the reasons that band directors do not?
2. All of Bruce's middle school jazz bands over the years have met before school, and Emily's first jazz band met during lunch. Such is often the case, in that schools do not feel they can offer jazz band as a class during the school day. Why is this the case when most schools offer concert band during the day? Is the assumption that concert band is a "legitimate" musical offering, whereas jazz band is an "extra?" Why not reverse the paradigm?

## Reference

Azzara, C. D., and R. F. Grunow. 2006. *Developing Musicianship through Improvisation*. Chicago: GIA Publications.

# PART II

# Language of Jazz

# 3

# Social Language of Jazz

## Andrew Goodrich

### Peer Interaction in the High School Jazz Band

Bruce believes that at the high school level his students learn as much from each other as they do from him and tend to elevate one another in rehearsal. While he leads the rehearsals and guides the group musically, his high school jazz ensemble relies heavily on the mentorship and motivation among more experienced peers within the group:

> My high school jazz band is not student-run and I am selecting the literature most of the time, but the kids are more hip to the literature than I am in a lot of ways. So, they are like "we should play Four Brothers. Here, listen to my iPod, listen to this tune, we should do this Woody Herman chart." I'm like, "great, put it on, let me hear it. We'll do it. I'll order it." Then the other kids say, "well here is what I have on mine" and they sit around and jam with each other after rehearsal. My jazz band is a two-hour block at the high school but I tell them we're going for an hour and a half as a big band and for that extra [half] hour I will hang around as long as you want and whoever wants to just sit around and play—do it. So, you see the kids that want to do that and the other kids who aren't so good at it sort of [sit] at the feet of the masters listening to what they do so it is kind of cool.

Interactions among students can provide the basis for them to learn from each other, even when directors like Bruce still maintain control of the ensemble rehearsals. For directors of jazz ensembles, though, the majority of rehearsal time is devoted to preparing students for an upcoming performance. In these rehearsals, directors are considered the sole source of knowledge as they rehearse their students to prepare for a performance. In addition to teacher-directed instruction, students can benefit greatly from mentoring. While there are obstacles to implementing mentoring, including limited rehearsal time, the benefits of mentoring for students will pay dividends in the end. Mentoring is often not used by jazz ensemble directors, for a variety of reasons. These may include lack of time to implement and maintain a mentoring system, limited rehearsal time, and the plethora of administrative duties that must be accomplished on a daily basis. Yet tapping into mentoring in its various forms—an important component of the early historic jazz culture—can increase the knowledge and comprehension of jazz music of both the director and the students. Mentoring is one of the best instructional practices that jazz educators can use to increase their own knowledge about teaching and performing jazz, as well as to help their students to teach each other in the jazz ensemble program.

Jazz musicians originally learned to play jazz in a variety of ways: listening to and transcribing recordings, listening to live performances, and asking questions of each other. From this aural and verbal communication with each other came the development of mentoring, or the social language of jazz. As jazz musicians hung out with each other, they shared ideas for learning that increased their knowledge of jazz music and elevated their level of musicianship. This type of conversation, both verbal and aural, occurred before, during, and after gigs. These conversations centered around how to learn what others were doing when they performed jazz music. For example, young players would listen to and emulate more established players. Perhaps the most famous mentoring relationship in the historic jazz culture is that of Joe "King" Oliver and Louis Armstrong. Oliver mentored Armstrong in New Orleans, and this relationship continued when Armstrong later joined Oliver's group in Chicago. Jazz musicians in the early days of the music did not go to school to receive a jazz education, nor did they take a jazz pedagogy course. They learned from each other.

Today, mentoring remains the social language of jazz; however, the mentoring process has changed somewhat as jazz music has entered schools. Mentoring can build and support strong social connections between directors, between directors and students, and between students, in addition to elevating the performance level of the students in the jazz ensemble. In addition to building strong social connections, the mentoring process can provide opportunities for additional instruction for students, support the ensemble director, provide a link to the historic jazz culture, and help to immerse students in a jazz culture.

In this chapter the various facets of the mentoring process are explored within the context of social interactions in jazz education. To provide a context for mentoring, this chapter begins with a discussion of the different types of mentoring and the knowledge that can be used during the mentoring process. The use of various types of mentors is explored, which include seeking out adult mentors and peer mentors for jazz ensemble directors and how these mentoring experiences can contribute to our own growth as jazz educators and performers. Further discussion includes how jazz ensemble directors can implement and use peer mentoring among their own students to increase their jazz knowledge and individual performance skills—including social aspects of peer mentoring and leadership.

# Mentoring

Mentoring typically entails a more experienced and knowledgeable individual (the mentor) helping out a less experienced and knowledgeable individual (the mentee). Various types of mentoring exist, including peer mentoring, cross-age mentoring, and lifelong mentoring. In peer mentoring, individuals share knowledge with their peers. An example of peer mentoring is a high school senior sharing information with a freshman. Cross-age mentoring occurs when an older peer helps a younger peer of a different age group. For example, a high school junior may help a seventh grader with how to play articulations. Lifelong mentoring entails a desire for adults to continue seeking out a mentoring relationship and the sharing of their experiences. Peer mentoring and cross-age mentoring embody a hierarchical relationship in which the mentor is more knowledgeable than the mentee. Lifelong mentoring is not necessarily hierarchical, as the peers may be similar in age as well as knowledge and skills.

Within the domain of peer mentoring, three types of social relationships exist: information peer, collegial peer, and special peer (Kram and Isabella, 1985). An information peer is one who solely shares information-type knowledge learned from personal experiences. Similarly, a collegial peer shares information-type knowledge with peers, but also includes advice and feedback along with the information. A special peer is someone who provides emotional support as well as advice and feedback during the mentoring process. Mentoring therefore involves the sharing of knowledge. But what kinds of knowledge are used in the mentoring process?

*Knowledge.* Different types of knowledge are shared in the mentoring process. These include foundational knowledge, nonfoundational knowledge, tacit knowledge, and explicit knowledge. Foundational knowledge is the sharing of basic information that has been learned from a teacher, for example, knowing how to accent quarter notes in the Basie style and sharing this information with a peer. Nonfoundational knowledge is "derived through reasoning, questioning, discussion, and negotiation of beliefs" (Dooly, 2008, p. 22). With this type of knowledge, students may ask questions and have a discussion with each other, such as how to interpret style in a 1920s-era Ellington composition. Tacit knowledge is learned from experience, and students are not always sure where they learned the information, nor are they always able to clearly articulate the knowledge to someone else. Students may know how to articulate a phrase from a Basie chart, but not really know how they are doing it or how they learned to do so. Explicit knowledge is knowledge shared through print and media. Charts in the jazz ensemble and recordings of these charts are examples of explicit knowledge. With explicit knowledge, it takes prior learning to be able to read these charts and to comprehend what one is listening to in the recordings.

When people share knowledge during the mentoring process, the term *mentoring* is often used synonymously with other terms, such as *coaching, guiding*, and even *teaching*. For the purposes of this chapter, mentoring entails the sharing of knowledge between two people who are open to the possibility of serving as a mentor or mentee. The sharing of knowledge in jazz can occur verbally—that is, explaining to someone how to articulate a quarter note—or aurally, such as modeling a phrase to help a person understand how it is supposed to sound. Mentoring occurs for musical and nonmusical reasons, and when used as an instructional technique it can help directors and students more fully comprehend the subject matter during the learning process when directing or playing in a jazz ensemble.

The following types of mentoring are discussed in the next sections: (a) adult mentoring, a form of lifelong mentoring, in which directors receive mentoring from fellow teachers, jazz musicians, and jazz educators; and (b) peer mentoring, in which directors guide and instruct their students in how to mentor each other with regard to teaching, learning, leadership, and social connections in jazz.

# Adult Mentoring

Music educators are not always prepared to go out and direct a jazz ensemble when they procure their first contracted teaching positions. Reasons for this vary and may include lack of experience performing, listening to, and learning about jazz in a degree program. Or, if a music educator does not play what is considered a jazz instrument (e.g., trumpet, saxophone), opportunities for learning jazz are sometimes limited. Even directors who possess jazz performing and teaching experience can still benefit from seeking out mentoring opportunities to improve their skills and their students' skills in jazz. Directors should consider learning from fellow elementary and high school directors with jazz experience—seeking out opportunities to work with directors of similar jazz teaching and performing abilities—and from university-level jazz educators and professional jazz musicians. Learning on the job and seeking out mentoring opportunities can help improve directors' jazz teaching skills and in turn improve the knowledge and performance level of jazz of their students.

**More advanced peers.** Mentoring opportunities in the context of jazz education can include networking with fellow music teachers who have a reputation as good jazz ensemble directors, but not necessarily professional-level jazz performers or jazz educators. The first step toward developing a mentoring relationship may include attending concerts (even with one's own students) to hear how other ensembles sound. This can provide an entrée into making the first offer to meet with teachers on an individual basis to ask them questions about how they direct their jazz ensemble, how they learned to teach jazz music, and any suggestions they may have for becoming a better jazz teacher. Finding a common meeting time to get together is certainly an issue, but during the course of a school year it is likely that time can be found to get together at least once for lunch and possibly to observe at least one rehearsal.

**Peers with similar abilities.** Another tactic for mentoring in jazz is to seek out fellow teachers who also wish to improve their jazz teaching skills. Learning together and mentoring each other throughout this process is a fantastic way to share information and to improve one's knowledge about teaching jazz, and possibly about performing jazz music. This can be difficult in terms of time and distance, but meetings could occur via Skype. Even sending email or text updates to update each other on current progress with learning jazz can help. Another option is to meet during the summer months. For example, get together and improvise, critique each other, and share ideas about jazz teaching that have been learned since the last meeting. This could become an annual get-together for a periodic "jazz checkup." In addition to seeking out mentoring relationships, additional opportunities for improving one's jazz teaching skills include attending clinics, workshops, and summer jazz camps. Work up a conversation with the clinician or jazz musician and be open to the possibility of being mentored by established jazz educators.

**University-level faculty and professional jazz musicians.** Bringing in university-level jazz educators and professional jazz musicians provides excellent opportunities for both students and directors to learn more about performing jazz music. Granted, this is not always an option due to time and/or limited finances. However, many adult mentors appreciate being asked to help. Reaching out to them sends the message that their input is valued and appreciated.

Bringing in jazz experts who can share information with both directors and students can be especially helpful help for directors who are not yet comfortable or do not have time to invest in developing their own jazz vocabulary. These mentors can be jazz educators and/or jazz musicians. Further, with university-level jazz educators, directors of elementary and high school jazz ensembles could "tap" into the university students as a resource for cross-age mentoring. In cross-age mentoring, directors could bring in area university jazz students to mentor high school or junior high school students. These university jazz students can run sectionals, improvise with the students in the jazz ensemble, and share knowledge with the students during rehearsals.

Local jazz musicians can come in and run sectionals or occasionally run clinics or rehearsals. Again, this may be difficult to do in rural locations, so this could become more of a once-per-semester or even an annual event. Bringing in established jazz educators to mentor students can help to increase the level of knowledge provided. The director will need to make a commitment of both time and finances. Bringing in jazz educators from the outside can help, especially if the mentor possesses knowledge beyond the director's skill set. For example, a director who is a trumpet player could bring in a guitarist or drummer to work with the rhythm section students in the jazz ensemble.

Not only can adult mentors help to elevate knowledge and the performance level of the jazz ensemble, but they can also help connect students to the "world" of jazz outside of the band room. These mentors can share information during the teaching process and through other ways of transferring knowledge, such as recommending recordings, which can include audio and video footage. The adult mentors can "show them the ropes" and can use guided listening to help students connect to the historic and current jazz culture. Adult mentors can also share information on various learning processes in jazz, such as transcribing recordings, and on fundamentals of jazz playing, such as groove. Throughout this process, directors can add what they learn from these outside mentors, expanding their own teaching repertoire.

Adult mentors can help directors in terms of making rehearsals more efficient. Ensemble directors do not have enough hours in the day to devote to the various ensembles they teach, not to mention all of the administrative duties associated with teaching in a full-time position. Using outside adult mentors can help jazz ensemble directors mentor and share knowledge with their students. As students learn from outside adult mentors, the students can bring their new knowledge into the jazz ensemble and subsequently elevate their individual performance level and ultimately the performance level of the jazz ensemble. In addition, the students can bring certain aspects of what they learn in terms of musicianship back into the entire band program (e.g., concert band). Adult mentors can serve as models for jazz sound and style and can influence and motivate students to perform at a higher level. Bringing in adult mentors to work with the students will help to inspire them and allow them to connect to the world of jazz outside of the classroom.

# Peer Mentoring

In addition to adult mentoring, directors can help students in the jazz ensemble learn how to share knowledge with each other through peer mentoring. As mentioned previously, peer mentoring is usually hierarchical in structure, but in jazz this does not necessarily translate to a hierarchy in terms of age. For example, a senior alto sax player could mentor a freshman about playing correct articulations in a specific chart. However, sophomores who are more advanced with their improvisation skills could mentor a less knowledgeable senior. Throughout the process of peer mentoring, students can share information with each other to help teach skills, instead of merely learning how to play specific tunes for a concert. Over time these skills can be shared from student to student, which in turn will elevate students' knowledge and skills in the jazz ensemble.

In addition to sharing knowledge with each other, students in the jazz ensemble can develop friendships, experience personal growth as musicians, and provide support for each other as they engage in acquiring more knowledge during the peer mentoring process. Peer mentoring in the jazz ensemble can occur for musical and nonmusical reasons, and similar to adult mentoring, can help to elevate the performance level of each student and ultimately the entire jazz ensemble. Peer mentoring occurs in the form of students sharing information with each other about how to play their parts, or help with other aspects of performing jazz, such as improvisation, chord voicings, and comping. Peer mentoring can help create an environment conducive to cooperation among students, instead of competition.

Peer mentoring can occur in various ways in a jazz ensemble program, for example, while students remain in their sections. The lead trumpet player can help members of that section with fingerings. Peer mentoring can occur across sections, too, with students moving around the band room to mentor outside of their sections. For example, the lead alto sax player can help a trumpet player with how to play the correct articulations in a musical phrase. Peer mentoring can also occur between ensembles. Jazz combo students can help mentor younger students in the big band jazz ensemble, or the students in the top jazz ensemble could help mentor students in the lower jazz ensemble. Cross-age mentoring may occur, in which high school students could mentor students in a junior high jazz ensemble, which would likely be a feeder program for the high school jazz ensemble. In turn, this creates opportunities to self-perpetuate knowledge among the students in the jazz ensemble program. Peer mentoring can occur on the fringes of rehearsals. For example, a nonverbal form of mentoring could entail freshmen being inspired as they listen to juniors warming up on their instruments before the jazz ensemble rehearsal begins. In addition to peer mentoring in the jazz ensemble among students, peer mentoring can occur outside of the band room. For instance, students can provide peer mentoring when they get together in their homes to help each other transcribe an improvised jazz solo.

*Social.* Peer mentoring occurs for social reasons. Research indicates that the friendships that develop during the peer mentoring process comprise the most important aspect of peer mentoring. Friendships can begin or evolve as students share information, which in turn can help students to feel more invested in the jazz ensemble program, as they become aware that peer mentoring can help continue the success of the program. (See ⊙ appendix 3.1, "List of Resources," for further reading.)

*Leadership.* Another important component of peer mentoring is leadership. Students in the jazz ensemble with leadership positions, such as a section leader, or who possibly hold a position such as band president, can serve as mentors. Leadership can entail peer mentoring for nonmusical reasons. Students who are peer mentors can assist with classroom management during rehearsals, at which they can help the jazz ensemble director to enforce discipline. In addition, peer mentors can assist the director with setting up the room. Although this aspect of peer mentoring does not necessarily entail the transfer of knowledge, teachers need to carefully monitor this type of mentoring, for students can sometimes get in the way as they try to help. The students who assist with classroom management may not necessarily be the most advanced jazz players in the room, but they are leaders, and students listen to them. Not all jazz ensemble directors will be comfortable with student leaders, however. For directors, it is important to meet frequently with those recognized as student leaders to make sure they are doing what the directors want them to do so they are consistent with expectations. It is important for students to treat each other with respect and not create problems. These student leaders are a work in progress. Leadership comes from the director, but students may learn leadership in other school activities; in extracurricular activities such as Students Against Destructive Decisions (SADD); or elsewhere, such as in drum major leadership camps.

These student leaders can also assist with attitudes in the ensemble and work toward maintaining a more positive learning environment. For example, Goodrich (2005) reported that a student leader in the jazz ensemble thought some of the students had bad attitudes, so when he made room assignments for the group's trip to a regional International Association for Jazz Education conference performance, he paired disgruntled students with positive, more engaged ones, with the intention of alleviating the problem.

The director needs to determine the extent of peer mentoring that occurs in rehearsals. That is, sometimes it can be difficult to determine if students are talking to assist each other with musical directives or are telling the latest joke. Each jazz ensemble program is different, so each mentoring system is unique to that particular program and needs to fit the director's style of leadership. Peer mentoring is an outreach of the director's teaching style, so directors need to work with students as part of the growth process. Ultimately peer mentoring is about the process of acquiring knowledge, which in turn contributes to the final product: typically, a performance by the jazz ensemble.

# Setting Up the Mentoring System

Directors serve a vital role in the peer mentoring process, for they must have an understanding of the capabilities of students and, more important, the learning styles of students, before assigning mentors to mentees. Research indicates that teachers should involve as many students as possible in the mentoring process. It is important for directors to actively implement and support the peer mentoring system in a jazz ensemble program. Directors who remain actively involved will help to keep themselves the ultimate authority in the room, instead of giving control of the ensemble rehearsal solely to the students. Research indicates that students do value what they learn from each other; however, students and the director involved in the sharing of information can help to deepen the understanding of content being taught in the jazz ensemble rehearsal. Peer mentoring involves leadership, and the relationships that emerge among students during this process can be the most important component of mentoring (Madsen, 2011).

Directors need to actively set up the peer mentoring system and meet with students on a frequent basis, which could be daily or weekly. For example, directors need to pair peer mentors and mentees with each other and monitor the mentoring process (for use of language and inappropriate comments), ensuring the students are effectively paired.

In the peer mentoring process, directors need to set goals and clearly articulate them to the students designated as mentors. When doing so, the director guides students through the process of how to share knowledge and how to explain this knowledge to mentees, such as specific aspects of performing in a particular jazz style. Directors should encourage two-way communication about goals for the jazz ensemble program. As student mentors share their goals with the director, they become more involved in the program and take on more ownership.

## Summary

Mentoring involves the process of sharing information to increase and enhance knowledge. Whether or not directors possess basic jazz teaching skills, seeking out more advanced peers can provide a fantastic way to increase one's knowledge about directing a jazz ensemble. Interacting with fellow directors, both with those considered jazz experts and those with a similar level of knowledge, can provide opportunities for growth in jazz teaching skills and learning how to perform jazz music.

With students, using adult mentors can assist directors in making rehearsals more efficient, in addition to bringing in areas of expertise outside of a director's comfort zone. Directors can establish peer mentoring among students in their jazz ensembles. Students who serve as peer mentors can help share knowledge with other students, bringing in knowledge that a director may not possess about jazz and also contributing to making rehearsals more efficient. Student leaders can also help make rehearsals more efficient and contribute to the growth of the jazz ensemble program. Mentoring in jazz, whether for musical or nonmusical reasons, provides a platform for both directors and students to share in the social language of jazz and contributes to the growth process in becoming better jazz educators and performers.

## Questions for Discussion

1. Bruce talks about how his high school jazz students learn as much from their peers as they do from him. Think back about your high school band experience: Was this the case with you? In what ways was learning from your peers more powerful?
2. Bruce rehearses his high school jazz band for an hour and a half and gives the students the last half hour to "just sit around and play." Is facilitating these kinds of interactions important to their musical development or a dereliction of "teaching" responsibilities?

3. How important is facilitating student leadership and peer interaction to the musical development of high school students?

4. In what ways do student leadership and peer interaction look different in the high school jazz band than in the middle school jazz band?

5. How can band directors help create a jazz culture within their groups? Why is facilitating this culture important to what we do as band directors?

# 4

# Pedagogical Language of Jazz

Russell A. Schmidt

## It Was Like Going Over a Cliff

Bruce played jazz in middle school and high school "stage band." In high school, stage band was neither a class nor a school-sponsored club, but rather just a group of students assembling once a week for rehearsals, led by the band director. The director was no jazz expert either. He was a former service band baritone player who had also performed in Revelli's band at the University of Michigan. Bruce's stage band experience included very little improvisation instruction:

> I don't remember being taught anything about improvisation in high school or middle school. It was, "here's the chart—play the chart" and then you had a saxophone player that was pretty good at improvising, so he would get all of the solos. And we might play around with it a little bit, but it was very much "what is on the page."

He continues, explaining that the improvisation instruction received usually came from mentoring by more experienced peers:

> We had some guys in that band who were jazzers—just independently sought it out themselves and could really play. But it was fun playing with them and I learned a little bit from them. I still remember [one]: Doug Ladney was his name. He played a really good alto and he did summer jazz workshops and talked about these different chords that I didn't understand . . . I got more from those guys than I really did from the director, who basically knew that [improvisation] wasn't his thing. [He] just gave us the charts to play and the guys who were ambitious about jazz could do something with it.

Similarly, the only instruction that Emily received was to "make something up" without any guidance abouts to how to do that:

> It was like here is a bicycle—you have never seen one before; however, you will ride down this hill. I remember a tune called "Template" by Torrie Zito, and it was one of these hot saxophone, 100 miles an hour pieces with change, change, change, change, and I didn't have a clue—I didn't have a chance, but I was still the best improvisor in the class and the director at the time said, "It's you—go." It was like going over a cliff. It was embarrassing and I thought, 'I'm going to figure this out.' I suppose it is kind of like when you made your first tree house. You said, OK, we can get up in it and it's not going to fall, but man it looks [awful], so we're going to make the next tree house better. That is sort of the way I was about it. I said, well, I have to refine this and figure out how to do it better.

Fortunately for present-day students, the pedagogical language of jazz continues to evolve. Changes in the art form itself, the gradual development of jazz education resources and techniques, the impact of our digital age on matters such as interpersonal communication and access to music, and other factors play roles in this continued evolution. Conversely, certain fundamental pedagogical theories of what constitutes effective instruction continue to prove true for each new generation of music students.

In this chapter, the means of reconciling those components—one ever-changing, the other rightfully stable—are presented: practical teaching techniques, framed in a way to be received most successfully by today's students, while still honoring foundational theories that have shaped outstanding music instruction for decades. With an intended goal of cultivating stronger rehearsal technique in ensemble directors, serious consideration must be given to rehearsal plan development, including improvisation studies, effective communication skills, and techniques to ensure student engagement.

## Consideration of Rehearsal Technique

In my experiences visiting schools and universities as a guest clinician, I have found that some ensemble directors value technical conducting skill development more than the refinement of their rehearsal technique. This is not to say that the technical elements of conducting are overrated. But from the vantage point of students, solid rehearsal technique from their ensemble director is more critical to success. In fact, jazz ensemble directors are in a unique position: the timekeeping presence of bass and drums often makes dictating a beat pattern unnecessary. With this being the case, developing one's rehearsal technique becomes all the more valuable. Thankfully, there are numerous ways in which one can work on becoming a more effective rehearsal technician.

# Develop a Rehearsal Plan

One way to cultivate greater effectiveness when leading a jazz ensemble is to set a priority scheme for each rehearsal. Predetermine what you hope to accomplish, having musical and educational intention for each piece. And make certain your developmental goals result from consideration of both short- and long-term educational planning.

**Short-term planning.** Plot out a schedule for each rehearsal, determining what pieces to work on and how long to spend on each one. In addition, consider how much time should be given to warm-ups and other possible rehearsal components, such as directed listening.

*Warm-ups.* Determining how much time to allocate to warm-ups, tone production development, and the building of other fundamental skills is completely dependent on context: the general performance level of your students, the frequency of ensemble rehearsals, the pacing of the group's performance schedule, whether it is an official (graded) class or more of a club, and other similar factors. But the primary factor shaping the degree of emphasis I give to warm-ups and tone production development is the age and experience level of the band. Generally speaking, the younger the band, the more I recognize the need for formalized warm-ups and exercises to improve basic tone production. (Jazz ensembles also have to build their collective rhythmic vocabulary. The rhythmic warm-ups found in chapter 5 in this volume are an excellent resource in this area.)

Ultimately, the most important consideration in apportioning rehearsal time for warm-ups, tone production development, and building fundamental skills is that you respond to what the students need. Do not hold stringently to a system that has worked in the past if it ceases to be relevant for your current group. Decide what *their* general, overall needs are, designing the initial portion of your rehearsals to improve the skills that most need attention.

*Repertoire.* When moving on to repertoire, determine your intention for each piece. Should you be working on more basic musical components such as pitch accuracy and rhythm? Should your goal be to improve other, less fundamental elements? As a practical matter in most situations, the ensemble director must proceed with a more nuanced, layered approach to improve a band's performance, prioritizing which musical components to work on initially. Making determinations regarding the questions posed here depends heavily on context. The most basic variable is familiarity, whether the chart is new to students or has already been rehearsed a few times. But there are other contextual factors. For instance, if students are playing repertoire that is less difficult than the grade level they are used to, the director can demand more right out of the gate. However, the most challenging piece in the folder will require painstaking attention to detail. And it is the ensemble director's obligation to prioritize all the work to be done.

Regardless of context, you should always be guided by an honest, accurate response to what you hear from the band. Identify problems first, then prioritize the order in which you choose to address them. This is the general priority scheme I use when rehearsing repertoire with jazz ensembles: focus on more basic elements before turning to subtler refinements.

*Focus on the basics.* The first one or two times we read a chart of sufficient difficulty to challenge the band, I tend to focus on improving notes (i.e., pitch accuracy) and rhythms. In follow-up readings of the piece (or portions of it), I begin to require greater accuracy in dynamics and articulations. However, I do not wait until notes and rhythms are perfect before making these next-level requests. The approach is more overlapping, like folding in different ingredients in a baking recipe.

*Turn to more subtle refinements.* Depending on what I am hearing from the group, and influenced by the particular qualities of the composition or arrangement, I might next turn to one or more other elements: expression, style, balance and blend issues, note releases, breathing, and so forth. To be clear, this is not to indicate that all these musical subjects can or should be broached during the *first* rehearsal of a piece. Hopefully one can go into ever-deeper levels of instruction during each subsequent rehearsal. But by setting a plan for any *particular* rehearsal, I try to anticipate what might need attention and how far in depth the group might be able to go when working on a piece. And that will inform how much time I allocate to each piece rehearsed that day.

*Addressing intonation concerns.* One final thought about the prioritization of musical components that require improvement: an ensemble's intonation needs continual and ongoing attention. Intonation problems defy simple categorization at some fixed level of priority. Sometimes intonation can be just as critical to address as notes and rhythms, even when sight-reading. But spending too much time on intonation, particularly early on in a rehearsal schedule, can derail momentum and cause focus to dissipate. As a result, there may be occasions when an ensemble director has to let a modest intonation concern go unattended, so as to address other matters. This approach to working on group intonation, while practical, is also highly situational. Remember that one can always amend the subsequent rehearsal schedule to allocate more time to address intonation concerns. See chapter 9 in this volume for exercises specifically intended to improve ensemble intonation.

*Directed listening and stylistic emulation.* As an ensemble director, it can become easy to zone in on improving notes, rhythms, articulations, and other fairly objective ways to make better music. But often the greatest communication between performing ensemble and audience results from paying close attention to more subjective qualities. A piece might be meditative, ebullient, melancholy, evocative, or even confrontational. Or a work might need to be performed in a way that honors unique, historical performance practices. How might a director develop greater expressivity and convincing style emulation skills within the jazz ensemble? And how much emphasis in rehearsals should be given to directed listening to achieve these particular goals?

Traditional notation has some limitations in communicating musical intent to jazz performers. As such, it is absolutely critical for a director to allocate directed listening time during rehearsals. Among other possibilities, students might consider style emulation (identifying performance practices unique to a particular subgenre of the music); interaction and communication between performers; or even more ephemeral qualities, focusing on emotion, drama, or the specific character of a highly programmatic piece.

While there can be great value in creating listening assignments for one's students outside of regular rehearsal time, it is also important to listen to recordings by historically significant jazz artists together as a group. By listening all together, an instructor can encourage focused, deeper consideration of a recording without any distractions. Such directed listening may lead to group discussions in which students reflect on what they have just heard, identifying important musical qualities and finding role-modeling opportunities that may shape their own performances. As an ancillary benefit of the continued use of this approach, students may bring heightened listening skills to whatever music they are exploring independently, outside of class. Given such potential benefits, every ensemble director should periodically set aside some rehearsal time for the purpose of directed listening. The focus can be on complete pieces or simply a few well-chosen musical excerpts that effectively illustrate a particular concept.

**Long-term planning.** Previously I recommended consideration of both short- and long-term goals in plotting out a rehearsal schedule. Turning now to factors impacting long-term planning, the director should identify pieces that will need more frequent rehearsal, determine when sectionals or other alternate rehearsal approaches should happen, and continue to develop students' improvisation skills.

**Rehearsal scheduling.** To help students understand long-term goals for the ensemble, I recommend creating and posting a month-long rehearsal schedule. Ideally, it should receive rolling updates every one or two weeks, showing which pieces will be rehearsed on what days. Posting and updating a month-long rehearsal schedule is not merely a courtesy; multiple benefits will result from announcing longer-term plans. Students will have the opportunity to create practice deadlines for themselves, knowing in advance when pieces will be rehearsed. And for charts requiring an expanded instrumentation, students will know what days to have woodwind doubles or flugelhorns available or when to set up a vibraphone or synthesizer (and keyboard amplifier). Having those ready to go, as opposed to waiting for someone to retrieve and set up an instrument during practice, ensures a more efficient rehearsal.

# Develop Improvisation Skills

As the experiences that both Bruce and Emily had as jazz students a few decades ago clearly indicate, another piece of long-term planning must be a more intentional development of improvisation skills within the ensemble. If students only have the opportunity to improvise when an arranger happens to provide solo space in their part, they will not develop these skills in a meaningful way. Exploring individual and collective creativity through improvisation should be a core component of any jazz performance experience, regardless of ensemble size. (In addition to abbreviated comments here, see chapter 8 in this volume for more thorough examinations of this subject.)

Periodically, a director might set aside rehearsal time for students to improvise on a blues form or a jazz classic like "Doxy" or "Tune-Up." Many different students in the band should have a chance to solo. In addition to providing lead sheets to the students (transposed as necessary), it will be helpful to offer access to play-along recordings of the pieces for follow-up improvisation practice at home.

In an attempt to develop a different type of creativity, I occasionally ask a small group of students to create a free improvisation that evokes the image of an especially programmatic noun, such as hummingbird, glacier, or kite. They are given only the title: no key or tempo, no indication of which student starts it or how it should end (see ⏵ video 4.1, Developing Communication through Free Improvisation).

When you ask four young musicians to play "Glacier" in front of their peer group—with a mutual understanding that the piece does not yet exist—they can sometimes achieve an amazing level of listening and interaction. After such a performance, there should be an opportunity for students to discuss the creative endeavor, with only modest (and encouraging) critique coming from the director. Commonly, students will make mention of how much harder they were listening during the free improvisation. And it is *then* that you can encourage all your students to employ that heightened level of listening every time they play and aim for that level of interaction every time they improvise. There can be tremendous learning opportunities for students in the absence of printed music, especially when the director commits sufficient time in the long-term plan to the development of students' improvisation skills.

## Communicate Effectively

It is a responsibility of any leader to clearly articulate goals and intentions. Certainly effective communication can lead to greater efficiency in managing rehearsal time (see ⏵ video 4.2, Vocalization Rehearsal Techniques in Ensemble Settings). Consider these two ways for an ensemble director to present a critique right after cutting off the band in the middle of a chart:

1. "That note . . . [sings a 2-bar phrase] . . . that note on the & of 2 is marked staccato and some of you are playing it long. Also, the note in the next bar is off on three." [A student asks where in the music the director is talking about.] "Letter G, starting in the fifth bar. Got it? Let's play this again." [Another student interrupts the count-off to ask if the band should start at letter G or at the fifth bar of G.] "Let's start right at letter G."
2. "Everybody find letter G [waits briefly]. Got it? Good. Now count up to the fifth bar of G. That note on the & of 2 is marked staccato . . . [sings a 2-bar phrase] . . . some of you are playing that note long. Also, let's be off on three in the next bar. Can we try this again? Let's start right at letter G."

Which version offers more effective communication? The *content* of the instruction offered is nearly identical. But the order in which that information is presented determines the clarity of the instruction. From the perspective of the students, the second example is far more helpful. They are first told where to look, then they are given a critique. In the initial example, the instruction comes first, then they are told where to look. Students are not going to process that information nearly as well (and a subsequent run-through of that section may be no better).

As a clinician and adjudicator, I see similar moments of ineffective communication from ensemble directors. No single stumble like this is especially critical, and I hold neither myself nor anyone else to an unattainable standard of perfection as communicators. But if one is consistently imprecise with one's choice of words, then moments like the first example accumulate over time, making the director less effective when addressing the band.

**Self-assessment.** How can an ensemble director improve communication skills in this area? Record rehearsals, then go back and listen closely to the way commentary is offered to the band. As a tool for self-critique, listening to rehearsals can help you identify more successful ways to provide information to students. In addition to analyzing the content and clarity of your critiques, you can also gain a sense of the rehearsal's flow, noting how often you stop the band. Part of effective communication can also involve finding the *best* moments to offer a critique.

## Sustain Student Engagement

Effective instruction cannot take place when students are not fully engaged in the educational process. Discussed here are suggestions to help ensemble directors maintain student engagement in rehearsals.

**Embrace a variety of instructional approaches.** Most veteran music educators will tell you student attention spans are shorter now than they were twenty years ago. This change in students is not cause for lamentation. It simply requires adaptability by the instructor. And using greater and more frequent variety in instructional approach is one way to help today's students reach their collective potential.

Variety can be created in a number of different ways. Certainly one should use variety in rehearsing a band. While it might be most common to speak about challenges in a piece using musical terms, one can also sing or clap to students, have students sing or clap back, ask a lead player to demonstrate a passage, listen to recorded examples, employ analogies, or explore other possibilities. It is vital for a director to be able to make a similar point in different ways, especially in settings where the students' skill and experience levels vary widely. Using different instructional methods in rehearsals will ensure better comprehension of one's intent by *all* the ensemble members.

There can also be variety in how the rehearsal schedule is designed. In addition to the traditional rehearsal format, one could separate the band for sectional rehearsals or turn the focus away from repertoire by committing an entire class period to improvisation study or directed listening. Variety can even be created in the way you have the band set up. I sometimes have my jazz ensembles set up in a box shape for a few rehearsals shortly before an upcoming concert (see chapter 2 in this volume for setup illustrations). The box layout, with all instruments facing inward toward a central point, gives musicians a better opportunity to hear each other and understand how their parts fit into the greater whole (see figure 2.12). And the variety often triggers a heightened interest in the music, enticing band members to listen more actively to one another.

**Continually evaluate engagement in the classroom.** How does one know when the time has come to bring more variety to the proceedings? Always make certain to "read the room." As ensemble directors, we frequently ask students to look up, to not have their eyes buried in the music stand. This must be a reciprocal act; we need to look up from our conductor's scores to evaluate the room continuously.

When students are asked to sing their parts, is everyone singing? When you are working with the trombones on the shout chorus, are the trumpets also paying attention? When explaining a new concept to the band members, do their facial expressions indicate a good sense of comprehension? Endeavor to read the room, then respond to what you have observed.

Also, try not to leave any section of the ensemble uninvolved for too long. While this may prove difficult at times, proactive planning with the schedule (such as focusing on a challenging saxophone soli during a sectional rehearsal) will work to your advantage.

Finally, consider limiting technology in the rehearsal space. Distractions created by electronic devices will negatively impact student engagement. If students are truly going to *be in rehearsal*, they cannot only be there physically. They must commit to being fully present, concentrating on the meaningful task of making music together.

**Meet your students where they are.** Make an effort to understand why your students are in the band room with you, why they are in the jazz ensemble. Having that perspective can change how you interact with them. And it can help you sleuth out the most effective ways to work with your students, sustaining a positive classroom environment and maintaining that critical engagement necessary for successful instruction.

We always need to remember that students are in our ensembles for many different reasons, and not all of them have a driving passion to achieve greatness in the art form. Many students may love the social aspects of being in a jazz ensemble as much as the actual process of making music. (Refer to chapter 3 in this volume for a thorough examination of this subject.) As committed educators, we must cultivate student growth and maintain a certain standard of excellence. But the particulars of that standard need to be appropriate for—and attainable by—one's current group of students.

One critical way to meet your students where they are involves programming. Set your students up for success by aligning your artistic desires with what your students *need* (developmentally) and what they can *achieve* (technically). Choosing repertoire specifically for your current group might seem obvious, yet I have seen directors program a favorite chart (think Bill Holman's arrangement of Ernesto Lecuona's "Malagueña") once every four years whether they have students capable of performing it or not. If young musicians sense they will never play a piece in a way that sounds convincing, they will likely feel deflated. And maintaining student engagement in such a situation becomes extremely challenging (see chapter 20 in this volume for many great insights on this topic).

**Speak with charity.** Previously I expressed the importance of effective communication, of speaking with clarity. As a companion to that thought, I also encourage ensemble directors to speak with charity. Addressing one's ensemble in an empathetic, supportive, *charitable* manner helps cultivate a positive learning environment and improves the level of student engagement.

While it is important for directors to be positive and encouraging with students as much as possible, demanding more from an ensemble is always appropriate. This is especially true when a rehearsal is progressing far beneath a group's potential. To offer false praise at such a moment will undermine the credibility of an instructor's words. Yet due to widespread cultural and societal changes, many of today's students are not used to accepting blunt or harsh critiques and are likely to tune out an educator they feel focuses too much on the negative.

I have found the greatest success in ensemble rehearsals by speaking with charity. Praise what truly deserves it, then couch subsequent criticism in uplifting language whenever possible. In choosing my words judiciously, I find I often use phrases such as "even better." Whether I am trying to elevate a student performance from poor to fair or from good to great, I can honestly offer constructive criticism by explaining "how we can make things *even better*." There is less judgment of the performance just completed in such language; instead, there is greater focus on the process of continual improvement. And valuing process over outcome in rehearsal settings often leads to wonderful productivity.

Another way to speak charitably and honor the educational process is to avoid unnecessary overstatement. Comments such as "you *always* speed up there" or "you *never* remember the key signature" are not helpful in establishing a supportive, creative environment. One should encourage students to aspire toward excellence; misplaced hyperbole places barriers before such a goal.

Finally, it is important for students to understand the aforementioned focus on continual improvement, though this may need to be articulated with care. Years ago, when I was directing a jazz ensemble at Bowling Green State University, my lead trombonist asked if I was ever really satisfied with the band. He wondered what more I could want, once the notes, rhythms, dynamics, and articulations seemed right. With a positive demeanor, I responded by offering these words: "I want infinity."

I went on to explain that there would always be more things to work on (balance, blend, stylistic emulation, communication between musicians, a more spontaneous shaping and shading of phrases, etc.) than time available to rehearse. And I explained that for me, making music does not truly begin until the point when he thought we should be finished: when all the notes and rhythms were right. He seemed satisfied with my response, and rehearsal continued along in a constructive manner.

But this young man also helped me realize that students needed to hear such goals explained. When communicated effectively, there can be charity in reframing demands as aspirations. The desire for continual improvement by the ensemble can be presented as a worthwhile goal, one that can lead to ever more satisfying experiences for students and teacher alike. However, such a critical reframing requires the ensemble director be highly skilled in the use of the pedagogical language of jazz.

## Questions for Discussion

1. Bruce and Emily both mention how little training they received in improvisation when they were students. How might a present-day music teacher who is a jazz novice use modern educational resources (and easier access to classic recordings) to successfully develop students' abilities as improvisors and jazz performers?

2. This chapter advocates a well-coordinated approach between short-term and long-term rehearsal planning. What strategies can an ensemble director use to develop the short-term schedule in ways that ensure long-term program goals are met?

3. A single rehearsal might include warm-ups, directed listening, repertoire, and improvisation study. How does one prioritize the time allocated to each? What factors impact such choices, including more spontaneous decisions to change course during a rehearsal?

# 5

# Internal Language of Jazz

Mike Titlebaum

## You Understand It Because You Heard It as a Youngster

One of Emily's earliest experiences hearing recorded jazz was through watching cartoons and hearing the Hoyt Curtin soundtracks that often accompanied them. People who grew up watching *The Flintstones*, *Johnny Quest*, and *The Jetsons* know these soundtracks and the jazz style that was so rich within them. Another one of Emily's early experiences hearing recorded jazz occurred through her parents' listening to their Benny Goodman record collection. Emily recalls this experience:

> My dad had a big thick volume of Benny Goodman's old 33s and that was like the Gospel, the Bible. It was so cool that we almost never heard it. He loved it so much. It was a big thick leather bound collection and he kept it up in the closet where it was this magical thing. I probably only heard it a few times 'cause it was too good to play. But it was something that you realized was very important to people who you thought were really important and that was maybe some of the connection.

While these early experiences with recorded jazz influenced Emily, hearing live jazz was what really hooked her. Emily grew up in Detroit right across from Rouge Park, where trust fund gigs were often held. She recalls "seeing them once in a while in the park and they were just so close that there was a connection there. [That is] the earliest [experience] where I thought, I like this beat, I like this genre, I like what's cooking."

Similarly, Bruce recalls growing up hearing the sounds of Louie Prima, Louis Armstrong, Sinatra, and others from that genre when his parents would have their records on in the background. In addition to hearing recorded music, Bruce recalls

> hearing live music when the local high school stage band would give a public performance: "They were kind of my heroes. They had a stage band that was actually really good. When you have some of that that you listen to, if you have musical sensitivity at all—the jazz phrasing and swing style and all—you understand it because you heard it as a youngster."

Edwin Gordon makes a distinction between executive skills and audiation skills.[1] Executive skills are those involved in physically manipulating the instrument (posture, hand position, breath support, embouchure, tone production, etc.), often referred to as *technique*. Audiation is the ability to hear and comprehend in one's mind sounds that are not physically present. Perhaps the most important aspect of jazz is that it absolutely requires inner hearing—audiation—to perform it effectively. The performers must hear the music inside their head at the moment of producing it; to only hear the music after it comes out of the horn is a recipe for certain disaster. This chapter presents activities for teaching rhythmic and tonal audiation in the jazz ensemble.

## Rhythmic Audiation Exercises

For the listener, the rhythm of jazz is likely the most compelling part of the music. The rhythms make people want to dance. It allows them to feel the music physically. To quote Duke Ellington, "It Don't Mean a Thing If It Ain't Got That Swing." Therefore, we as jazz educators must stress to our students that rhythmic groove is the most important aspect of the music, and it is what makes it unique and beautiful.

When a concert band or symphony orchestra plays a collective warm-up, they often do it with scales or chords—exercises that emphasize some of the most important aspects of the tradition of those groups: tone quality, intonation, blend, and dynamics. Those musical aspects are certainly not unimportant to jazz, but it's more fitting to warm up a jazz group with exercises specific to jazz and to use ones that focus the students' attention on internalizing rhythm, time feel, and groove.

The following warm-up exercises are important to all members of a jazz group, including winds ("horns"), rhythm sections, and vocalists. Wind players cannot simply rely on the rhythm section to "provide" the beat for them; every member of a jazz group must have the same level of dedication to the time feel. Do these exercises at a quick yet comfortable tempo of quarter = 160. In order to ensure that all students feel all the beats as a single unit, play a metronome aloud at quarter = 40 while placing the click on beat 4. This will require the students to "fill in" the remaining beats in their own minds. The act of practicing rhythms in this fashion forces all students to internalize the groove themselves—to feel the beats that nobody else is playing. This internalization of rhythm is the foundation of groove.

Start by writing (or perhaps projecting, if you have a smart board) several straightforward, one-measure rhythms on the board. For this introductory exercise, make sure that each rhythm contains a rest on beat 4, because that is when the click will be heard, and everyone

**FIGURE 5.1** Rhythmic Audiation, Introductory Set

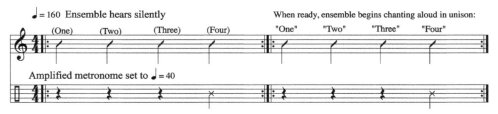

**FIGURE 5.2** Establishing Tempo with the Click on Beat 4

needs to hear it clearly. I like to make sure to use a Charleston rhythm (number 1 in figure 5.1), since that is one of the foundations of swing feel. You can then fill out the board with a few more, tailoring the difficulty and complexity to the age level of the group. The nine rhythms in figure 5.1 work quite well for a young group.

It is important to include some rhythms that outline similar contours. For example, the first four rhythms all end on the & of 2. Those are important because they get everyone comfortable with small variations on a simple pattern. Rhythms 5 and 6 on that line are a bit different. Since both of those rhythms rest on beat 1, students must audiate beat 1 because it is not being sounded by anyone. Rhythms 7, 8, and 9 are more challenging because they are sparser and require even more internalization and independent counting skills to perform them correctly and comfortably. Start the metronome at quarter = 40 and ask the students to "find" the tempo by counting "1-2-3-4" aloud, placing the click on beat 4 (see figure 5.2). This may be tricky the very first time they try it, but after a few sessions they should be able to get the hang of it and be able to find the quarter = 160 tempo readily.

Once the count and click form a steady rhythmic groove, ask the students to play/sing the rhythms on the board on a single pitch. You should point to the various rhythms you want them to perform, before beat 4 of the previous measure, which gives the students suffi-cient preparation time before each rhythm.

At first, have them play/sing one measure at a time, leaving a measure of rest in between each. Once they're ready to progress a bit, leave out the measure of rest so they will play con-tinuously. You can treat this in something of an improvisatory fashion, moving around the board. If the group struggles on any particular rhythm, or if a rhythm does not feel steady, repeat that problematic rhythm multiple times and return to it often. You should drill the rhythms students have trouble with more often than the others, but it is also helpful to regularly return back to number 1, the Charleston rhythm, to ensure that all the students feel well-grounded in the fundamental swing groove.

Sometimes drummers will ask if they can play a complete drum groove along with the horns. This might help at the beginning to get things started, but keep in mind that the purpose of the exercise is to allow everyone in the band to begin to feel the pulse internally without the rhythm section providing it to them. Therefore, as soon as possible, ask the drummer to play only the same rhythms as everyone else without playing any underlying groove.

The next step is to gradually increase the complexity of the exercise, while consistently reminding students that they need to focus on the rhythm and time feel above all other concerns. This increase can occur in a single session or can be spread out over multiple sessions as the group's groove improves. Increasing complexity can take several forms, including (a) adding a melodic element; (b) adding a formal element, such as a blues or another song form; (c) using more challenging rhythms; and (d) using rhythms from a chart you are about to rehearse.

It is important to note that these exercises can be exhilarating, but also mentally tiring for young people. Spend only as much time on these as your students' age and energy level allow. With my college students, I can spend 20 minutes. With high school kids, I only spend 10 minutes on this warm-up. With middle school students, I usually spend no more than five minutes before they start to get antsy. But the person who knows your students best is you; do not let these warm-ups tire them out, because that will not set them up well to have fun and play the music after the warm-up. This is just a way of setting the mood for a great rehearsal.

## Adding a Melodic Element

Once the students feel comfortable with the basic concept, change the exercise slightly by adding some small wrinkle. The objective now is to require them to consciously think about some aspect of music other than rhythmic groove, such as melody or harmony, which they would normally find very easy, and add it to the existing rhythmic exercise. When the rhythmic groove gets worse by adding this melodic element (which it inevitably will), point out to them that rhythmic groove is the most important aspect of jazz, and we can never let our attention to other musical aspects diminish the rhythmic groove or push our attention to groove into the background of our musical minds. One way to add a very small melodic element is to have the students change pitches with each new measure, ascending through the first 5 pitches of a B♭ major scale for the first 4 bars, then descending back down to B♭ for the next 4 bars, while alternating pointing between rhythms 1 and 4 (see figure 5.3).

Pay attention to the students' rhythm. If the rhythmic groove becomes unsteady as a result of adding the scale fragment, or if they make more rhythmic mistakes, stop for a moment and remind them that the entire point of this exercise is to increase the sense of their *rhythm and groove*. Jazz musicians should never let anything—melody, harmony, improvisation, or

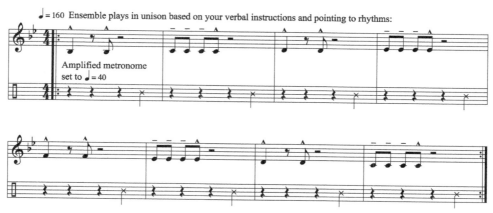

**FIGURE 5.3** Wrinkle 1, Changing Pitches

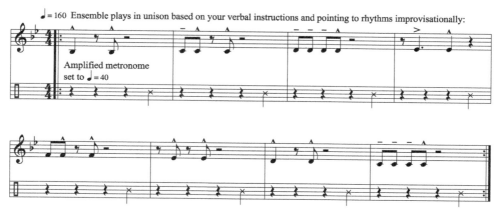

**FIGURE 5.4** Wrinkle 2, Less-Predictable Rhythms

clothing or hairstyle—cause the groove to break down. At any time, if the exercise breaks down, or the group loses track of the click, immediately stop the exercise and return to chanting the "1-2-3-4" count with the click on beat 4.

Once the groove is steady and you determine that the class can successfully navigate the scale fragment with a regular alternating rhythmic pattern, then you might alter the rhythmic pattern to something less predictable (see figure 5.4).

# Adding a Formal Element

A group that has begun to master these rhythms could blend this rhythmic exercise with learning other fundamental aspects of jazz. For example, you could teach students a common jazz form such as the 12-bar blues. Other song forms are also possible, but the 12-bar blues form is so central to jazz that it is a good place to start. Have your group play rhythm 1 on the roots of each chord in a simple blues progression. It will only take a few minutes to aurally teach your group a simple I-IV-V form of the blues (see figure 5.5).

**FIGURE 5.5** Wrinkle 3, Adding the Blues Form

If some students seem to have trouble remembering the roots in the form, you can give them some assistance by holding up one, four, or five fingers, corresponding to each root, one or two beats before each bar to remind them of the root motion. You will not have to do this for long before they all know it well, but as before, remind students that improving the rhythmic groove is still the primary focus.

Learning the root motion is only the first part of learning a form. As soon as the group feels comfortable with the roots while keeping a good rhythmic groove, it is time to give them another exercise. A good exercise that teaches compelling melodic voice leading (guide tone motion) starts with MI, the third note of the tonic chord. This melodic pattern follows the chords of the form by dropping to ME in the 2nd bar, the seventh of the IV chord. It would not take long before the students could follow this guide tone line through an entire blues chorus (see figure 5.6).

Once your students have learned this pattern, it's a good idea to remind them that jazz improvisors use lines like this to "guide" them through the harmonies as they build their solos. If they improvise using nothing but the blues scale, ignoring guide tones completely, they are not capturing some of the key harmonic and melodic devices of the blues that jazz musicians have utilized for a century.

## Adding More Challenging Rhythms

One of jazz musicians' most compelling techniques is rhythmic displacement: moving a rhythm ahead or behind by varying amounts. This can be practiced using the same metronome techniques as those already established, by writing a rhythm of two marcato quarter notes that are subsequently displaced by an eighth note in each bar (see figure 5.7).

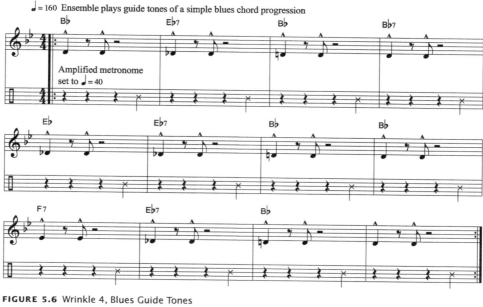

**FIGURE 5.6** Wrinkle 4, Blues Guide Tones

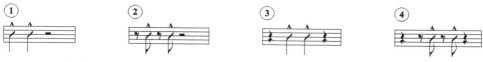

**FIGURE 5.7** Wrinkle 5, Rhythmic Displacement

**FIGURE 5.8** Wrinkle 6, Crossing Over the Bar Line

As you point to the rhythms, you can move sequentially forward or backward through the pattern to create a feeling of a $\frac{7}{8}$ or $\frac{9}{8}$ cross rhythm. For an additional challenge, you can utilize rhythms that start before the downbeat (see figure 5.8).

# Adding Rhythms from a Chart You Are About to Rehearse

The rhythms you use for this rhythmic audiation warm-up can be derived from a piece that you are planning to rehearse during that session. You might even opt not to tell the students at first that this is how you selected these particular rhythms. In one example, the opening melody for a famous big band chart can be distilled down into three distinct rhythms (see figure 5.9).

**FIGURE 5.9** Rhythms from the Tune You're About to Rehearse

**FIGURE 5.10** Rhythms from a Popular Jazz Tune

Can you figure out which famous chart these rhythms come from? If not, perhaps you could identify it once you have assembled the rhythms into a pattern from a song (see figure 5.10).

This is Neil Hefti's classic swing chart "Cute," written for the Count Basie orchestra in the 1950s. You might even get that "aha" moment with your band once they realize what you have done. This method could easily be applied to other pieces, too, and would allow students to focus on the rhythms of a chart outside the context of any potential difficulties they might have playing the right pitches. A video demonstration of me teaching rhythmic audiation using the process outlined in this chapter can be found at the website related to this text (see ⊙ video 5.1, Rhythmic Audiation Exercise).

# Tonal Audiation Exercises

At a recent New York School Band Directors Association (NYSBDA) symposium, I had the privilege of directing the honor jazz band through two days of rehearsals, culminating in a Sunday afternoon performance. The ensemble performed music in a variety of styles, utilizing arrangements that ranged from a simple head/solos/head configuration, to pieces with more complexity and harmony. The arrangement of Dizzy Gillespie's "Night in Tunisia" was so complex that the band was performing in two meters simultaneously: $\frac{5}{8}$ and $\frac{6}{8}$. Afterward, the audience gave the band a rousing standing ovation, and we heard many compliments on the high quality of the performance. This might have been unremarkable, except for the fact that the students performed the entire concert without reading a note; no music stands were even present on stage. Why did we perform this way? And how was it even possible with only two days of rehearsal?

When Tim Savage approached me to direct the honor band, I proposed a novel idea to him and the rest of the NYSBDA executive board: I would prepare the entire concert without sheet music. All the students would learn the melodies to the songs, memorizing them along the way, and we would put together straightforward arrangements that were well-rehearsed and allowed space for individual expression through improvised solos. The process has come to be known as doing "head charts." The meaning of the term is twofold: melodies are often referred to as the "head," and arrangements ("charts") done with this process are often organized into a simple "head-solos-head" structure often used with combos. But in addition, the pieces are taught by ear, and once fully memorized, they are completely kept in the performers' "heads."

Learning music aurally is a long-standing tradition in jazz. Historically, the best jazz players have learned much musical vocabulary by ear. They mimicked the older/wiser generations of players, learned the standard songs from recordings, and worked on improvising in the style of the masters long before setting off on their own to become unique stylists in their own right.

In addition to individual soloists learning their craft by ear, some entire bands have also worked aurally. Kansas City riff-oriented bands like the Count Basie Orchestra often "grew" their arrangements organically. The players learned the melodies, added some simple riffs, perhaps to be used as backgrounds behind a soloist, and even came up with simple shout choruses. Over time they worked up complete arrangements this way. The benefits of this approach are many, but I believe three of the most important ones are (a) ear training, (b) retention, and (c) getting students' eyes and ears out from behind the music stand.

*Ear training.* We want our students to audiate before they play, but we know that all too often, some students just "push the buttons." Learning by ear forces them to hear the notes inside their heads first, only producing them from their instruments after they have heard the melodies. This reasoning extends to improvising solos, too, because we cannot reasonably expect aspiring improvisors to learn to do it successfully without audiating.

*Retention.* Students will retain the melodies for much longer than they might by only playing their own written parts. I believe their lives will be enriched forever by memorizing and thoroughly internalizing the melodies.

*Getting their eyes and ears out from behind the music stand.* We often find that students are so focused on reading their parts that they have a hard time listening to the rest of the ensemble while they play. Using the head chart approach, the instant the arrangements are memorized, students can focus much more of their attention on aspects of ensemble playing, which fall into the category of "making music": things like blend, intonation, good tone, rhythm, and time feel.

## Head Charts

We didn't start completely from scratch. Before the symposium, I selected songs I thought could be learned in approximately an hour or less. I gave students and band directors access to a Dropbox folder in which I posted lead sheets of the melody and chord changes, along with several classic jazz recordings of each song. When the group finally assembled, the songs were not completely foreign to them.

Once we began rehearsals, I had the rhythm section establish the key center by playing the tonic chord. Then I played the first note of the song on my instrument and asked the entire band (including the rhythm section) to sing and play that pitch. Next I quieted them down and played the first two notes of the melody to see if they could successfully navigate the first interval. Sometimes I would have them sing rather than play first, depending on how complex the melody was.

Slowly, over the course of several minutes, we learned the first complete phrase of the song. We then repeated it multiple times, having the rhythm section play the groove and chords of the song. Often we would "loop" a few bars for a more effective memorization exercise. Many kids today who use GarageBand or other audio software inherently understand looping, so this familiarity can be used to speed up the process. We continued on, learning more phrases of the melody, always doubling back to the beginning to make sure the band did not forget the portions already learned. It is important to end each rehearsal with a review of what was learned during that session.

Once the ensemble had memorized the melody, we started putting together an arrangement. I have found that the most clear arranging ideas are often simple ones, such as having (a) one instrumental section play the melody for half a chorus, then a different section for the second half; (b) one section play a background (for a soloist or the melody) of guide tones in half or whole notes; (c) an improvised solo section be played, with possible backgrounds; and (d) one player improvise a bluesy riff, which can be repeated for rhythmic/propulsive backgrounds and then be played louder or higher or be harmonized simply for a shout chorus.

One fun blues to learn is Thelonious Monk's "Misterioso." The melody is comprised of a pattern of straight eighth notes that outline the blues harmony using ascending 6ths. It has three things going on simultaneously: a simple bass part of chord roots and 5ths in whole notes, a lower melodic line, and an upper melodic line. It is fairly straightforward to teach the three lines separately, one bar at a time, assigning them to the various instruments based on their tessitura (see figure 5.11). A video demonstration of me teaching this blues head can be found at the website (see ⊙ video 5.2, Teaching a Blues Head Aurally).

The harmonic progression for this blues is comprised entirely of I, IV, and V chords, so I held up fingers indicating the root to remind the students which chord they were about to play. The entire song can be taught in about 15 or 20 minutes. Many other blues heads can also be taught and arranged fairly quickly; Charlie Parker's "Now's the Time," Sonny Rollins's "Tenor Madness," Monk's "Blue Monk," and Oscar Pettiford's "Blues in the Closet" are all relatively easy to work with in this context.

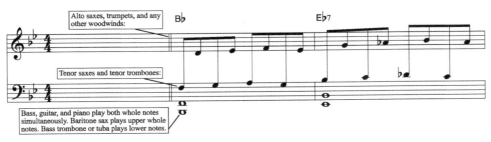

**FIGURE 5.11** "Monk Tune"

# Coda

Even though I strongly feel that the aural traditions of jazz are integral to learning the art form, I do not believe that teaching music by ear is the only way to direct a big band. In fact, there is a tremendous amount of beautiful, historic, and intricately arranged jazz ensemble music that is perhaps almost never played from the written page. The great works by master writers like Duke Ellington, Thad Jones, Sammy Nestico, Neil Hefti, and Bill Holman are almost always performed as head charts. But that should not stop us from engaging our students in purposeful, active audiation training, and incorporating the rhythmic and tonal audiation exercises suggested in this chapter is a great way of helping to ensure that when our students do perform written notation, they are doing so in tune and in time.

# Questions for Discussion

1. What are some challenges of having students listen to jazz? What are some possible solutions?
2. What are some elements of musicianship common to concert band and jazz band? Are there elements that do not overlap?
3. What are the relative benefits and drawbacks to ear-based instruction?
4. What are the differences between executive skills and audiation skills? How can we teach for each?
5. From a music education perspective, how do you feel about the author's statement, "The performers must hear the music inside their head at the moment of producing it; to only hear the music after it comes out of the horn is a recipe for certain disaster"?

# Note

1. Edwin E. Gordon, *Learning Sequences in Music: A Contemporary Music Learning Theory* (Chicago: GIA, 2007).

# PART III

# Teaching Beginning Jazz

# 6

# Beginning Woodwinds and Brass

Bruce Dalby

**Everyone Is Welcome vs. Oboes Need Not Apply**

Bruce believes that students should have the opportunity to play jazz regardless of their instrument, and without regard for having a set number of each instrument. For Bruce, allowing all students to participate in jazz ensemble on their primary instrument is important because his primary goal is nonexclusionary participation, rather than traditional instrumentation. Such participation increases students' musical enjoyment and, he hopes, encourages them to continue into his high school ensemble:

> We have clarinets and flutes. I even have clarinets in my high school jazz band just because they want to play. I used to get into arguments with my friend Paul, who would say, "How can you let clarinets into a big band?" I was like, "well, because they want to, you know." I don't care. The bassoon and oboe don't really lend themselves, I suppose, but there is jazz everything. The function of jazz band for me, especially at the middle school level, is just for the kids to play because it is fun and they want to play.

> Emily, on the other hand, notes that if she were only teaching improvisation, then she would be more apt to allow nontraditional big band instruments (e.g., oboe, bassoon, horn) into the class. However, the focus of her jazz ensemble is as much on big band literature as it is on improvisation; consequently, she limits the instrumentation to that for which "traditional" big band literature is written: "I think it all depends on the scenario that you are given. If you are saying that you are doing it as an exploratory and everyone gets a feel for jazz, it's another thing. If you are doing it in the real world where you are going to go out and play a lot of events, I think you have to be a little more selective about what is written there for jazz band."

Many school jazz programs in North America do an impressive job of developing their members' technical and music-notation-reading skills, necessary to perform jazz big band literature with polish and precision. In my view, however, the list of skills many jazz students lack is as notable as those they possess.

At its core, jazz is a vernacular tradition, yet many school jazz students are as dependent on notation as they are in the concert band. Although the young jazzers may take improvised solos in jazz band performances, they may be unable to negotiate chord changes or incorporate characteristic jazz vocabulary. At the end of several years of instruction, the number of jazz tunes the jazzer can play by ear is few—possibly even zero (and forget about transposing to other keys!). Finally, although jazz is fundamentally a chamber music genre,[1] with members of the jazz combo collaboratively directing their music making, our typical jazz student remains dependent on the teacher to meaningfully make music with others.[2]

In light of this, I identify three foundational topics for the reader to consider in fashioning an authentic and effective jazz curriculum: (1) establishing a listening foundation, (2) developing ear-playing ability, and (3) developing a personal repertoire of jazz tunes. Following these sections I address (4) style and articulation and (5) rhythm.

## Establishing a Listening Foundation

Jazz educators have emphasized the importance of listening since for a long time, but developing in students the disposition to listen to jazz on their own initiative is enormously challenging. It is many decades, after all, since jazz could be considered popular music; recent market research puts it at 1.4 percent of music consumption in the United States.[3] Therefore, it is reasonable to assume that the majority of jazz students start their instruction with little familiarity with the art. Most are probably attracted to the jazz program because of social[4] and perceived "coolness" factors.

Still, the jazz educators must do their best to foster the development of students' listening habits. Directed listening[5] in class has the potential to spark self-initiated listening and also allows the instructor to deepen understanding by providing musical and cultural-historical context. And as the band room is a second home to many students, they should regularly hear jazz tracks being played on the band room sound system before school, at lunchtime, and after school. Finally, although students' musical tastes are formed by multiple factors—including pervasive music media—music teachers are often among their most admired role models. Make the most of your influence by modeling your passion for jazz during listening episodes and describing your own jazz listening experiences and priorities.

## Developing Ear-Playing Ability

The skills needed to play by ear are of two types: aural and executive. The student must first audiate[6] the music to be played, then connect that audiation to the physical manipulation of the instrument. The goal is for the instrument to become an outer extension of the inner audiation instrument.

In my view, two tools are essential:

1. Singing. This is not a new idea, of course. Influential wind instrument educators have long advocated that students learn to "sing" through their instruments. Consider the renowned brass pedagogue Arnold Jacob's motto: "Song and wind."
2. Tonal solfège syllables. Solfège syllables facilitate the retention of tonal patterns in students' long-term memory. They also help simplify transposition complexities associated with wind instruments built in various keys.

Following are suggested sequential procedures for introducing ear-playing activities with wind instrumentalists who have undergone a period of traditional notation-based instruction. Notice that I recommend simple traditional tunes for initial instruction. Jazz tunes are typically unfamiliar and often too complex for the beginner. Consider delaying the introduction of jazz heads until ear-playing skills have begun to develop.

1. Start by playing—and singing—something familiar: A B♭ concert scale (see ⊙ video 6.1, Scale with Singing and Tonal Syllables).
2. Learn a simple melody by rote (see ⊙ video 6.2, "Rhody" in B♭).
3. Teach the root melody of the tune in the same fashion (see ⊙ video 6.3, Root Melody to "Rhody").
4. Play the same melody in a different key (see ⊙ video 6.4a, E♭ and A♭ Scales, and ⊙ video 6.4b, "Rhody" in E♭ and A♭).
5. Introduce minor tonality (see ⊙ video 6.5, C Minor Scale).
6. Learn a simple tune in minor (see ⊙ video 6.6, Minor "Rhody" in C).

With this foundation established, numerous further steps beneficial for aural and ear-to-hand musicianship development can be implemented in good sequence. For example:

- Teach more tunes.
- Teach more tonalities, such as Dorian and Mixolydian.
- Teach more keys (see ⊙ video 6.7, Minor "Rhody" in F).
- Teach *si* (raised *so*), the leading tone in minor tonality. The melody of "Joshua," for example, a tune students love to play, uses the leading tone. ("Joshua" is also an ideal tune for introducing swing rhythm and style.) (See ⊙ video 6.8a, Harmonic Minor Scale; and ⊙ video 6.8b, "Joshua" in C Minor.)
- Teach basic harmonization practices (see ⊙ video 6.9a, Tonic and Dominant Arpeggios in Major Tonality; ⊙ video 6.9b, Major Scales and Arpeggios in Five Keys; and ⊙ video 6.9c, Harmonizing "Rhody").
- Teach more tonal functions (chords) and associated tunes.
- Introduce improvisation.

# Developing a Personal Repertoire of Jazz Tunes

School music programs in North America have a long and glorious history of emphasizing performance quality. Thousands of bands, choruses, orchestras—and yes, jazz bands!—across the land regularly achieve standards of excellence that are the envy of the world.

In my view, however, our programs achieve much less with the flipside of quality: quantity. Six or more weeks of an organization's rehearsal time may be spent intensively polishing just a few selections. Competitive marching bands are particularly notable in this regard; they may rehearse 10 minutes of music for three or four months or more. As a result, students may finish six or more years of school music instruction with exposure to a rather narrow range of musical material. Might this have something to do with the limited level of musical independence and initiative with which the average school musician graduates from high school? I believe so.

Jazz musicians, on the other hand, are musical hoarders; they learn as many tunes as possible. Ask accomplished lounge pianists how many tunes they know and the answer—after a quizzical pause, eyes looking skyward—is likely to be "I have no idea!" No doubt the number is in the thousands, though.

In a perfect world, all wind instrumentalists would come to their first day of jazz instruction able to sing and play by ear numerous melodies: traditional melodies; music they've heard around the home and in church; favorite examples of popular, rock and movie music; and more. In the real world in which most of us live and teach, it may be necessary to begin ear-playing instruction and tune repertoire building activities in the fashion just described, with simple traditional melodies rather than jazz literature.

At some point in your program it will be appropriate to start teaching jazz heads. Many, of course, require technique beyond the beginner's ability, so choices should be made with care. The primary criterion for inclusion is the technical difficulty of the melody. The associated chord changes are not necessarily appropriate for beginning improvisation instruction. ⊙ Video 6.10a, Learning a Jazz Head by Rote 1; ⊙ video 6.10b, Learning a Jazz Head by Rote 2; ⊙ video 6.11, Root Melody and Guide Tone Line Processes; and ⊙ video 6.12, Improvising Around Blues Guide Tone Lines all involve learning jazz heads and harmony (root melodies and guide tone lines) by rote, with no notation. See also ⊙ appendix 6.1 for a list of tunes appropriate for beginning improvisation. This list is not meant to be exhaustive or authoritative—there are certainly many other possible choices—but could serve as a good starting place, especially for a teacher with limited jazz experience.

## Style and Articulation

Many of the technical challenges beginning jazz students face are associated with style and articulation. Wind articulation in jazz style differs from classical[7] articulation in several crucial ways. As with all facets, listening to and rote copying of authentic jazz performances should provide the foundation for the beginner's learning. In addition, though, analysis and systematic drill have a valid role to play in enhancing the efficiency of skill development work. Videos addressing style and articulation include ⊙ video 6.13, Legato and Accented Legato; ⊙ video 6.14, Extended Scale Exercises in B♭ Major; and ⊙ video 6.15, Extended Scale Exercise with Up-Down Tonguing.

# Stylistic Chanting of Figures

Begin instruction of each new articulation concept without the instrument. Many of the excellent method materials now available include recommended syllables for chanting jazz figures. A commonly used method, Mike Steinel's *Essential Elements for Jazz Ensemble*,[8] starts by distinguishing between classical and swing treatment of a basic rhythm (see figure 6.1).

Steinel advocates the use of a variety of consonants for conveying accent and inflection characteristics, hence his use of the "b" consonant for accented upbeats. I side with other authors, who recommend chanting with only the "d" consonant used to start notes on the instrument (see figure 6.2). Enactive experience—students immediately echoing your chanted models—is most important, but if you choose to provide written examples of chanted figures, consider putting unaccented notes in lowercase and accented notes in uppercase, highlighting this essential distinction (see figure 6.3). Choosing from among the various style syllable systems—some of which seem to me to be overly complex—will likely take some study. In the interest of simplicity, I offer a system that requires only four primary syllables.

**For notes followed immediately by another note, with no break in sound.** May be as short as an eighth note, or may be elongated:

doo (unaccented)
DAH (accented)

**For notes followed by a break in the sound.** The break may be a notated rest or the silent part of a note played shorter than its rhythmic value, such as a staccato or marcato

Tah Tah Tah Tah Tah    Doo Bah Doo Bah Dot

**FIGURE 6.1** Classical and Swing Treatment of a Basic Rhythm

Doo Dah Doo Dah Dot

**FIGURE 6.2** Using "D" Consonant to Start Notes

doo DAH doo DAH DOT

**FIGURE 6.3** Accented Notes in Uppercase

("housetop" accent; see figure 6.4 for an example of these syllables applied to jazz rhythms) quarter note:

>   dit (unaccented; typically, a staccato quarter note on beat 1 or 3)
>   DAHT (accented; eighth notes, quarter notes, and various elongations)

# Classical and Jazz Articulation Compared

A good place to start in analyzing jazz style is to compare jazz and classical articulation. I identify four primary jazz articulation characteristics here.

**1. Extensive use of connected articulation.** Connected articulation is also important in classical playing, of course, but it has a uniquely distinctive and rather pervasive role in jazz. While learning the distinction between separated and connected style is a standard part of beginning classical wind instruction, many students do not develop good connected articulation by the time they begin jazz studies, so remedial work may be needed. Begin by vocalizing for your class three pairs of connected straight eighth notes followed by a quarter note ("doo-doo, doo-doo, doo-doo, doo"), and on beat 4 of the 4-beat pattern provide a preparatory conducting gesture to signal students to echo your pattern without any break.

When adding instruments to the mix, a scale exercise is an appropriate first step. Although contrived and nonidiomatic, scale exercises can be beneficial in that they provide students the opportunity to focus attention on one issue at a time, and they make for lots of needed repetition. Further, because scales are familiar, they help facilitate the introduction of new concepts and skills *without* notation.

Start by doing multiple repetitions of each note in a familiar scale (see figure 6.5). Then do the same exercise with swing eighth notes. Follow this with patterns having two notes per scale degree (see figure 6.6) and one note per scale degree (see figure 6.7). Scale and arpeggio exercises from band methods or instrumental technique publications are excellent vehicles for further work in developing connected style.

dit doo DAH    doo DAH doo DAHT    DAHT    DAHT DAH doo doo DAHT    doo DAHT DAHT

**FIGURE 6.4** Sample Jazz Rhythms with Recommended Articulation Syllables

**FIGURE 6.5** Connected Articulation, Exercise 1

**FIGURE 6.6** Connected Articulation, Exercise 2

**FIGURE 6.7** Connected Articulation, Exercise 3

**FIGURE 6.8** Accented Connected Articulation, Exercise 1

**FIGURE 6.9** Accented Connected Articulation, Exercise 2

**FIGURE 6.10** Accented Connected Articulation, Exercise 3

**2. Accented connected articulation, especially on off beats.** As stated previously, connected articulation is a technique fundamental to both jazz and classical styles. Unique to jazz practice, however, is the use of accents on connected notes, a technique *never* needed in classical playing. And for the beginning jazz student, the challenge of performing accented connected notes correctly is magnified by the rhythmic context; accents usually occur on off beats.

As always, begin drill instruction with chanting. For pairs of swing eighth notes in the typical unaccented-accented relationship, use the syllables "doo-DAH." The first exercises with the instrument might be as previously shown, with a 4-beat pattern on each step of a familiar scale in a swing rhythm (see figure 6.8), followed by two notes per scale degree, also in swing (see figure 6.9), followed by one note per scale degree, also in swing (see figure 6.10).

Expect to work on exercises such as these over an extended period. In my experience, even diligent, high-achieving students rarely have immediate success with these new skills. They typically struggle with one or both of two issues:

1. Putting a slight separation before the accented off-beat eighth note. Emphasize that connected swing eighths must be completely "shoulder to shoulder"; even the slightest space degrades style unacceptably. We touch the airstream with the tongue without actually stopping it.
2. Difficulty maintaining the off-beat accent scheme. An extended sequence of eighth notes with off beats accented is counterintuitive to a student brought up in the strong-weak accent scheme of classical music literature.

Scale exercises such as these should soon make way for more rhythmically idiomatic studies. Jazz method books provide many excellent exercises. Even more valuable are genuine

doo DAH doo  DAH    etc.

**FIGURE 6.11** "Blue Monk" Example

**FIGURE 6.12** Hard Accents with Charleston Rhythm

jazz heads such as those listed previously, preferably learned and played by rote. "Blue Monk" is an ideal vehicle for novices to work on accented connected off beats. The first measure is shown in figure 6.11 with appropriate style syllables.

**3. Harder articulation.** Turn on a recording of one of the great jazz big bands playing the shout section of a heavy swinger and listen carefully for their use of accent. They accent *really* hard, don't they?! Classical large ensembles such as band and orchestra, of course, can also play very loud—and they likewise make use of accent—but there are important distinctions between the two styles that the jazz novice must learn.

In classical playing, the loudest part of an accented note is not at the very beginning; the accent follows the consonant by a microsecond, as in "ta-HAW." Then the volume of the body of the note is usually tapered, with the end of the sound dissipating into silence (the "Tah" from Steinel's example).

Accents in jazz and related styles tend to be more pressurized, explosive; the air gushes forth immediately upon release of the tongue. Furthermore, the ends of notes that precede space also get a harder treatment; note the consonant "t" at the end of "dot" and "DAHT" in our jazz-style syllables. Wind players often stop the note with the tongue, a practice rarely if ever implemented in classical playing.

A good way to practice hard accents would be to drill variations of the Charleston rhythm (see figure 6.12).

Finally, keep in mind that the aural impact of an accented note is only partially a function of its absolute volume. Contrast also plays a crucial role. Immature players sometimes make the mistake of playing every note in a shout passage accented. But if everything is accented, nothing is accented! If you want accented notes to really "pop," make sure they are surrounded by unaccented notes that are considerably softer.

**4. Articulations are frequently dependent on tempo.** Let's look again at "Blue Monk." Play the first figure at an appropriate medium tempo (quarter = 124), tonguing all four accented and unaccented connected notes as previously described. Now play the figure repeatedly, increasing the tempo each time. At some point, it becomes impractical to tongue all four notes. But put a slur between the second and third notes, as shown in figure 6.13, and you will find that the figure "lays" nicely.

This technique of "slurring across the beat" is used extensively by jazz players; many authoritative sources recommend it, sometimes using the term *up/down tonguing*. The tongued upbeat note gets some degree of accent, and the slurred-to note on the downbeat

doo DAH oo DAH    etc.

**FIGURE 6.13** Articulation at Faster Tempos

**FIGURE 6.14** Slurring Across the Beat, Exercise 1

etc.

**FIGURE 6.15** Slurring Across the Beat, Exercise 2

**FIGURE 6.16** Slurring Across the Beat, Exercise 3

is unaccented. As always, scale exercises can be beneficial for drilling this new skill (see figure 6.14).

A good way to extend this exercise is to play the same pattern starting on multiple scale degrees (see figure 6.15). Wind players of intermediate level and above can learn this exercise, by rote, up to scale degree 5 and back, in multiple keys; Bb, Ab, and C work well for the various wind instrument registers. It will take repetition over a period of weeks to get all members of your jazz band up to speed, but the benefits to jazz articulation skill development—as well as general wind instrument technique—will be significant.

Note that the "slur across the beat" technique is not universally applied. Melodic contour also plays a role, with accents (tongued notes) usually occurring on melodic high points, which may be on downbeats instead of off beats. Figure 6.16 is an example of a passage in which an accented downbeat (beat 1 in measure 2) would be preceded by three slurred eighths. Typically, none of these slurs would be notated. The example shows how such a line—at a brisk tempo—would likely be performed by an experienced player. So, regarding where to tongue and slur, three rules apply to the majority of up-tempo cases:

1. Tongue the first note of a figure.
2. Slur across the beat, accenting most tongued upbeats, except where melodic contour suggests an exception.
3. Tongue the last note of a figure.

When I clinic or adjudicate young jazz groups, rule 3 almost always comes up. Students often know that the last note of a figure requires an accent, but it is difficult, if not impossible, to execute the accent effectively with a slur. When the slur is replaced by the tongue, the "punch" of the accent is significantly enhanced. This sort of error may sometimes be the result of inappropriate slur markings; an entire phrase may reside under a slur's graceful arch. The editor's intention may be to convey a general sense of flow and connectedness, but if the student takes the slurs literally—and does not use the tongue to accent appropriate notes—the drive of swing will be lost. Note that slurring and tonguing issues specific to trombone are addressed in chapter 15 of this volume.

# Rhythm

Rhythm in jazz and related styles differs from classical music primarily in the extensive use of syncopation. The complexity of these rhythms poses demanding challenges to the young learner, so teaching procedures and sequence must be carefully considered. A thorough analysis of the content of jazz rhythms is beyond the scope of this chapter. Instead, I briefly describe three general pedagogical principles the reader may find conducive to the delivery of effective and efficient rhythm instruction.

## Teach One Thing at a Time

Educators from all disciplines agree that "information overload" is detrimental to learning. When introducing new rhythm content, consider first the "sound before sight" principle. Music notation reading should be a process of recognition, not decoding, so experiences of listening to and performing new rhythms should come first. During initial stages, reduce the complexity of the learning task further by also removing the instrument from the equation. Appropriately sequenced chanting and movement activities, as described later in this chapter, provide the readiness for presenting the notation (symbolic association) for new rhythms being studied, then later reintroducing the instrument to the process.

## Use Rhythm Syllables

Used appropriately, rhythm syllables help students build a vocabulary of rhythm patterns in long-term memory by exemplifying the similarities and differences among patterns. Many rhythm syllable systems exist, so choosing well is crucial. The "1-e-&-a" system is common in instrumental programs, but I find that students brought up in that system are typically not fluent with the syllables. They may be able to analyze rhythms—for example, "play that note on the 'and' of 2, not beat 3"—but struggle to chant with the syllables from notation or to apply the syllables to heard rhythm patterns.

I recommend the Gordon rhythm syllables for their performability, among other merits.[9] In the Gordon system, beats—what he calls macrobeats—are performed with the syllable *du* (pronounced "doo"). When the basic division of the beat is duple (simple meter),[10] the syllables are *du-de* ("doo-day") (see figure 6.17). For triple subdivision (compound meter), *du-da-di* ("doo-dah-dee"), see figure 6.18. When duple beat subdivisions are divided, the syllable used is *ta* ("tuh") (see figure 6.19).[11]

**FIGURE 6.17** Simple Meter Rhythmic Solfège

**FIGURE 6.18** Compound Meter Rhythmic Solfège

**FIGURE 6.19** Simple Meter Rhythmic Solfège with Subdivision

**FIGURE 6.20** "Blue Monk" Example, Written

**FIGURE 6.21** "Blue Monk" Example, Performed

**FIGURE 6.22** Up-tempo Rhythmic Figure, Written

**FIGURE 6.23** Up-tempo Rhythmic Figure, Audiated

Swing is pervasive in jazz and must be accounted for. At slow to medium tempos, the duration relationship of eighth note pairs is two to one, so triple syllables are called for. Our motif from "Blue Monk" is notated as in figure 6.20, but is performed as in figure 6.21, so its assigned rhythm syllables would be as shown.

As tempo increases, the swing of eighth notes evens out, but—perhaps serendipitously—so does the need for the jazz musician to audiate bigger beats. At all tempos, most jazz literature is notated in $\frac{4}{4}$,[12] but experienced players feel fast tempos in $\frac{2}{2}$, or "¢." Observe an advanced jazz big band playing an up-tempo chart, and you will notice that those players who move to the beat—by tapping the foot, swaying, or nodding—move to half notes. Quarter notes are too fast; they are audiated as beat subdivisions. So a rhythm such as that shown in figure 6.22 is audiated as in figure 6.23, with the indicated macrobeat-microbeat-division syllables.

## Use Rhythmic Movement

Music educators agree that movement is an essential tool for teaching rhythm. Although rhythmic relationships can be analyzed mathematically, such analysis doesn't help students internalize and retain rhythm patterns in long-term memory. Effective instruction focuses on how rhythm is *felt* through bodily movement.

There are various systems for combining movement with rhythm syllable chanting. I agree with Gordon that it is essential for students to concurrently and enactively experience the three essential elements of rhythm: beats, beat subdivisions, and melodic rhythm. The following sequence works well. Depending on the circumstances, you may find it appropriate to have students put their instruments aside, look away from their notation, or both.

- With students seated, establish an appropriate tempo. For duple beat subdivisions (up-tempo jazz in 2/2 and straight eighth note genres such as rock, funk, and Latin), quarter note = 100 or so is good. For triple beat subdivisions (slow or medium swing), quarter note = 80.
- Put beats in the heels. Movement should be steady and relaxed, without stomping.
- Put beat subdivisions in the hands, "patching" lightly with the fingertips on the thighs just above the knees.
- Chant rhythm syllables corresponding to the rhythm being studied.[13]

The extent to which you engage both types of movement may depend on your circumstances. For example, when a slow or medium swing rhythm pattern is particularly challenging to students, it makes sense to slow the tempo to the point where they can patsch triple beat subdivisions without straining to keep up. On another occasion, if you are confident that students audiate the triple beat division competently, it might be fine to have them patsch only to the swing eighth notes, omitting the middle triplet ("du-di, du-di," etc.), or perhaps just moving their feet to beats.

A final point about movement in relation to jazz groove is warranted. Jazz teachers often advocate that students tap their feet on beats 2 and 4 of each measure, the "backbeat." This is fine advice for promoting good swing feel, but it takes audiation and coordination, so getting students to execute the skill accurately will likely require sequential steps. Consider the following:

1. In initial instruction students, move one or both feet to quarter note beats, as previously described.
2. When they have developed sufficient coordination, they alternate feet to the beat, marching style; left, right, left, right, and so on. (Leading with the left is chosen because many students are likely to be in marching band, where that practice predominates.)
3. The next step is go to bigger beats. Drop the right foot and keep the left foot going on 1 and 3.
4. Finally, reverse step 3. Drop the left foot and move the right foot on 2 and 4.

## Putting It All Together

Coordinated chanting and moving activities are effective for rhythms encountered in jazz literature as well as those found in curricular materials such as jazz method books or rhythm flash cards. For patterns that are unfamiliar to students, appropriately sequenced rote call-and-response activities are needed. The teacher chants a pattern—often 4 beats, but sometimes longer—and students echo in time, without a break between patterns. Ideally, a neutral syllable stage ("bah" works well) would precede the use of rhythm syllables, but many teachers are apt to skip that stage due to time constraints. At the least, though, have the patience to allow patterns to "sink in," to be audiated and stored in students' memories, before proceeding to notation reading.

# Conclusion

The technical, stylistic, and rhythm reading skills that students typically develop as members of school jazz ensembles provide them access to deeply meaningful and motivating experiences of a wonderful art form. Jazz educators should feel proud of the high standards achieved by many school performing groups. By putting a high priority on the aural and ear-to-hand skills addressed early in this chapter, teachers can assist their students in gaining the musical independence and initiative necessary for a fulfilling jazz life after graduation.

# Questions for Discussion

1. At the middle school level, Bruce values participation more than instrumentation in the middle school jazz band and thus allows students with all instruments to join. Where do you stand on this issue?
2. Emily says that if she were only teaching improvisation, she would be more inclined to allow students with "nontraditional jazz instruments" into jazz ensemble. Why might this be the case?
3. What are your views regarding instrumentation in the high school jazz ensemble? Are they different than your views regarding instrumentation in the middle school ensemble?

# Notes

1. Chapter 8 in this volume also addresses the chamber music character of jazz.
2. This paragraph describes my considerable experience, but of course there are exceptions.
3. http://s0.thejazzline.com/tjl/uploads/2015/03/nielsen-2014-year-end-music-report-us.pdf.
4. See chapter 3 in this volume for an elaboration on this topic.
5. See chapter 4 in this volume for a more in-depth discussion of class listening activities.
6. *Audiation* is Edwin E. Gordon's term for thinking music in the mind, with comprehension. For further information visit www.giml.org.
7. Other terms sometimes used to characterize the world of music outside of jazz and related styles (rock, fusion, Latin, commercial, pop, etc.) are *symphonic* and *traditional*. Perhaps no single word is ideal, but let's at least agree to banish forever the term *legit*. What could be more legitimate, after all, than North America's most significant contribution to art?!

8. Mike Steinel and Michael Sweeney, *Essential Elements for Jazz Ensemble: A Comprehensive Method For Jazz Style and Improvisation* (Hal Leonard Corp., 2000).

9. For a description of Gordon's rhythm syllable system, including some suggested adaptations, see Bruce Dalby, "Toward an Effective Pedagogy for Teaching Rhythm: Gordon and Beyond," *Music Educators Journal* 92, no. 1 (September 2005): 54–60.

10. Gordon's term for beat subdivisions is *microbeat*.

11. We won't concern ourselves here with divisions of triple beat subdivisions.

12. Genres with a triple component to their meter, such as jazz waltzes and $\frac{12}{8}$ Afro-Cuban, are beyond the scope of this discussion.

13. Some teachers have students perform melodic rhythm by clapping. Among the drawbacks to this practice, in my view, is that there is no way to perform note durations, and expressiveness through vocal inflection is lost. Further, students struggle to keep up with fast passages, whereas with an appropriately performable syllable system they have little difficulty chanting fluently and in time.

# 7

# Beginning Rhythm Section

Chad West, C. Michael Palmer, Michael Grace,
and Daniel Fabricius

## Driving the Car and Making the Horns Sound Good

The rhythm section at Bruce's middle school consists of "whoever shows up" for jazz band on a given Monday morning at 7:30. This year that most often consists of a bass player and a drummer. This year there is no piano player; consequently, Bruce plays piano with the group each morning. Being a trombone player and identifying primarily as a "concert band" director rather than a "jazz band" expert, Bruce is less familiar with the instrumental pedagogy of the rhythm section instruments normally found in a jazz band than he is with "traditional" concert band instrument pedagogy. Nevertheless, Bruce is a sensitive musician and knows what he wants to hear stylistically from the rhythm section. When asked what he wants to hear from that section, Bruce became a bit self-conscious as if he were about to give "the wrong answer" and admitted that he teaches the rhythm section that their job is little else than to "provide a harmonic foundation for the horn players and to make the horn players sound good."

> Rhythm. Rhythm and chords. This is probably terrible. You are probably going to use this as the example of everything not to do, but their function is to make [the horn players'] jobs possible. I'm much more interested in what the saxes and trumpets and trombones are doing. And your job is to make their job possible and I'm going to pay attention to [the horns] and you guys just function. I'm the offensive genius and you're the left tackle. It's your job to block so that my incredible quarterback can do his job.

Emily dedicates a lot of rehearsal time to teaching the rhythm section. Part of the reason is that Emily feels that the role of a rhythm section player is more difficult and takes longer to develop than the role of a horn player within jazz ensemble. To help them understand what their roles are in the ensemble, Emily tells the rhythm section that they are the engine of the car:

> "The saxophones, they're the cool paint job and everyone else is the rims and the 'bling,' but man, you're it—you're the car." I joke about [the TV show] *Pimp my Ride*. I say, "what do they do on *Pimp My Ride*, they go and they give some guy a brand-new exterior, but underneath, man it's not happening. That car will look beautiful, but in two months it's going to be in the dumpster because it doesn't have the inner workings to make it work every time."

These two vignettes point out the essential role of the rhythm section in the jazz ensemble: to maintain time by playing a steady groove (i.e., bass and drums) while providing sufficient harmonic support to the ensemble and soloists (i.e., guitar and piano). Learning how to do this requires an understanding of the role of each instrument in the section and what basic rhythmic and harmonic techniques are expected. This chapter addresses the teaching of the rhythm section with regard to (a) interpreting rhythm section notation, (b) bass, (c) piano, (d) guitar, (e) drum set, (f) auxiliary instruments, and (g) rhythm section rehearsal strategies.

# Interpreting Rhythm Section Notation

Due to the growth of jazz programs in schools since the 1960s, the music publishing industry has produced a wide variety of sheet music for jazz ensembles. Jazz music published in the 1960s, as well as many recently published professional-level charts, include loosely notated rhythm section parts, often consisting of just chords and other nonstandard notation markings. However, in the last 10 years nearly all school jazz charts have been published with fully notated rhythm section parts. While these fully notated parts will get the young jazz player through the tune, they are often written in a way to minimize executive skill demands and are therefore often a bit uncharacteristic.

## Adjusting Fully Notated Charts

Often the written piano voicings are notated as whole notes (with chord symbol notation above). To help your piano player create a more characteristic sound from the printed page, have the student use the written chord voicings, but add characteristic rhythms. Many entry-level pieces will have simple comping rhythms to show an example of the style. Nearly all guitar parts for entry-level charts are only chordal. We find that guitar parts are often the most challenging to read if the publisher does not suggest or supply chord frames with the set of parts. In these instances, jazz directors often need to supply this information for the student or edit the parts. Entry-level bass charts are almost always fully notated with notes and rhythms that have chord symbols included. Bass players who do not read well often respond well to tablature provided by the jazz teacher and eventually could function reading notated parts supplied by the publisher. Many entry-level charts have vibe and percussion parts. If not, the teacher can easily write these out, drawing from melody instrument lines as well as piano and guitar parts. Finally, various publishers range from supplying too much notation to too little notation for drum charts; therefore the director needs to have a vocabulary of fixes based on common jazz drum sounds.

Although the availability of fully notated charts requiring only slight adjustments is certainly good news to jazz teachers and young students learning jazz, it is still important that young rhythm section players also learn how to read loosely notated charts; while most contemporary big band charts are fully notated with traditional notation markings, most lead-sheets are not, and if students are going to play in a combo setting, or one day in a professional-level big band, they will surely encounter loosely notated rhythm section charts. At the very least, jazz teachers and students should be aware of them.

## Loosely Notated Bass, Piano, and Guitar Charts

In the case of piano, bass, and guitar, loosely notated charts often take the form of chord symbols (see figure 7.1). As we can see from this example, jazz charts for these instruments often just indicate the chord, and it is left to the performer to interpret the pitches, voicings, and rhythms. To further complicate matters for the beginning player, there is often inconsistency in how chord changes are notated (see figure 7.2).

## Loosely Notated Drum Set Charts

In the case of the drum set (sometimes referred to as the "drum kit" or "trap set"), charts are usually notated indicating the style to be performed and providing horn cues, from which the drummer is supposed to provide fills, setups, and/or accented hits. The drummer reads four types of lines: (a) symbols that indicate keeping time, (b) symbols that *suggest* a rhythm to be played, (c) symbols that indicate a specific rhythm to be played, and (d) symbols that indicate important horn entrances for which the drummer is to provide a setup (see figure 7.3).

FIGURE 7.1 Bass/Piano/Guitar Notation

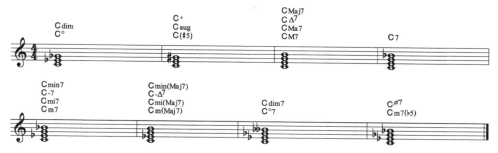

FIGURE 7.2 Chord Symbols

Drums — Keep Time — Suggested Rhythm — Play as Written — Horn Entrance

**FIGURE 7.3** Drum Notation Patterns

The typical instrumental music education curriculum in college programs does not prepare us to teach drum set, bass, guitar, and piano. Even if we have learned these instruments in our undergraduate programs, we often have learned how to play them according to standard concert band notation rather than by reading chord changes and interpreting what is expected when presented with horn cues. This can present a challenge for students entering ensembles as well as for the band directors who are charged with teaching them this new way of interpreting what is on the page. There are, however, some basic ideas and skills that band directors can teach their rhythm section students to help them perform using this type of notation. These are explored here as we provide an overview of each instrument in the rhythm section.

# Bass

There are two types of instruments used to play the bass part in the rhythm section: the upright acoustic bass and the electric bass. For an authentic jazz sound, we recommend using an upright acoustic bass with a pick-up and amplifier. If this is not available, an electric bass and amplifier will be adequate. The latter may also be an instrument that some of your students already play and is a great doubling instrument for rock and funk charts. Having a bass player in the rhythm section is a must. A band is sorely lacking without a bass player, making it difficult to create a cohesive-sounding group. If you are unable to find a student to play bass, find someone to play the bass part on another instrument, such as the tuba, baritone sax, or electric keyboard. This part cannot be omitted from the rhythm section because it functions as both a harmonic instrument, outlining chord tones, as well as a time keeper, playing steady quarter notes when "walking" (i.e., playing swing-style music).

To develop an authentic walking sound on the upright bass, make sure that the students are using the side of their right index finger when plucking the string. The more flesh comes in contact with the string, the deeper and richer the tone will be. After plucking the note, the player should allow the right elbow to fall into the body so that the weight of the arm draws the sound out. Naturally the hand will turn to the right as this happens. If your students are playing the electric bass, be sure they are plucking the strings by alternating the first two fingers of the right hand. Avoid using a pick for this style of music.

## Walking a Bass Line

**Playing roots.** One of the first forms a beginning jazz bass player needs to learn is 12-bar blues, since much beginning and standard jazz literature is written in this form. (We suggest first making sure that your bass students are familiar with their scales and/or providing them

**FIGURE 7.4** Bass Line on the Root

**FIGURE 7.5** Bass Line Adding Chord Tones

with scale sheets for reference.) Begin by developing a basic understanding of how to "walk" on the bass by playing steady quarter notes on the root (see figure 7.4).

**Adding chord tones.** When your bassist understands the 12-bar blues form by playing roots, it is time to add in other chord tones. Have your bassist play quarter note roots on beats 1 and 2 and the 5th of the chord in quarter notes on beats 3 and 4 (see ⊙ video 7.1, Bass Roots and 5ths). Then have students learn the chord tones 1, 3, and 5 (see ⊙ video 7.2, Bass Roots, 3rds, and 5ths, Example 1; ⊙ video 7.3, Bass Roots, 3rds, and 5ths, Example 2; and ⊙ video 7.4, Bass Roots, 3rds, and 5ths, Example 3). To help bassists learn to pick out guide tones, we suggest having them work on this daily in the warmup (see ⊙ appendix 7.1, "Bass Guide Tone Warm-up"). A good beginning approach to teaching students to "walk" a bass line in a 12-bar blues style is to have them play the chord tones 1,2,3,5 or 8,7,6,5 (see figure 7.5).

**Adding chromatic passing tones.** This is a very basic construction and a good way to get young students started. As your bass player progresses, it is a good idea to introduce chromatic approaches to make the line more interesting and avoid repeating notes. A good first step is to apply a chromatic approach to the instances in the 12-bar blues progression where a note would otherwise be repeated, such as in the 6th bar and 8th bar (see figure 7.6). As your bass players get comfortable building bass lines in this fashion, encourage them to start exploring other less-formulaic ways of constructing bass lines that are more idiomatic to jazz. Finally, have your bass players learn more sophisticated walking bass lines (see ⊙ video 7.5,

**FIGURE 7.6** Bass Line Using Chromatic Passing Tones

**FIGURE 7.7** Sample Beginning ii⁷-V⁷-I Bass Line

**FIGURE 7.8** Sample Beginning ii⁷-V⁷-I Bass Line Alternating 5ths and 3rds

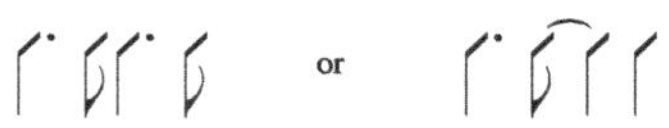

**FIGURE 7.9** Latin Bass Rhythm Patterns

Creating Sophisticated Walking Bass Lines, Example 1, ⊙ Video 7.6, Creating Sophisticated Walking Bass Lines, Example 2; ⊙ video 7.7, Creating Sophisticated Walking Bass Lines, Example 3; ⊙ video 7.8, Creating Sophisticated Walking Bass Lines, Example 4; ⊙ video 7.9, Creating Sophisticated Walking Bass Lines, Example 5; and ⊙ video 7.10, Creating Sophisticated Walking Bass Lines, Example 6). Also, see chapter 18 in this volume for information on constructing more sophisticated bass lines.

## ii⁷-V⁷-I Bass Lines

Another common progression in jazz is the ii⁷-V⁷-I, which requires a different approach than that for a 12-bar blues progression. We suggest having students start with what is referred to as a "2-feel" or a "2-beat" pattern, just playing roots and 5ths (see figure 7.7). A next step in teaching a 2-beat pattern over a ii⁷-V⁷-I progression might be to have the bass player play the root on beat 1 and alternate playing the 5th and the 3rd on beat 3 (see figure 7.8).

Latin styles typically require variations of the 2-beat pattern. The pitches would stay the same, but the bass player would simply use different rhythms (see figure 7.9) (⊙ video 7.11, Latin Bass Comping Patterns). When the piece calls for a "walking" bass line over ii⁷-V⁷-I changes, we suggest

**FIGURE 7.10** Sample Beginning ii⁷-V⁷-I Bass Line with Chromatic Approach

**FIGURE 7.11** Sample Written Piano Block Chords, Voicings, and Comping Rhythms

having the bass player play chord tones 1, 3, and 5 on beats 1, 2, and 3, and using beat 4 to chromatically approach the root of the next chord (see figure 7.10).

# Piano

## Jazz Piano Written Notation

The piano serves as a melodic and harmonic instrument in the rhythm section. We recommend using an acoustic piano, although electric keyboards with piano patches will suffice. When playing with just the rhythm section or a small combo, the piano needs no amplification; however, positioning a microphone near the sound board and patched into a sound system with monitors for the large jazz ensemble is recommended. This ensures that all musicians can hear the harmonic foundation the piano provides. As previously mentioned, beginning jazz charts will often provide standard notation for the pianist. Although this is helpful, simply reading the block chords, voicings, and comping rhythms written for these charts may be new to the classical pianist (see figure 7.11). The first hurdle is for the pianist to become accustomed to this style by playing the written notation and paying attention to the sound of the chords and rhythmic comping. Then encourage students to mix and match rhythms. Pair this early learning with listening to jazz recordings so that the young pianists understand their role in the ensemble.

## Reading Chord Changes

Most beginning pianists enter jazz band with some classical training and can read standard notation at a functional level. With pianists, we have found that they are often *too dependent* on notation and need to become less attached to the page. We encourage them to memorize the form of songs and the chord changes and then help them find places in the arrangements where the piano can fill a space left by the horns. When the pianists have developed a basic understanding of chord structure and how to comp from written notation, it is time for them to learn how to read the changes (i.e., chord symbols). When introducing this concept,

**FIGURE 7.12** Sample Piano 3rds or 7ths

**FIGURE 7.13** Sample Piano 3rds and 7ths

**FIGURE 7.14** Sample Piano 3rds, 7ths, 9ths, and 13ths

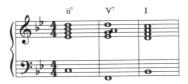

**FIGURE 7.15** ii⁷-V⁷-I Piano Voicing

stick to one key (e.g., F or B♭) so that the students can learn to recognize patterns for chord voicings. We recommend starting off your piano students by having them find either the 3rd or the 7th of each chord and place it in the left hand (see figure 7.12). Have them comp on this note with the rhythm section. Once students can do this, have them locate and place both the 3rd and the 7th in the left hand and repeat the comping exercise (see figure 7.13). To help pianists learn to pick out 3rds and 7ths, we suggest having them work on this daily in the warm-up (see ⊙ appendix 7.2, "Piano Guide Tone Warm-up"). Next, have students add the 9th or 13th in the right hand (see ⊙ video 7.12, Sample Piano 3rds, 7ths, 9ths, and 13ths). Teach your students to observe the basic rules of voice leading, moving easily between chords by keeping chord tones or moving to a neighboring tone (see figure 7.14).

## Voicing ii⁷-V⁷-I Chord Changes

The process of learning to voice chord changes described in the preceding subsection works well for 12-bar blues progressions. These voicing techniques do not apply so well for ii⁷-V⁷-I progressions; a different approach is needed (see ⊙ video 7.13, ii⁷-V⁷-I Piano Voicing, Example 1; and ⊙ video 7.14, ii⁷-V⁷-I Piano Voicing, Example 2). Again, most beginning charts will write out the voicings, but when students begin reading ii⁷-V⁷-I chord changes in intermediate and professional charts, they will need to know how to identify and characteristically voice them (see figure 7.15). When students are comfortable with this, you can introduce them to the ii⁷-V⁷-I tritone substitution chord voicing to add variety (see figure 7.16).

**FIGURE 7.16** ii⁷-V⁷-I Piano Voicing with Tritone Substitution

**FIGURE 7.17** Sample Piano Swing Comping Patterns

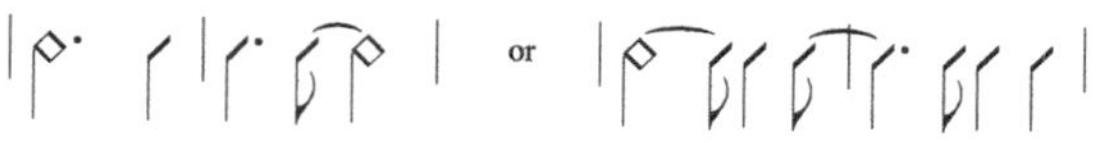

**FIGURE 7.18** Sample Piano Latin Comping Patterns

## Piano Comping Patterns

One of the piano player's jobs is to fill rhythmic and harmonic holes while not covering up the melodic line. This requires *comping* (meaning "to accompany" or "to complement") rhythms using the chord tones previously described. Depending on what is happening within the ensemble, a beginning piano player can learn to choose from different swing patterns and apply them where appropriate (see figure 7.17). Latin style requires different rhythmic patterns, but the same voicing guidelines for swing can be applied (see figure 7.18).

# Guitar

The guitar serves the same function as a piano, in that it provides a harmonic and rhythmic complement to the ensemble. The experienced guitarist in your ensemble likely comes from a rock background and is used to playing power/sustained chords and solos. Knowledge of pentatonic and blues scales will be helpful when learning jazz. The guitarist may only read tablature and will now need to learn to read chord symbols and notation. In addition, the sound of the guitar should be simple and clean, with no effects. This is best achieved on archtop/hollow-bodied guitars or semi-hollow-bodied guitars. The student's right-hand finger style and use of a pick will be the primary influence in creating an appropriate sound for the ensemble. Listen to recordings of great jazz guitarists to become familiar with this type of sound.

## Jazz Guitar Notation

One of the many difficulties with teaching guitarists to read traditional staff notation is that the same pitch can be played in multiple places on the guitar; learning to read tablature can alleviate this problem. Many of the beginning and intermediate jazz ensemble charts published today come with guitar chord sheets. Guitarists are also encouraged to use guitar

**FIGURE 7.19** Sample Jazz Guitar Notation

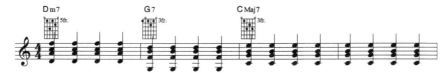

**FIGURE 7.20** Sample Freddie Green Rhythm

**FIGURE 7.21** Sample Freddie Green Rhythm on Beats 2 and 4

chord apps and chord books for additional reference. Jazz guitar parts feature chords for comping as well as traditional staff notation (see figure 7.19).

In learning jazz chord voicings, guitarists should be mindful that the bass will be responsible for the root, so playing rootless chords is recommended. As with piano, first have your guitar players find 3rds and 7ths and then add 9ths and 13ths when they are comfortable. To help guitarists learn to pick out 3rds and 7ths, we suggest having them work on this daily in the warm-up (see ⊚ appendix 7.3, "Guitar Guide Tone Warm-up"). Then have students learn the basic shapes to all basic chord types in C (i.e., Maj7, m7, half-dim7, dim7, and aug7), paying attention to the shape of the fingers on the fretboard. From there, chords in other keys become instantly possible by simply moving the hand up the neck of the guitar to the appropriate fret using barred chords. Chord shapes will also help with smooth transitions and voice leading.

## Rhythm Guitar and Comping Patterns

**Rhythm guitar.** When playing with the full band, a good swing pattern for a rhythm guitar is what many refer to as the Freddie Green rhythm, wherein the player plays chords using a quarter note rhythm while emphasizing beats 2 and 4 (see figure 7.20). When the guitarists are comfortable, have them omit the chords on beats 1 and 3 and focus on playing with the drummers' hi-hat (see figure 7.21). Next, work on upbeat syncopated patterns (see figure 7.22). Playing these percussive chords builds excitement and intensity in the music.

**Comping.** When playing in the rhythm section, the guitarist has responsibilities similar to those of the pianist: to comp for the band and soloists, play improvised solos, and play the melody with the horns. Due to this similarity, it is important to pay particular attention to defining the guitar and piano roles in each piece to avoid cluttering the melody and texture.

**FIGURE 7.22** Syncopated Chords

Generally, the guitarist should play more sparingly than the pianist, while trading comping responsibilities during solos. Additional rhythms can be used, such as those mentioned for piano. Regular listening to jazz recordings will help the young guitarist develop an aural understanding of how the guitar sounds in a rhythm section.

# Drum Set

The first task with the drum set is ensuring that you have the basic components and that they are set up properly so that the drummer can easily access them. At a minimum, the drum set should include a snare drum and stand, bass drum with kick pedal, two toms (one small tom attached to the bass drum and a floor tom), hi-hat cymbals and stand, ride cymbal and stand, medium crash cymbal and stand, and drum throne/seat. Every part of the set should be within easy reach. The bass drum and hi-hat pedals should be equidistant from where the drummer is seated, with the snare drum and stand positioned between the knees. The height of the hi-hat should allow enough space for the left hand to play the snare when playing hi-hat with the right hand. Position the music stand on the left-hand side of the drum set so that the drummer can keep the full ensemble and director in sight while playing. Finally, place the drum set between the piano and the band near the bass player's amp. This will allow for good communication between other members of the rhythm section and the rest of the band.

Beginning drummers often have a more difficult time reading and keeping track of where they are in the chart. This is a problem even if they are otherwise competent readers on snare drum. They are usually good with playing time but often default to playing the correct rhythm with the wrong balance; for swing they are usually too heavy on the bass drum and usually play uncharacteristic backbeats on 2 and 4. As with the piano, we encourage drummers to memorize the form and learn when they need to really read the chart as opposed to just "checking in."

## Rock and Funk Beat Patterns

Many young drummers may have some drum set experience, which helps in overcoming initial problems of coordination between the hands and feet. Typically, those with experience will have played rock (see figure 7.23) and/or funk music (see figure 7.24). These styles emphasize a straight-eighth feel and feature a regular bass drum pattern on beats 1 and 3.

## Swing Patterns

In swing, the fundamental style and "feel" of the music places emphasis on beats 2 and 4 subdivided in triplets. To begin learning this style, a beginning jazz drummer should learn to

**FIGURE 7.23** Rock Beat Pattern

**FIGURE 7.24** Funk Beat Pattern

**FIGURE 7.25** Hi-hat and Ride Cymbal Notated vs. Performed

play the hi-hat (using the foot pedal) on beats 2 and 4. This is a fundamental source of sound ("chink") for keeping time in swing music, which the band and other rhythm section players rely on. It is helpful to teach drummers to use a rocking motion with the left foot so that it goes back on the heel on 1 and 3 and down with the toe on 2 and 4. This helps the drummer maintain a steady beat while playing the hi-hat on 2 and 4.

Once the drummer is comfortable keeping a steady 2 and 4 on the hi-hat, it is time to add swing quarter and eighth patterns on the ride cymbal. The students can start out playing straight quarter notes, focusing on maintaining a horizontal stick position when hitting the cymbal with the stick tip while drawing out a clear, crisp sound. When the students are ready, have them add eighth notes on beats 2 and 4. As previously mentioned, this is often not written out, but only marked using slash marks to signal the drummer to keep time (see figure 7.25).

**Snare and bass drum.** Once the basic hi-hat and ride cymbal swing patterns are established, the drummer can start implementing hits on the snare drum and occasional thumps on the bass drum. Unlike rock or funk, the bass drum's role in swing music is less integral to the groove and used more sparingly. Similarly, the snare drum hits are brief, improvised patterns that fill in the sonic space between the cymbals. The best way to understand the role of each of these components is to listen to recordings and watch professional jazz drummers.

## Bossa Nova Patterns

Another style that we teach beginning drummers is a basic bossa nova pattern. Latin grooves can get incredibly complex; one size does not fit all, so to speak. But for the purposes of equipping the beginning drummer with a basic pattern that can be used on many beginning "Latin" charts, we suggest first teaching a basic bossa nova pattern. Whereas swing

**FIGURE 7.26** Drum Set Bossa Nova Pattern

**FIGURE 7.27** Drum Set "Cheater" Bossa Nova Pattern

**FIGURE 7.28** Drum Setups

grooves are 1-bar patterns, a bossa nova is a 2-bar pattern. We suggest first having your drummer keep steady eighth notes on the hi-hat played with the right hand while playing dotted-quarter-eighth patterns on the bass drum. Once that groove is comfortable, have your drummer provide rim clicks on the snare drum (see figure 7.26). If this proves too challenging at first, you can utilize a less-complex, 1-bar pattern often referred to as the "cheater" bossa (see figure 7.27).

## Setups

When your drummer is keeping steady time in these basic styles, you can introduce another important responsibility, setups, which are rhythmic gestures that signal or *set up* a horn section entrance. We suggest teaching two types of setups to beginning drummers: for horn entrances that occur on the downbeat and on the upbeat. For those horn entrances on the downbeat, an appropriate setup for a beginning drummer would be to kick the bass drum on the beat prior to the entrance. For entrances occurring on the upbeat, an appropriate setup for a beginning drummer would be to provide the two eighth notes on the snare prior to the entrance (see figure 7.28). (see ⏵ video 7.15, Setups.)

# Auxiliary Percussion

In addition to the drum set, various auxiliary percussion instruments can be used to highlight particular jazz styles. If you have multiple drummers, this is a good way to keep everyone involved in making music. Instruments such as the conga, bongos, timbales, and guiro are used for Latin charts. The notation for these instruments is similar to drum set notation, specifying particular rhythms to be played and solo fills. Encourage players of these instruments to listen carefully to the rest of the rhythm section, particularly the drum set, to lock into the established groove in order to provide a new, balanced rhythmic texture.

The vibraphone or "vibes" is another keyboard instrument that can be used in the rhythm section, albeit on selective charts. It functions as harmonic support by comping like piano/guitar, as a solo instrument, or by playing the melody with the horns. It is important to determine the scope of the vibraphonist's role in the ensemble so that the texture does not get muddied. If a part for vibes exists, it is often written in standard notation. In other cases, vibraphonists create their own parts using the piano part (i.e., chords) and horn parts (i.e., melody). The vibraphonist typically uses four mallets when comping and two mallets for soloing.

## Rhythm Section Rehearsal Strategies

It is always a good idea to set up some rhythm section rehearsals apart from the full jazz ensemble to work on establishing a firm rhythmic/harmonic foundation (see ⊙ video 7.16, Working with the Beginning Rhythm Section). If the rhythm section is unable to play well as an autonomous unit, that will have disastrous consequences for the rest of the band. The first order of business is to set up the instruments so that the students can see and hear each other clearly. This ensures that students will be able to learn how to communicate throughout a song and performance. Encourage them to look at one another as they play. Avoid letting them bury their heads in the notation (see figure 7.29).

Make sure to stress with young rhythm section players (a) becoming competent at reading, (b) memorizing song forms while keeping their place in the music, (c) comping effectively in each style, (d) checking in with the other rhythm instruments to stay in time and in balance, and (e) improvising fills (rhythmic on drums and melodic on piano). It is good

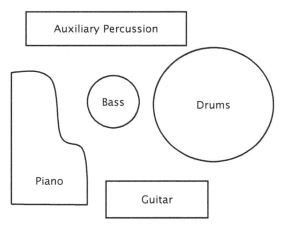

**FIGURE 7.29** Typical Rhythm Section Configuration

for jazz teachers to remember to (a) not ignore the rhythm section, (b) plan something to say to someone in the rhythm section at every rehearsal, (c) encourage rhythm section players to come in for extra help when needed, (d) practice each of the instruments so that they can play the parts they want students to play, and (e) listen to more jazz.

When you begin rehearsing the music, the focus should first be on keeping good time. Playing through a medium-slow blues form is an excellent way to work on groove. The drummer can focus on the hi-hat on 2 and 4 and a clear swing rhythm on the ride cymbal, while listening intently to the walking bass line. The bass player should align the walking quarter notes to the steady "ping" on the ride cymbal. The pianist/guitarist/vibes can take turns playing a blues head (i.e., standard blues melody) and comping. As the group plays through several choruses, strive for a strong bass sound, steady time in the bass and drums, clear/percussive comping patterns in piano/guitar/vibes, and a clear melody. With time your rhythm section will function as a cohesive unit in swing and Latin style (bossa nova) (see ⊙ video 7.17, Rhythm Section in Latin (Bossa Nova) Style). Apply these same principles to the other styles of jazz you wish to play, and before long you will have a rhythm section capable of "driving the bus!"

# Questions for Discussion

1. Bruce talks about how the rhythm section's job is to "make the horn players sound good." Is this oversimplifying, or is this really the essence of their responsibility?
2. If you had to choose, which rhythm section instrument would you most want to not be without and why?
3. Bruce, an expert 30-year veteran band director, admits that teaching the rhythm section still intimidates him. Do you think this is true for most band directors who play brass or woodwind primary instruments? Is it a cause for not having a jazz band, or is the director's job more about teaching style and musicianship anyway?
4. Emily talks about how the roles of the rhythm section players take more time to learn than do the roles of the horn players. What are their different roles, and why does one type take more time to learn than the other?
5. Emily talks about the rhythm section being the engine of a car and the horn players being the exterior. In what ways is this an appropriate analogy?

# 8

# Beginning Improvisation

Michael Treat

## Competence or Confidence

In jazz ensemble, Bruce is more focused on his students having fun and enjoying playing their instruments than he necessarily is on the students becoming solid *jazz* musicians. The same is true regarding his beliefs about middle school jazz improvisation. He would rather the students develop confidence and comfort improvising than necessarily a high level of proficiency:

> Just doing it and not worrying about whether it is right or wrong. What I want to hear from them is a lack of self-consciousness. I don't want them to feel nervous about it. I want them to be free to make all the mistakes they feel like making. For me, that is the most important thing that they just feel like they can do it without fear. I'll never tell anybody, "wow, that was a terrible solo."

Like Bruce, Emily values the opportunity students get to improvise. "You get to lay out what you feel this piece is about. You can interpret the piece, where you don't get to do that in band—the conductor does." These musical choices allow students a greater opportunity to interact with the other ensemble members:

> I think our society is becoming more of a, "Here is the information and we give you the information." But in jazz, you get to take what your drummer is doing and as a soloist, you get to do it. As a piano player, you get to talk to somebody. Isn't that amazing that you can be in a performing situation and you have some discourse with someone else?

Have you ever heard really great storytellers? Storytellers can capture an entire room not only with a great plot, but also by how they deliver it. Through humor, anticipation, and unexpected twists, listeners will find themselves captivated. If the storytellers told the same tale again, it would likely be a different version from what listeners had already heard and equally as entertaining. Such is the nature of jazz improvisation. Great soloists will captivate you by telling a musical story. They can develop musical ideas to create a sense of anticipation and deceive expectations to create twists in a musical plot. What is more, there are multiple dimensions of improvisation in jazz. While the soloists create a melody, the rhythm section is responding harmonically and rhythmically in a way that enhances the solo, all within the structure of a preexisting tune.

So how do you teach someone to become a great storyteller? You can teach the stories, but can you teach someone how to be engaging or humorous and how to ad-lib? Teaching jazz improvisation presents the same challenges. You can teach tunes and licks, but how can you teach students to be creative when improvising? Like teaching any subject, it is essential to implement a well-developed sequence of instruction that develops fundamental skills and allows students to implement those skills authentically.

Consider the case study presented at the beginning of the chapter. Bruce is correct that young improvisors need confidence to improvise. However, to be musically effective they also need to play with harmonic and rhythmic accuracy. Emily is correct that improvisation allows players to be expressive and collaborate. However, they need to learn how to play using phrase structure and contour before they can be expressive improvisors. This chapter outlines an approach to teaching beginning improvisors that can develop both confidence and competence.

## Beginning Improvisation

Improvisation is inherently different from reading precomposed music. To read notation is to interpret someone else's musical creation after it has been created, much like reading a book. Improvisation is creating, performing, and responding to musical ideas in real time, much like having a conversation. When we converse, we recognize the topic of conversation and have a set of vocabulary we use to create our responses. What would you say if someone came up to you and said, "Excuse me, do you know how to get to the coffee shop?" You might respond, "Yeah, it's down three blocks on the left." If that person replied, "Oh, so it must be by the parking garage," you might then say, "yeah, and the daily fee for that garage is outrageous!"

When you were first asked directions, you knew what to say, but you did not know how the other person would reply to your answer. When that person responded, you could immediately reply appropriately and propel the conversation forward. Jazz improvisation works the same way. Jazz tunes are like a topic of conversation in which musicians use melodic, harmonic, and rhythmic vocabulary to interact with, and respond to, other musicians. More advanced players have more vocabulary and improvise more interesting solos, like someone who can speak intelligently and at length on a certain topic. Young players, however, need to first learn how to play simple musical vocabulary in a coherent fashion before trying to utilize advanced jazz vocabulary. The videos for this chapter on the website illustrate how a sequence of improvisation exercises can guide students through learning some of the fundamentals of jazz improvisation.

# Step 1: Conversing in Jazz (Developing Call and Response, Rhythm and Contour)

**"Hi. Hello."** The first step is utilizing the dynamic of social interaction. After explaining the parallel between improvising and conversing, the teacher says "Hi" to a student. The student responds with "Hello." Using the syllable structure of that call and response, the teacher assembles these words into a 2-bar rhythm. The students play that on a concert F over a 12-bar blues progression in F so they can begin to feel how call and response is incorporated into a musical context. With three notes, they have captured the essence of improvisation (see figure 8.1). (See ⊚ video 8.1, Hi Hello.)

**"Hi. How are you?"** The teacher reinforces the conversational dynamic by having another student offer a different response. Still only using concert F, the students find the natural rhythm of that speech and play it on their instruments. The teacher sings it again in a rhythm that is stylistically correct. The students repeat it several times to establish the feel of this rhythm (see figure 8.2). (See ⊚ video 8.2, Hi How Are You?.)

**Questions.** Here, the teacher uses the idea of asking a question to introduce a new pitch. By ending the musical idea on a concert Ab, the lick imitates the human voice rising when asking a question. By introducing only one new note, students can more accurately maintain rhythmic integrity and contour in their early improvisations (see figure 8.3). (See ⊚ video 8.3, Questions.)

**Variation.** Using the "question" idea from video 8.3, the teacher introduces another pitch that encloses the final note by jumping from F to Bb and then stepping back down to Ab. The students are now using their original idea to execute a more sophisticated contour (see figure 8.4). (See ⊚ video 8.4, Question Variations.)

FIGURE 8.1 Hi. Hello.

FIGURE 8.2 Hi. How Are You?

FIGURE 8.3 Questions

FIGURE 8.4 Question Variations

FIGURE 8.5 Question and Answer

FIGURE 8.6 Improvising Questions and Answers

FIGURE 8.7 Solos with Questions and Answers

**Question and answer.** The teachers now remind students that questions need answers. They ask the students for an answer to the question "How are you?" The answer offered is "Doin' good." The teachers show them that starting on the upper note (A♭) and descending back to F imitates the human voice descending when answering a question. Once again, they set this to music. The result is a four-measure phrase that sounds great over the blues progression (see figure 8.5). (See ⊙ video 8.5, Question and Answer.)

**Improvising questions and answers.** This is the first time the students are improvising free of setting their ideas to words. Their task is to listen for contour by alternating who is improvising a "question" and who is improvising an "answer." With their first attempt to improvise a short phrase, almost everyone uses strong rhythm and the correct contour (see figure 8.6). (See ⊙ video 8.6, Improvising Questions and Answers.)

**Solos.** Students are now invited to play longer solos by improvising a question and following it with an answer. As a result of the preceding activities, these solos have strong rhythmic integrity and contour. The fact that each student is waiting until 4 bars have passed to play a solo demonstrates that the students are starting to hear phrase structure while they improvise (see figure 8.7) (See ⊙ video 8.7, Solos with Questions and Answers.)

**Adding another pitch.** Up to this point, the "question" concept has meant moving upward away from the tonic. The teachers present the idea that moving down from the tonic pitch can have the same effect. The new pitch is a concert E♭. After a quick musical application of this idea, they do another round of solos, asking the students to use this new pitch. Notice how eager the students have become to try this and improvise with more material (see figure 8.8). (See ⊙ video 8.8, Adding Another Pitch.)

**FIGURE 8.8** Adding Another Pitch

Can you see how these introductory activities lead to students playing coherent rhythms and phrases? The pitches suggested (F, A♭, E♭) are some of the defining colors of a minor pentatonic scale. This is a sound that is heavily employed by many jazz musicians, especially when playing the blues. By starting with just these three pitches and using an accompaniment in a jazz style, students can easily move away from or gravitate back to a tonic pitch, creating melodic tension and release. They are beginning to *hear* melodic structures and rhythms used in jazz rather than *thinking* about the notes in a scale.

## Step 2: Further Developing Phrase Structure and Introducing Form

Jazz musicians hear formal structures on a large scale and create their melodies accordingly. Whether a tune is a 12-bar blues, 16-bar form, or 32-bar AABA or has an unusual form will affect what musicians play and how they develop their solos. It is therefore essential that a sense of form be established early on. The videos in step 1 demonstrate how students can learn to improvise 4-bar phrases. If those phrases are played and repeated over a blues progression, they are called riffs. By turning phrases into riffs, the students can create a stylistically appropriate blues melody based on their own improvisation.

**Creating a riff.** After explaining the idea of a riff, the teacher recalls the opening phrases based on spoken words. By playing this riff three times, students are playing a blues melody that reinforces phrase structure through repetition (see figure 8.9). (See ⊚ video 8.9, Creating a Riff.) Guiding students to create their own blues melody is a great way to wrap up the introductory phase of teaching beginning improvisation. The resulting tune can be used as a vehicle for improvisation itself, and the first jazz tune in students' repertoire is their own. Don't forget to have students give their own tunes titles!

**Riff tune with one-phrase solos.** At this point the teachers introduce the idea that this repeated riff fits into a larger 12-bar form called the blues. They then review how individual solos would be played following the melody. In this rendition of the tune, students play the melody, each student improvises a one-phrase solo, and they all play the melody again. During the solo the teacher helps the students know when their solos start (see ⊚ video 8.10, Riff Tune with One-Phrase Solos).

**Riff tune with two-phrase solos.** This is each student's first chance to play two successive phrases. The teachers remind the students that phrases are often separated by space and demonstrate how this is implemented with their own improvisation. The resulting student solos have coherent rhythms, contour, and phrase structure (see ⊚ video 8.11, Riff Tune with Two-Phrase Solos).

The case study at the beginning of the chapter summarized two philosophies for teaching improvisation, confidence and competence. After listening to the students in these

**FIGURE 8.9** Creating a Riff

videos, you can see that it is possible for young improvisors to acquire both. Throughout the process, you see students who are engaged in and confidently creating, developing, and performing their own ideas. At the same time, they are developing their sense of phrase structure and contour and eventually improvising ideas that are harmonically and rhythmically accurate.

## Additional Improvisation Activities

Once your students have developed a basic level of confidence and competence, have them continue to improvise new phrases and share ideas. Keep using call and response and add variations to the licks and phrases they create. Use different keys, create new tunes, and have students take longer solos. Like the sequence demonstrated in the videos, these activities should be continued until students can improvise rhythmically and melodically coherent phrases.

## Rhythm Section

This chapter is not intended to focus on the instruments of the rhythm section. However, in the context of introducing young players to jazz improvisation, players of rhythm section instruments should be developing their skills alongside players of single-line instruments. Take time to have the rhythm players do all the same activities described in this chapter and have the single-line players learn the role, vocabulary, and nuance of each of the rhythm section instruments.

## Prerequisites for the Teacher

In order to effectively teach students how to improvise jazz, the teachers must be comfortable improvising. This doesn't necessarily mean they have to have the chops of an active jazz performer, but the teachers do need to be familiar with artists and recordings and have the ability to improvise using basic jazz idioms. Much as an English teacher reads students' writing and offers suggestions for improvement, jazz educators need to be able to do the same with their students' improvised melodies.

Fluency on the keyboard and the ability to improvise stylistically appropriate accompaniments for your students are invaluable skills. In the absence of keyboard skills, there are numerous resources with play-along recordings that can be used. Some of the most readily available are listed here:

- **The Jamey Aebersold Play-a-Long Series**: This is a series of over 100 books of standard tunes and exercises. Each book includes a play-along CD. The series is published by Jamey Aebersold Jazz.
- **The Real Book Play Along**: The Real Book is a widely accepted source of notated standard jazz tunes and is available with play along CDs. It is published by Hal Leonard.
- **Apps**: There are play-along apps available for use on devices such as smartphones and tablets. These apps have a large bank of tunes. Some offer the flexibility to change the tempo, key, and style of the play-along track. Some of these apps only offer chord symbols as a visual aid and do not provide a noted melody for the tune being played.

The downside of the play-along option is that the students lose a dimension of jazz improvisation that only exists when accompaniments are created based on melodies that are being simultaneously improvised. The upside is that familiarity with these resources can provide students with valuable practice tools.

## Next Steps

Having developed a concept of call and response, rhythmic structure, melodic contour, phrasing, and formal structure, beginning improvisors have the tools they need to begin to explore the music and some of its creative possibilities on their own or with others. The teacher should give them opportunities to play standard tunes, listen to jazz artists, transcribe solos, and study advanced harmonic and rhythmic concepts. One of the most effective and authentic ways to expand on these introductory steps is for students to start playing in jazz combos. Other chapters in this book provide more information on these topics.

In addition to working in ensembles like combos and jazz bands, teachers may find it most beneficial to create an additional time and place to introduce jazz improvisation as its own art, such as an improvisation class or club. In this model, students can learn the etiquette for improvisation as well as develop the ability to play tunes by ear and improvise stylistically appropriate solos. These skills can empower them to participate in teacher-led or student-led combos and/or be strong soloists in a jazz band.

## Conclusion

Almost anyone can learn to improvise on any instrument. In teachers' efforts to serve students, they should make the opportunity available to as many students as possible. Let every child have the opportunity to hear jazz music and explore the act of creating melodies on an instrument in a safe and supportive environment.

This process of learning to improvise will inspire some students to become more serious jazz players. Those individuals will need to learn more tunes, more vocabulary, and more chords and scales; transcribe solos; and study numerous recordings. A strong foundation in the basics of improvisation will help yield students who are better prepared to do so.

Furthermore, because of the foundation established, your students will be stronger musicians, more versed in creativity, and have an appreciation for jazz music. They will have participated in an experience that is social and collaborative and strikes at the very center of why music improves our quality of life.

## Questions for Discussion

1. What do you think is the right balance between confidence and competence when getting students to improvise?
2. What do you think are the most fundamental musical skills students need to begin to be effective improvisors?
3. What would you need to hear in your students' improvisation to know they are ready to begin to develop more advanced concepts in their playing?
4. What skills do you need to develop as a teacher to effectively teach beginning improvisation?

# PART IV

# Teaching High School Jazz

# 9

# High School Woodwinds and Brass

Andrew Goodrich

## Grabbing the Style Baton

Bruce does not perceive many differences between teaching and learning in concert band and teaching and learning in jazz ensemble. "I don't really have any differences. My teaching all stems from what I do in my concert band. There are stylistic differences to talk about, but other than that, mash the right button, play the right partial, and when it says 'p' don't play loud."

Emily feels that jazz ensemble allows students another opportunity to function in different ways within the ensemble. "You compromise in different ways. You agree in different fashions. Depending on the ensemble, you listen to and take cues from different players." Jazz ensemble allows students to function in ways different from what they are used to in concert band. "If I'm playing bass trombone in orchestra, I know that my buddy and pal is the tuba player and everyone else I might talk a little bit to, but basically I'm going to do whatever he says to do. In jazz band you have a different set of people that you listen to." One of the main differences in roles is that in jazz ensemble there are "lead" players, and students in that role develop an increased sense of musical leadership:

> Do I really have to do it the same way that lead alto player does? Well, yes. Yes, you really should. It's cute. Sometimes, you'll have a group that will get led from the alto spot. Sometimes you'll have a group that will get led from the trumpet spot. Once in a great while you'll have some great bone player that wants to grab the style baton and do it their way.

When rehearsing the high school jazz ensemble, it is important to guide high school students toward becoming musicians who can make independent musical decisions. Doing so will ultimately make the jazz ensemble experience more enjoyable for both the students and the director. As students elevate their level of musicianship, more options for repertoire will be available to them.

To provide context for this chapter, references are made to instrumentation for a traditional big band jazz ensemble that includes five trumpets, five trombones, five saxophones (two altos, two tenors, bari), piano, bass, guitar, and drums. These jazz exercises, however, can be used with any type of instrumentation and are intended to serve as a basic "roadmap" for directors, who should adapt these exercises for their own jazz ensembles. The exercises are not intended for use only once during the school year. Rather, with slight modifications they can be used throughout the school year and during a student's four years in high school. These exercises contribute to and support the notion that listening is a process, not an event.

In addition, the exercises in this chapter can be used at any time within a rehearsal. They can also be used to set up fundamental components (e.g., rhythm) of a specific composition. Students can thus get in "the zone" during the warm up and experience a higher degree of success in the rehearsal, which in turn moves them forward toward weekly, concert sequence, semester, and yearly goals.[1]

This chapter includes a discussion on the various roles students have with their instrument parts in the jazz ensemble and how to teach students to listen to the lead trumpet player and to the instruments scored in the low ranges. Additional ear-building exercises include how to teach students to improve their listening skills for intonation and how the use of basic scales can improve listening skills among them. The concept of groove is addressed later in the chapter with exercises for how students can learn to practice with a metronome and with each other. Finally, discussion and exercises include how to teach students to use their air more efficiently to improve their sound and groove when playing in the jazz ensemble. Overall, the exercises in this chapter can help directors teach their students to elevate their individual levels of musicianship as well as that of the entire jazz ensemble.

## Roles in the Jazz Band

In a traditional big band jazz ensemble, each member has a specific role to play that contributes to the overall sound, style, and groove within an arrangement. Major roles in the winds and brass sections include the lead trumpet player (who sets the overall style, including articulations and dynamics), the lead trombone and lead alto players (who also set the style within their respective sections, but need to match the information given to them by the lead trumpet player), and the bass trombone player and the bari sax player (who lay down the foundation for all of the winds and brass). Subroles in the traditional big band jazz ensemble include 2nd, 3rd, 4th, and 5th trumpet and trombone players; lead tenor sax player (who plays solos in addition to soli lines); and 2nd alto and 2nd tenor players (who can play a major role with intonation).

Teaching students to understand their roles in the jazz ensemble in terms of their instruments and parts will contribute to a deeper understanding and comprehension of a

**FIGURE 9.1** Listening to the Lead Trumpet Player

composition when they perform jazz music. The following exercises will aid with teaching and guiding students to focus on and engage with active listening of their own volition instead of the director always telling them whom to listen to.

**Listening to the lead trumpet player.** The most important role in the horns is that of lead trumpet. The lead trumpet part usually contains the highest notes and the melody, which makes it easier for members of the entire jazz band (including the rhythm section) to hear the style, articulations, and dynamics for how a phrase is performed. Listening to the lead trumpet player, therefore, is one of the most important aspects of performing in a jazz ensemble. For more information on the trumpet in jazz, please refer to chapter 14 in this volume.

Working with lead trumpet players is part of the growth process for the student selected to play lead. It is the responsibility of the director to teach lead trumpet players to correctly articulate their parts, to phrase musical passages, to set the style for each particular chart in the repertoire, and to become a leader in the jazz ensemble. In addition, directors need to teach everyone in the jazz ensemble how to listen to the lead trumpet player (see figure 9.1). This first exercise is one that Sam Pilafian often uses; it serves as a great warm-up exercise for the jazz band (see ⊙ video 9.1, Listening to the Lead Trumpet Player).

It typically requires just a couple of minutes. In this exercise (which can be performed with any two scales that are a perfect fourth apart), two different scales are played simultaneously as the lead trumpet player plays a perfect fourth (P4) interval above the rest of the members of the jazz ensemble. Because the P4 interval is an easy one for people to hear, it makes it easy for everyone to hear the lead trumpet player and helps to place responsibility on the lead trumpet player to set the style and dynamics while playing the scale. When playing the scale, it is helpful for everyone in the jazz ensemble to ascend to the 9th of the scale before descending down to the root of the scale. Because many chord voicings in jazz charts are often stacked up to the 9th, playing scales like this helps students become used to hearing the 9th. The director should count off the band for this exercise, and for the first few times this exercise is used, the lead trumpet players should play legato quarter notes so the members of the jazz band get used to hearing them. Having the lead trumpet play a soft dynamic, such as piano, in this exercise can help to make the members of the jazz ensemble listen intently, for the lead trumpet is playing an interval of a fourth higher than the rest of the jazz band. This is an exercise that the lead trumpet player leads the jazz band with during rehearsal.

Once the jazz ensemble can play this exercise, the next step is to add articulations and dynamics to the scale. The first time the exercise in figure 9.2 is used, the director may wish to count off the jazz ensemble, then allow the lead trumpet player to begin leading this exercise. Figure 9.2 demonstrates a potential way for the lead trumpet player to play this exercise. (See ⊙ video 9.2, Adding Articulations and Dynamics.)

**FIGURE 9.2** Adding Articulations and Dynamics

**FIGURE 9.3** Bari Sax and Bass Trombone Playing the Root

As lead trumpet players become more comfortable leading the jazz ensemble with this exercise, they begin to develop leadership skills for dictating how this exercise will be played. The lead trumpet player dictates the articulations and dynamics, and because the lead trumpet is making musical decisions in the moment, everyone in the jazz ensemble has to listen to and immediately implement the information provided. This exercise is done aurally and is not written down. By adding a repeat sign, the jazz ensemble can cycle through this scale exercise several times to provide ample opportunities for the lead trumpet player to play a wide variety of articulations and dynamics, etc.

In addition to playing a quarter note on each scale degree, different rhythms can be used as an exercise, including phrases from a tune in the current repertoire of the jazz ensemble. It is also important for students to listen to their respective section leaders in addition to the lead trumpet player, so this exercise can be used with the lead trombone player playing a P4 above everyone else, or the lead alto player leading the band, to help these section leaders develop their musical leadership skills. Ultimately, using any member of the jazz ensemble as the leader in this exercise helps to develop musical leadership among the students in addition to developing listening skills. This exercise works in any type of jazz ensemble situation where listening to a particular player is needed and also works well in sectionals.

**Listening to the bottom end.** A variation of the exercise in figures 9.1 and 9.2 is to focus listening toward the bottom end instruments of the band: the bari sax and bass trombone players. To guide students in the jazz ensemble toward focusing on listening to these two roles, the exercise in these figures can be used, but with either the bass trombone or bari sax player playing the scale up a P4. Another variation of this exercise is to have the bottom end players continuously play the root of a scale while the members of the winds and brass sections play the particular scale. This helps to establish the bari sax and bass trombone players as two important roles for creating foundations for intonation, balance, and melody and countermelody lines. In addition to the bari sax and bass trombone players, the bassist can also join in with this exercise (see figure 9.3). (See ▶ video 9.3, Bari Sax and Bass Trombone Playing the Root.)

Even though the bass trombone player and bari sax player are playing one pitch, continuously playing the root is a highly important contribution to the intonation and balance of the ensemble. When students become more comfortable with this exercise, encourage the bottom end players to make their own decisions with dynamics to help train the members of the jazz ensemble to really listen to these players.

# Intonation

It is (obviously) important for directors to guide students through the tuning process. However, this often entails the director using a tuner and telling the students whether they are sharp, flat, or in tune. Although using a tuner is beneficial in jazz ensemble rehearsals, directors need to be careful that they (a) do not always dictate the status of intonation at the expense of not teaching students how to listen for intonation or (b) teach students to develop 20/20 vision by staring at the needle on the tuner. It is important to guide students through the process of learning how to really listen to each other in the jazz ensemble. Because many jazz arrangements are voiced in a manner so that intervals range from a minor 2nd (m2) to a perfect fifth (P5) interval, using scales can help students improve their intonation and develop their listening skills in the jazz ensemble setting.

**Scales.** Scales can be a great way to improve balance, sound, and intonation in the winds and brass sections in a jazz ensemble. For balance and listening, playing scales in separate groups to create chords is a great way to refine listening skills among the members of the jazz ensemble. Warming up the jazz ensemble with a scale in unison in the key of the first tune in the rehearsal, or possibly multiple scales in the keys of the tunes for the rehearsal that day, helps to not only get students focused on listening but also get them familiar with the keys they will play in that day. This will ultimately make it easier for the members of the jazz ensemble to navigate through the tunes, especially if they are in a key they are not used to playing.

To begin the exercise in figure 9.4, the students no longer play scales in unison, but rather in succession, so they can practice hearing intervals. Group 1 begins playing the scale in whole notes, and then group 2 begins when group 1 is on the fourth note of the scale. Finally, group 3 begins when group 2 is on the fourth note of the scale. As each group returns to the root of the scale, the students continue to play the root of the scale. The various intervals of the fourth (e.g., perfect fourth, tritone) form the basis for this exercise. As the scale progresses, additional intervals are created (e.g., minor 2nd), creating many opportunities for students to play and listen for intonation with different intervals that they will encounter as they play jazz charts. (See ⊙ video 9.4, Scales [Concert Key].) Variations exist for the exercise in figure 9.4 in how to group students together. One example is for each section in the winds and brass to comprise a group. For example, the trumpet section is group 1, the trombone section is group 2, and the saxophone section is group 3. In addition to forming groups by section, the director can designate the lead players (trumpet, trombone, alto sax) as group 1, the middle players (2nd–4th trumpet parts, 2 and 3 trombone, 2nd alto, lead and 2nd tenor) as group 2, and the low-sounding parts (bari sax, bass trombone, bass guitar) as group 3.

Another option is to have someone improvise over these scales, such as the lead tenor, who often has many of the solos in the jazz ensemble. A side benefit of this approach is that the jazz band students will take their mastery of scales back to their other ensembles (e.g.,

**FIGURE 9.4** Scales (Concert Key)

**FIGURE 9.5** Major 2nd Scales (Concert Key)

concert band), which will greatly improve the ability of the members of other ensembles to play their scales.

Another scale exercise used by Sam Pilafian that helps students to hear and be able to tune intervals is playing two scales concurrently that are a major 2nd (M2) apart (e.g., concert B flat and concert C major scales). Playing these two scales together at the same time will definitely sound odd to students, for they are used to hearing more consonant intervals such as a P4 or P5. Playing scales concurrently in major 2nds will help to improve their listening skills, as many jazz charts are voiced with one part an M2 interval away from the other part (e.g., 3rd and 4th trumpet) (see figure 9.5). (See ⊙ video 9.5, Major 2nd Scales [Concert Key].) In this example, half the band plays the concert B♭ major scale, while the other half plays the concert C major scale. Various options exist for dividing the jazz ensemble into two groups. For example, divide the jazz ensemble in half, literally down the middle, creating two groups, or have certain players (e.g., lead players) play one scale while the rest of the band plays the other, etc. With this exercise use whole notes at first so the students can really get used to the sound of these two scales played together at the same time. Jazz ensemble directors will likely discover that students will try to open up the M2 interval to make it sound more like a minor 3rd, an interval they are often naturally more comfortable with hearing and playing. With this exercise, though, students will learn to hear the interval of an M2 and play it in tune.

It is important for the director to guide students through this process in terms of playing in tune. One option is to always have the bottom end instruments, or a group of students, play the root of the scale (in this example, concert B♭ major scale) so that the students have a reference point while they play this exercise. This exercise can be used with any two scales where the roots of the scale are a major 2nd apart and works well as a warm-up activity or during a rehearsal. For example, in the middle of a rehearsal it can help to use the exercise in figure 9.5 to improve intonation if jazz ensemble members are not in alignment with intonation. It can help to get the students listening to each other and getting them to make independent musical decisions regarding intonation. In the heat of a performance, the director cannot stop the jazz ensemble and tell the students how to correct their intonation.

After the students in the jazz ensemble begin to improve their ability to hear the intervals in these scales, the next step is to practice hearing and subsequently tuning smaller intervals. In the example in figure 9.6, the jazz ensemble members once again play two scales simultaneously, but with this exercise the scales are a minor 2nd apart. (See ⊙ video 9.6, Minor 2nd Scales [Concert Key].)

Similar to the major 2nd scale exercise, this minor 2nd scale exercise helps the students get used to hearing smaller intervals, often present in voicings in their respective sections and within the jazz ensemble. For example, a 4th trumpet part may contain an A♭ and the 3rd trumpet part could have a G♮. As the jazz ensemble becomes comfortable playing these intervals and the director hears them being played in tune, additional intervals, such as a tritone, can be used in this manner to help develop the ears of the students.

**Tuning exercise.** An activity used by Sam Pilafian specifically for tuning that helps students develop their ears and make independent decisions about intonation is the exercise in figure 9.7. (See ⊙ video 9.7, Concert B♭, Concert B Tuning Exercise [Concert Key].) In this exercise, half of the jazz ensemble members play a concert B♭ while the other half play a concert B. There is no time meter with this exercise. The director conducts the first pitch, then indicates when to change to the next pitch in measure two, and there is a third indication for everyone to play a unison concert B flat in measure 3. That is, the jazz ensemble

**FIGURE 9.6** Minor 2nd Scales (Concert Key)

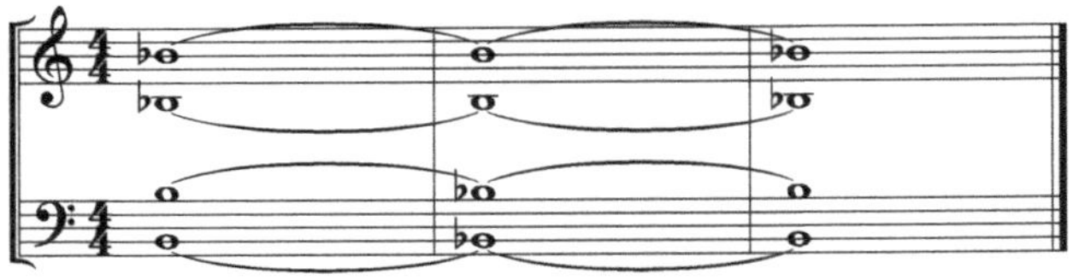

**FIGURE 9.7** Concert B♭, Concert B Tuning Exercise (Concert Key)

members who play concert B♭ then play a concert B, and vice versa, before everyone plays the unison concert B flat. Another way to think of this is:

Group 1: (1) Concert B♭, (2) concert B, (3) concert B♭.
Group 2: (1) Concert B, (2) concert B♭, (3) concert B♭.

When the students all play the unison B♭, it is easy for them to hear any discrepancies with intonation after playing the minor 2nd intervals. Although the director may have to do some fine tuning and guidance with the band, the students almost always correct any issues with intonation of their own accord. This exercise helps with the old adage that tuning is not an event; it is a process. Doing this exercise helps students make tuning decisions on their own, not solely with a director telling them whether they are sharp, flat, or in tune.

Similar to previous exercise groupings, the director can decide how to form the two groups. For example, the jazz ensemble can literally be divided down the middle, or the section leaders could comprise group 1 and everyone else group 2.

## Groove

While the development of higher quality sound for the jazz ensemble becomes established with proper balance, blend, and intonation, it is important to work on the groove, or time feel, of the jazz ensemble as well. Groove aids with style and getting the jazz ensemble members to play together. Similar to intonation, it is important for directors to teach their students to be able to make musical decisions regarding groove on their own.

**Organic groove.** Ultimately all jazz ensemble members are responsible for groove; however, teaching the winds and brass players to listen to the rhythm section will help improve groove during both rehearsals and performances. To help teach students to generate groove themselves, directors can guide the winds and brass players to listen to the bass player and the drummer. Listening to the bass player and the drummer (playing the ride cymbal) places the focus on two of the most fundamental components of groove in a jazz ensemble (see figure 9.8). (See ▶ video 9.8, Bass and Ride Cymbal Exercise [Concert Key].) To begin the exercise in figure 9.8, the director has the bass player play a low F on the e string concurrent with the drummer striking the ride cymbal. The bass player and drummer play at the same time (the director can conduct this), and it is important to let the sound decay naturally. Guide the students in the jazz band to listen to what is happening to the sound (it decays at the same rate). The bass player and drummer repeat this process so the jazz ensemble members can really hear the decay in sound. After playing this exercise a couple of times, the jazz ensemble members begin to focus more intently on the bass player and the

**FIGURE 9.8** Bass and Ride Cymbal Exercise (Concert Key)

**FIGURE 9.9** Bass Player and Drummer Playing Quarter Note Blues Groove

**FIGURE 9.10** Blues in F Groove with Elaborations

drummer playing the ride cymbal—two critical components of setting up the groove in the jazz ensemble.

Next, the directors count off 4 beats at a tempo of their choice. The bassist repeats quarter notes on the low F while the drummer plays quarter notes on the ride cymbal (see figure 9.9). The director needs to actively guide the bassist and drummer so they really listen to each other and line up their quarter notes. The director will need to reinforce the notion that the bass player and drummer need to play only quarter notes and no other rhythms at this point. A metronome can be used to assist with groove and to get the students to focus on a fixed pulse. In addition, doing without a metronome helps to make the students more responsible for really listening to each other and generating their own time. (See ▶ video 9.9, Bass Player and Drummer Playing Quarter Note Blues Groove.) Once the bass player and drummer play a solid quarter note groove, the bass player can begin walking a bass line in F blues, using only quarter notes while the drummer plays quarter note rhythms on the ride cymbal. Again, keeping the groove simple really helps to get these two players listening to each other. Make sure the winds and brass (not to mention the piano player and guitarist) are listening as well. Once the director feels that a solid time feel is established, the bass player and drummer can begin emphasizing beats 2 and 4, then adding any sixteenth note or eighth note elaborations to the groove at this point (see figure 9.10). (See ▶ video 9.10, Blues in F Groove with Elaborations.)

Now that a solid groove has been established, the winds and brass players can participate. For example, the jazz ensemble members can play a quarter note on the downbeat of each measure on an F blues scale. This can help the winds and brass players to really focus on the bass line and ride cymbal while being responsible for placement of the quarter note. The director can modify this exercise for a particular tune in the repertoire, so it does not always have to be a blues. For example, a medium swing Basie chart would have a different feel than a bossa nova chart. As members of the jazz ensemble begin to master this exercise, the winds and brass players can play on different parts of the measure (e.g., beat 2, beats 2 and 4), and then different parts of the beat (e.g., upbeats). Simplifying the groove with this exercise really helps to get the jazz ensemble members to listen to each other and helps them to establish, play, and correct as needed for any fluctuations in groove on their own without the director always having to stop and tell them what to do.

## Summary

When playing jazz music, it is highly important for high school winds and brass players to develop the ability to really listen to not only themselves but each other in the jazz ensemble. With the exercises presented in this chapter, directors can actively guide their students through the process of developing their musicianship to a higher level. In turn, this provides a solid platform for them to grow as musicians, capable of making independent musical decisions when they perform jazz music.

## Questions for Discussion

1. The exercises in this chapter are designed for a big band jazz ensemble. How can you adapt the exercises in this chapter for use with different types of jazz ensembles, such as a jazz combo?
2. How might you adapt these exercises if students play what are considered nontraditional instruments (e.g., oboe) in the big band jazz ensemble?
3. As a director of a jazz ensemble, how might you guide your students through the process of teaching each other to make musical decisions and listen to specific players (e.g., lead trumpet) in the jazz ensemble on their own?
4. Given that these exercises are intended to help directors of high school jazz ensembles teach their students how to listen to each other and whom they should listen to, how would you adapt these exercises for use with different age levels and in different ensembles, for example, concert band, middle school jazz band, or beginning band?
5. How might you take a chart, such as a Basie chart, and adapt it so that musical phrases from the chart could be used as playing and listening exercises similar to the ones presented in this chapter?

## Note

1. In chapter 3 in this volume, mentoring is described as an important process for directors to learn more about teaching jazz music. During the course of my career I have been fortunate to have fantastic mentors who were generous with their time and taught me a lot about directing a jazz ensemble. Two mentors stand out: Gary Gillett and Sam Pilafian, both of whom instilled in me the concept that we need to teach students to be musicians, not simply robots who can play a specific jazz chart not for note for a concert. Sam Pilafian has designed and used some of the exercises presented in this chapter. Although I have modified them somewhat over the years, Sam uses some versions of these exercises when he rehearses jazz ensembles.

# 10

# High School Rhythm Section

Daniel Fabricius

## Don't Trust Me; Trust That Hi-Hat

Just as Bruce thinks that instrumental pedagogy instruction is best delivered in the concert band setting, he also admits that he does not spend much time, if any, teaching the rhythm section. The reason behind this is rooted as much in his relative unfamiliarity with the rhythm section instruments as it is in the fact that there is not enough time in jazz ensemble (30 minutes a week) to delve heavily into instrumental pedagogy:

> I think the rhythm section thing is really intimidating—it still is for me. My thing when the kid comes in with a guitar over his back, I just tell him, "If you can't read, I can't help you. I could probably tune your guitar if I had to, but I don't really know much about the guitar. Piano kid, you know, here's the chart—figure it out." The rhythm section stuff—they're pretty much on their own.

While the rhythm section functions in a variety of different roles, Emily teaches her rhythm section students that their number one job is to keep steady time, because the time has to be in place before anything else can be achieved. To help her rhythm section players develop their sense of steady time, Emily continually reminds them that the hi-hat should never stop. "It's funny how little kids when they get excited they lose that hi-hat. That hi-hat just stops, but you got to tell them 'that hi-hat is the only person you really trust—don't trust me; trust that hi-hat to lock it in."

I believe that the most significant factor in my own musical development as a jazz musician was the process of learning, watching, listening, copying what I heard, and asking questions. Although I did not realize it at the time, I actually learned the nuances of playing jazz the same way that young apprentice jazz players learned in the early twentieth century in New Orleans, through the "aural tradition." Young jazz players at that time were often "schooled" as apprentice musicians by listening to the music and watching their mentors. Fortunately, my teachers stressed music literacy along with their encouragement to attend concerts, listen to recordings, and jam with my friends.

Today, music educators and students have many resources available to study the specifics of playing any instrument. However, as educators it should be our job to guide students to use their ears along with all of the other resources. Although the notation of traditional Western art music seems complete, musicians still need to learn "common practices." The notation of jazz music is not always as precise as in Western art music—and this music is also filled with common practices that players need to know. For example, the jazz rhythm section is comparable to the use of continuo during the baroque era, when a cello or bassoon supplied the bass line and a harpsichord supplied the harmony by reading figured bass notation and adhering to the common practices of the era. We have the same expectation of jazz rhythm section players. Jazz players need to know the style of the music, the form of the composition, and the harmonic progression of the piece. By adding in a knowledge base of common practices, jazz musicians can create artistic performances using minimal or even no written notation. This chapter focuses on ways that the jazz ensemble conductor can coach high-school-level-rhythm section players to make rehearsals more beneficial to all and to attain more authentic performances. The chapter includes details on various jazz styles, instrument-specific tips, and remedies for common issues within the rhythm section. It is divided into six main sections: (a) player profiles, (b) teaching jazz ensemble concepts, (c) awareness of other players, (d) improvisation, (e) chart reading, and (f) self-directed learning. Readers should find the information in this chapter helpful in developing their own rehearsal techniques that will fit their specific teaching situations.

## Player Profiles

While the majority of jazz instruction for rhythm section players may reside with the jazz ensemble conductor, it is common for students playing these instruments to also receive instruction from teachers specializing in them. Therefore, it is also possible that some directors may never need to address instrument-specific issues with each of the players. However, all teaching situations are different, so I recommend that all conductors have a solid background in each of the instruments and have the tools to address "teaching the instrument" during rehearsals. This chapter does not address all instrument-specific issues within the rhythm section; please consult applicable chapters of this book for more in-depth information.

The amount of jazz ensemble experience that members of a typical school band have can be quite varied. Some students may have already had years of jazz ensemble experience before high school. However, less-experienced players in school jazz ensembles often still have adequate skills on their instruments. I suggest that before starting any lesson planning, directors evaluate the potential of the group by creating a profile of each of the players. I encourage readers to use a tool such as the "player profile" (see ⊙ appendix 10.1, "Jazz Ensemble Player Profile").

## Setup and Instrumentation

The typical rhythm section should have a minimum of these three elements: drums, bass, and at least one instrument to supply harmony. Most jazz ensemble arrangements are written for four players—piano, guitar, bass, and drums—and many also include the option of using vibraphone and additional percussion instruments in the rhythm section. I suggest using a setup that keeps the rhythm section players compact so that the players can see and hear each other.

**Vibraphone.** The vibraphone is usually considered an optional instrument for both melodic and harmonic playing. Many published charts will not include a vibraphone part, so the director may need to give the player a piano, guitar, and/or flute part so that the player can supply harmonic accompaniment and also play any important melodic lines. Many directors also create their own vibraphone parts, using a mixture of significant melodic material and harmony notes that fulfill the same role as piano or guitar. The player will usually use four mallets when playing harmony. This is considered an advanced technique for high school students and may require some specialized instruction for the player.

The balance of this instrument can be adjusted by using mallets with various weights or hardness. Vibraphone mallets are generally cord-wound, while marimba mallets are yarn-wound. Make sure that the player is striking the bars so that a resonant tone is produced. Playing over the nodes (where the cord runs through the bar) will produce an inferior tone that is not resonant. The use of the motor to provide vibrato is really not often done in a jazz setting. Parts will usually indicate if and when to use the vibrato effect. Directors and players are encouraged to decide on this factor by researching common practices in the literature they are playing. Balance issues in performances can be rectified by using a microphone on the vibes for melodic playing and for solos.

**Auxiliary.** The literature for the contemporary school jazz band can also include parts for auxiliary percussion instruments. Sometimes specific parts are included with the set of music. However, players and conductors can often use their creativity to tastefully add appropriate instruments to add more interesting colors or to add rhythmic reinforcement. Historical use of auxiliary percussion in the swing style is a bit limited, but starting in the 1960s, it became more common to use conga or bongo drums to enhance swing-style jazz compositions. Rock- and world-music-style compositions are often more easily adaptable to adding extra percussion sounds. Tambourine, shaker, cowbell, and conga drums are common additions to many jazz compositions, but there are many other percussion instruments that may also be suitable. I suggest making notes on the score to keep track of any additions. Make sure that the density or volume of rhythm instruments will not overshadow the rest of the band.

# Teaching Jazz Ensemble Concepts

Our task as high school educators should be to guide and coach the rhythm section students *along with* the students playing other instruments even though the role of the rhythm section instruments is far different from that of the others. There is often a tendency for directors to pay less attention to the rhythm section or to address the section once the winds have learned their parts. The other problem with teaching the rhythm section is that each of the instruments is uniquely different in terms of its role in the ensemble and playing technique. Please consult each of the instrument-specific chapters of this book for more in-depth information. It is up to the director to address *all* elements of the band by providing the proper instruction and feedback for each section and each part within each section. Several important concepts apply to every member of the band: (a) balance/blend/intonation/tone quality, (b) pulse, (c) precision, and (d) style. Following is a summary of useful information and strategies that address the rhythm section in these four broad concepts (see ⊚ video 10.1, Warming Up the Rhythm Section; and ⊚ appendix 10.2, "Video Clip Guide").

## Balance/Blend/Intonation/Tone Quality

We must expect that each instrument will produce a characteristic tone quality first, so conductors may find it necessary to remind rhythm section students of proper playing techniques in this regard. Student musicians sometimes lose a sense of their own sound, especially when they are challenged with more difficult music. We also need to remind students of intonation issues in their performance. During rehearsal, conductors often ask smaller groups of wind players to play through short passages. Try adding one of two rhythm section players so that all can hear the intonation between the winds and rhythm instruments. The blend of individual rhythm section instruments playing soli parts with other instruments is another important consideration. Again, isolating melodic lines in rehearsal gives all players a chance to focus on this aspect of playing. Rhythm section instruments often serve two roles in an ensemble as they switch from providing the rhythm or harmonic accompaniment to playing melodic lines with other instruments. The conductor may need to provide feedback to students to make them aware of their roles and to help them adjust to the various playing situations.

The most common issue may be finding the proper balance of each rhythm section instrument. The rhythm section players must also be aware of balancing their volume with the rest of the band. For instance, it is common for the drummer to be unaware of saxophone section volume because this section is normally seated in front. Also, guitarists who are assigned to play a unison melodic line with saxophone or trumpet may need help finding the proper dynamic to balance. Section players need to hear the proper balance with their own ears and must develop a sense of playing with attention to proper balance as musical situations change within a composition. One of the most obvious changes must occur when a chart transitions from a full ensemble sound to a soloist. The players must learn to instantly adjust their volume to respond to these role changes (see ⊚ video 10.2, Knowing Your Role in the Ensemble; and ⊚ appendix 10.2, "Video Clip Guide").

## Steadiness of Pulse

While steadiness of pulse is a concern for all members of the ensemble, the wind players generally listen to the rhythm section to guide them. All musicians need to spend some time practicing individually with a metronome, and using an amplified metronome in the jazz ensemble rehearsal can shed light on steadiness issues for all players. Please consult chapter 5 in this volume for more in-depth information.

The main "pulse instruments" in the jazz ensemble are the bass and drums, and these players need to have a great awareness of "time" as they play. All players may become distracted from time if a passage is difficult to play. The ensemble may experience an undesired tempo change if there is a sudden change in the texture, since the "resting instruments" may not be feeling the pulse before they make their entrance. The most common reason for individuals playing out of pulse is that they are not paying attention to the entire ensemble as they play. Directors will often need to rehearse sections alone but constantly remind everyone to *listen across the band*. Again, try adding one or two rhythm section instruments when rehearsing wind sections separately. I find that adding a rhythm instrument often helps everyone hear outside of their own section and also allows the rhythm section players to hear how their parts fit with the wind sections.

## Precision of Pitches and Rhythms

The director needs to hear pitches and rhythms accurately as the full ensemble plays. It is common for any musician to "misread" rhythms, and younger players may lack the confidence to fix problems themselves. Sometimes the players who were right assume that they were wrong and just go with the majority. Directors need to keep track of errors and make corrections before the players grow accustomed to playing rhythms incorrectly. There are several common reasons for wrong pitches. Key changes, playing in unfamiliar keys, an abundance of accidentals, or returning accidentals in a measure are probably the most common reasons. The harmonic instruments of the rhythm section face an additional challenge if they are attempting to play unfamiliar chords. The players may not yet have extended chords and altered chords in their vocabulary. These players will need to read the notation carefully, make the connection between what they see on the page and how to play it, and become familiar with the quality of any unfamiliar chords. I suggest that directors have resources available to assist players with finding suitable voicing on piano, guitar, or vibes. Books such as *The Chord Voicing Handbook* by Matt Harris and Jeff Jarvis will be a valuable resource for conductors.[1]

## Presentation of Style

The ability to perform in a variety of jazz styles is a common expectation of high-school-level rhythm section players. It is possible to narrow the styles to just three broad categories: swing, rock, and world music. There are certainly many specific stylistic variations within these main styles, and it is important that the conductor and the players have at least a basic understanding of the type of sound needed for whatever style the ensemble is playing. There are countless resource recordings available to assist directors with understanding the specifics of various jazz styles. Please consult chapter 20 in this volume for more in-depth information.

**Swing.** Swing is a general term that suggests a triplet feel on each beat expressed as swung eighth notes. A large portion of jazz ensemble literature is written in this style, and the tempo will often dictate particular elements to address in rehearsals. The *shuffle style* uses the same rhythmic feel and interpretation as the swing style; however, due to influences from rhythm and blues (R&B), it is often presented with a more aggressive pulse on every beat. There is less subtlety in the shuffle style, with the most noticeable difference being in the drum part. The backbeat used in the shuffle will create more of a rhythmic "groove" than in jazz. The *jazz waltz* is another common groove within the swing style. Directors can find many suitable audio examples or various swing styles and should emphasize the essential differences and similarities to each player in the rhythm section.

**Rock.** Rock is a style in jazz ensemble music characterized by the same elements as the popular rock music that evolved starting in the mid-twentieth century. The rhythms are played in a straight eighth-note feel, *not* in a swing style. Although syncopation is an important element in jazz music, rock compositions do tend to be more simplistic in terms of rhythm. Layering simple rhythms can create a "feel" or "groove" that provides a strong foundation for a rock style composition. The bass and drums provide a more noticeable pulse in rock music. The funk genre is a mixture of soul music, jazz, and R&B. Funk music de-emphasizes melody and harmony and instead highlights a strong rhythmic groove of electric bass and drums in the foreground. Funk often uses the same extended chords found in bebop jazz. However, unlike bebop jazz, with its complex, fast chord changes, funk songs are often based on extended "vamps" on a single chord. Although the funk style is similar to rock (straight eighth notes, electronic instruments, backbeats), funk can be a more rhythmically complex music. The individual parts are more rhythmically independent, and the music lends itself to more instrumental virtuosity.

**World music.** World music is a general term that encompasses the utilization of rhythms of various cultures around the world. Many styles of music have been absorbed into jazz, ranging from African drumming ensembles, to Caribbean salsa, to the Brazilian bossa nova. Musicians now have many resources available to learn essential rhythmic elements for an endless list of world music styles. For the jazz ensemble conductor, a good place to start learning about world music styles is drum set method books. I suggest *Groove Essentials* by Tommy Igoe and *Studio and Big Band Drumming* by Steve Houghton as very useful resources.[2] (See ⊙ video 10.3. Another Warm-up; and ⊙ appendix 10.2, "Video Clip Guide.")

**Ballads.** A jazz ballad is a composition presented in a lyrical style and usually performed at a slow tempo. The jazz ensemble repertoire includes many popular songs that were first presented by vocalists. These songs make up the "Great American Songbook" and are considered standards that are known by most serious jazz players. The jazz ballad can be a composition in *any* of the styles previously discussed. Ballads provide a change of pace to any concert program. Jazz ballads usually contain several impressive elements: (a) solo or voice feature, (b) orchestration featuring a variety of instrumental colors, (c) more opportunity for rhythm section players to interact with the melody due to the slower tempo and thinner scoring, and (d) an opportunity for greater emotional intensity.

Rhythm section players can become prominent in ballads because a slower tempo creates more "space" to fill. Any of the rhythm section instruments can supply tasteful improvised fills to enhance the featured melodic material. The harmonic instruments can explore a wider range, and the drummer can utilize beautiful cymbal colors.

It is important to maintain an interesting sound in the rhythm section on ballads; this can be accomplished by looking first at the form of the song and the overall structure of the arrangement. For instance, rhythm section players can change the mood of the song by altering rhythms during the bridge section of the song. Using different registers or different colors of the instrument can also create more interest. Adding more rhythmic activity for the comping instruments can fill up space, and lessening the activity can put the attention back onto the melody. The director can identify what role each will play and also help the players to make artistic decisions on their own. One of the most difficult challenges for drummers is to play with brushes for slow swing-style ballads. There are many available resources for directors and students to study various brush techniques used in ballads. Learning jazz ballads can be very difficult for less-experienced players and challenging for directors. However, playing ballads provides an opportunity for all ensemble players (but especially the rhythm section) to display a mature understanding of jazz (see ⊙ video 10.4, Rhythm Section Common Practice; and ⊙ appendix 10.2, "Video Clip Guide").

## Awareness of Other Players

One of the main challenges for rhythm section players is to always be aware of what others in the section are doing. Each of the instruments has a different role to play as the section accompanies the rest of the ensemble. We can look to the African drumming ensemble as a comparison. In this type of ensemble, each voice plays a repetitive rhythmic pattern, and each of those rhythms together forms a polyrhythmic texture. A well-balanced ensemble playing perfectly aligned rhythms can have a mesmerizing effect on listeners. The same holds true for the jazz rhythm section. Players must be taught to constantly listen to each other and react to what they hear. The director needs to have a great awareness of all aspects of performance and should help the rhythm section learn to play with better clarity.

Student musicians can learn a lot from observing how professionals play; hopefully they will notice that professionals often look at each other for visual cues and that they respond to what they hear from each other. It may almost seem that the players are mind readers. In reality, experienced players have developed an intuition about what other players will play as well as their own way of responding to what they hear. These rhythm section "conversations" demonstrate maturity and a great depth of understanding that high school players should be developing.

Awareness and "musical conversation" skills are even more important when the rhythm section is accompanying a soloist. Although we are teaching jazz through playing in a large jazz ensemble, a lot of jazz playing in the world is done in a small group or "combo" setting. At a bare minimum, the rhythm section players will provide the framework for the soloist: pulse, bass line, and harmony. Real artistry can occur when a good soloist is accompanied by musicians who are really paying attention to the soloist. The rhythm section can serve as a catalyst, causing the soloist to play with great expression. Or the soloist can lead the section to play with more or less intensity.

Encourage students to study recorded performances that emphasize this element of playing in a rhythm section. In rehearsal, try giving the players a specific direction about intensity throughout a solo section. Try instructing one of the players to be the proactive leader. Try having students take turns leading. Allow them to "converse" and respond to what they hear others playing.

Probably the most important role for supporting the ensemble is that of the drummer. While sometimes all that is needed is a steady rhythm by the drummer, an arrangement can be greatly enhanced when the drummer *sets up* tutti ensemble rhythms. The drummer playing short setup fills should assist the winds by identifying exactly when to play syncopated rhythmic figures. Some composers/arrangers write specific rhythms that drummers can play as fills or setups to support the ensemble. This is often the case with charts written at the easy and intermediate levels. Advanced and professional-level charts will be notated with just the ensemble rhythms notated on drum parts, leaving it up to the player to tastefully interpret what to play. Charts like this may require the director to assist the player by providing additional guidance. (See ⊙ video 10.5, Listening and Interacting; and ⊙ appendix 10.2, "Video Clip Guide.")

## Improvisation

Although the main task of rhythm section players is to accompany, each of the players also needs to be able to improvise. Providing an authentic jazz accompaniment requires the more advanced musicians to create their own parts, similar to baroque musicians reading figured bass. More advanced high-school-level arrangements may have rhythm section parts that are completely notated. Yes, the chart should be fine if the musicians "play the ink," but the performance will be more artistic and characteristic of the style if the players can add their own touches. Whether by creating tasteful melodic fills, creating a walking bass line, or creating interesting drum setups for the ensemble, the rhythm players should feel comfortable improvising their accompaniment to the other instruments.

Jazz ensemble arrangements also include sections for improvised solos, and the rhythm section musicians should experience being the featured players in addition to always playing the supportive role. Students playing the harmonic instruments are already reading the chords and may be quite familiar with the concept of soloing. Some students are hesitant to solo if they are not secure with their technique or if they lack a vocabulary of jazz motives to play. Encourage them to try improvisation, but remind them that this is a skill that must be practiced. Students will get better and more secure as they study and practice. Students may require extra coaching sessions to become proficient with improvisation. This book includes chapters related to improvisation.

## Chart Reading

Although teaching the aural aspects of playing jazz was presented at the start of this chapter, the rhythm section players must also come to terms with printed notation. Depending on the past experience of the players, the students may need to learn about repeated sections, interpreting written comments concerning techniques that are idiomatic to their instrument, and jazz-specific terminology. Players may also require some instruction about music theory as it pertains to their own performance. Bass, guitar, piano, and vibes players may need to learn how to interpret chord symbols so that they know exactly which notes are chord tones. They will also need to learn appropriate voicings for chords. Bass players will need to learn how to construct a walking bass line by just reading the chord symbol notation. Drum parts for jazz ensemble music can range from too much information to minimal directions. Student musicians will need to learn to decipher the notation and mark their music in a way that provides simple indications to clarify the notation. Please consult chapter 2 in this volume for more in-depth information.

The individual parts for jazz ensemble compositions are sometimes referred to as "partially notated." For instance, the pianist might find that the part includes suggested chord voicing for the player to use. These are usually written in "whole note" values. Composers do not intend that the pianist should play only whole notes and half notes. Rather, it is up to the player to use the suggested voicings (if needed), but more important to create appropriate comping rhythms to fit the ensemble. Guitar music will probably indicate many measures with only chord symbols and "slashes" on each beat. Again, the player is expected to comp rhythms that are appropriate to the style.

Even with just two instruments comping, the players will need to listen to each other to make sure that the result is a clear mix of each instrument. Using three comping instruments at the same time usually produces a cluttered sound unless the players understand how to make each instrument fit. It may be best for the director to assign which players will comp in each section of an arrangement until the players learn how to make those decisions. Always encourage the players to communicate with each other concerning the texture when comping.

Although notation reading is a very desirable skill for rhythm section players, I suggest that directors coach their students to read but also be able to play *without* constantly looking at the page. Once the players know the form of the composition, they can break it down into sections that contain a specific number of measures. For the bass and harmonic players, they will then need to memorize the harmonic "changes" of the composition. For a piece written using a 32-bar song form of AABA, each section is eight measures long. There are three A sections and just one B section to learn. Memorizing just 16 bars does not seem so bad. It should be even easier to keep track of the three 4-bar sections of a traditional 12-bar blues. Memorizing the form and the changes allows players to become more aware of other musical elements as they occur. They will certainly experience a much more fulfilling musical experience when they can add this type of maturity to their playing.

# Self-Directed Learning

At the very least, all band members should occasionally practice their jazz ensemble music outside of rehearsals. High school musicians are capable of playing with outstanding technical proficiency, but there is little chance of this happening if the student only plays during rehearsals. Students need to study their *instrument* if they want to become better jazz ensemble players. They should be encouraged to work on technical exercises and solos that will advance their playing skills. Serious jazz students should also practice jazz etudes, transcriptions, and improvisation. It is up to the director to encourage students or to provide additional learning opportunities for them. Recommending good private teachers who are master players on their instruments can inspire students to learn more advanced techniques and lead them to become self-directed in their learning.

Rhythm section players should be encouraged to play together in situations other than just with the jazz ensemble. They can be the core of a jazz or rock combo. Encourage them to jam with each other and other musicians or find a way to provide some extra playing opportunities. There are many resources that will be helpful to students who want to learn more without the guidance of a teacher or their jazz ensemble director. Provide the encouragement and resource information, and you can help your students become the best players they can be.

# Questions for Discussion

1. Bruce, an expert 30-year veteran band director, admits that teaching the rhythm section still intimidates him. Do you think this is true for most band directors who play brass or woodwind primary instruments? Is it a cause for not having a jazz band, or is the director's job more about teaching style and musicianship anyway?
2. What are your thoughts and rationale regarding leading a jazz ensemble with an *expanded* rhythm section?
3. Brainstorm ideas for executing a short lesson on *awareness of other players* using short rhythmic motives.
4. Examine drum set parts to several charts and identify opportunities to *set up ensemble figures* played by other instruments.

# Notes

1. Matt Harris and Jeff Jarvis, *The Chord Voicing Handbook* (Kendor Music, Inc., 1994).
2. Tommy Igoe, *Groove Essentials* (Hudson Music, 2006); Steve Houghton, *Studio and Big Band Drumming* (C.L. Barnhouse, 1985).

# 11

# High School Improvisation

Michael Grace

## Blues Scales—Boy, Do Those Get Old!

While some school jazz teachers may use the blues scale when teaching improvisation, Emily does not because she has found that students use it as a crutch and don't ever move beyond its use:

> I think that you really limit your creativity when all you can do is play a blues scale. A lot of [students] are like, "that's the only scale I want to play forever" and boy, does that get old.

As students have success with and become comfortable improvising over vamps, Emily begins to add tunes with simple chord progressions. To have success improvising over these progressions, Emily first drills the students on a variety of different scales, beginning with major scales. She simplifies the changes for the students by helping them find the key area within which the chord changes occur and improvise within that key area. For instance, Emily will have students improvise using the notes from the tonic scale over $ii^7$-$V^7$-I changes. Later, she helps students make more choices about which notes to play and when, but in the beginning students will have success playing just the tonic scale notes over the $ii^7$-$V^7$-I changes:

> Basically, for a long time, you're going to find pieces that are $ii^7$-$V^7$-I and they can either play $ii^7$ and V7 and I or they can just play I and it's gonna work. Eventually you start to say, "well, this chunk of the piece is in this key and the next three bars are in a different key."

If you were to ask jazz musicians how they think about improvisation, you would probably get as many different answers as there were individuals whom you asked. However, there is one guiding principle to which almost everyone would agree, especially when teaching beginners: express the tonality of the piece. This chapter outlines a sequential process, termed *tonicization*,[1] for learning to express the tonality of pieces that use ii[7]-V[7]-I progressions and the 12-bar blues progression.

## ii[7]-V[7]-I Progressions

Since much of the jazz repertoire contains this basic ii[7]-V[7]-I chord progression (often shortened to ii-V-I), it is important that jazz teachers have a sequence for teaching students to improvise within these chord changes. Within this progression there are three families of 7th chords: major, dominant, and minor. Since there are 12 major keys, one could then say that there are 36 basic scales and 36 basic sets of chord tones that present 72 basic applications that students can practice for facility with the ii[7]-V[7]-I chord progression.[2]

## Learning Scales and Chords

First, I like to have students learn and practice the chord roots of three families of 7th chords: major, dominant, and minor (see ⊙ video 11.1, Circle of 4ths Major Chords, and ⊙ play-along recording 11.1; ⊙ video 11.2, Circle of 4ths Dominant Chords, and ⊙ play-along recording 11.2; and ⊙ video 11.3, Circle of 4ths Minor Chords, and ⊙ play-along recording 11.3). Then have students learn the scales that correlate to these three families of 7th chords: Ionian for major, Mixolydian for Dominant, and Dorian for minor and practice them in all 12 keys using the circle of 4ths.

It will take time for students to learn all major, minor, and dominant scales/chords in all 12 major keys, so be patient and allow them time to get these under their fingers. One good routine is to just work on major scales/chords one key at a time until the majority of the class has this relatively well in hand. If necessary, begin in quarter notes until eighth notes become comfortable for a majority of the class's melodic players. Keep adding keys to the drills until students can perform all 12 major scales in the circle of 4ths. Vary styles like swing, bossa nova, funk, reggae, double-time bossa nova, etc. Then use the same process to have students learn the dominant and minor scales/chords around the circle of 4ths (see figure 11.1). (See ⊙ video 11.4, Circle of 4ths Major Scales, and ⊙ play-along recording 11.4; ⊙ video 11.5,

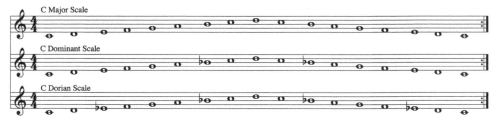

**FIGURE 11.1** Three Families of Seventh Scales

Circle of 4ths Dominant Scales, and ⊙ play-along recording 11.5; and ⊙ video 11.6, Circle of 4ths Minor Scales, and ⊙ play-along recording 11.6.) Having these scales and chords under their fingers in all 12 major keys is essential because it equips students with the foundational tools for expressing the tonalities of the piece (playing within the various ii⁷-V⁷-I changes).

## Tonicization

When students have these families of scales and chords under their fingers in all 12 major keys, it is time to introduce them to tonicization. Students now need to understand that a chord progression of Dm7–G7–CMaj7, for instance, represents a key area of C major *even if it is temporary and the overall key of the tune is different*. Since this represents C major, one could play a C major scale over all three chords, and though it would be a very basic approach, there would be no "wrong" (nondiatonic) notes. An improvisor could also apply a G mixolydian scale or a D minor scale across all three chords, and these scales would likewise contain only diatonic pitches within C major.

With this understanding, teachers can help students apply appropriate chords and scales to ii⁷-V⁷-I changes. A good first step would be to have them play the corresponding major chords and scales over all of the ii⁷-V⁷-I changes in the circle of 4ths (see ⊙ appendix 11.1, "ii⁷-V⁷-I Practice Sheet," as well as ⊙ video 11.7, ii⁷-V⁷-I Major Scale Applications, and ⊙ play-along recording 11.7). Then have students play the corresponding dominant chords and scales, and finally the corresponding minor chords and scales over ii⁷-V⁷-I changes in the circle of 4ths. This process not only reinforces students' technical ability to play the scales they previously learned, but more important, it shows them how to identify and target key areas represented by ii⁷-V⁷-I progressions.

Once students are comfortable targeting ii⁷-V⁷-I key areas with a single chord or scale, they can then target each key area with two and then three corresponding chords/scales. For instance, in a Dm7–G7–CMaj7 progression they could play the Dm7 scale over the ii⁷ and the V7, and play the CMaj7 over the I chord (see ⊙ video 11.8, ii⁷-V⁷-I Minor/Major Scale Applications, and ⊙ play-along recording 11.8). Another combination would be to play the G7 over the ii⁷ and the V7, and play the CMaj7 over the I chord (see ⊙ video 11.9, ii⁷-V⁷-I Dominant/Major Scale Applications, and ⊙ play-along recording 11.9). A final step would be to have students play the Dm7 over the II⁷, the G7 over the V7, and the CMaj7 over the I chord. Keep in mind, though, that a lot of repetition and patience will be needed. It may not be advisable to directly ask individuals to improvise at this point. This is a tricky time, and you do not want to scare anyone away from eventually trying to improvise. If you just continue on for a few short weeks, there will be a day when everyone is really swinging and you can pleasantly surprise the class by asking: "Would anyone like to take a solo?" Rest assured, if the groundwork has been laid, one or more (maybe all) students will want to take a shot at it.

## Applying ii⁷-V⁷-I Applications to Repertoire

Now is a good time to take a look at an example of how to apply some of the scale and chord tones that we investigated previously. At this point the students will probably understand the value of having scales and chords under their fingers. Using the tune "Opportuneistic" (see ⊚ appendix 11.2, " 'Opportuneistic' by Mike Grace"), have students play the head through a few times to make sure everyone understands the form (see ⊚ video 11.10, "Opportuneistic" by Mike Grace, and ⊚ play-along recording 11.10). The horns (saxes, trumpets, trombones, flutes, violins, violas, cellos, etc.—yes, you will have them all someday!) should know the melody well, and the rhythm section should play the chords and comp correctly in whatever style you choose to play.

**Major scale applications.** Once students have learned the tune, a good next step is to have them tonicize the key areas using corresponding major scales. Since the first key area is D major, begin by having them play a D major scale over the ii$^7$-V$^7$-I chords for the first 4 bars. Proceed in this fashion throughout the tune, targeting each key area with its corresponding major scale/chord (see ⊚ appendix 11.3, "Tonicizing 'Opportuneistic' with Major Scales," as well as ⊚ video 11.11, "Opportuneistic" with Major Scale Applications, and ⊚ play-along recording 11.11).

**Minor-major scale applications.** It is now time to make more advanced applications, and probably the next step is to have students apply the minor (Dorian) scale to the first 2 bars and then resolve that to the major scale for the last 2 bars of each line (4-bar phrase, still one key per line). It is a good time to begin pointing out a premise: what works for ii$^7$ also works for V7 and vice versa. Note that the chords change per bar, but that the scale sounds good over both chords. This application can be called the minor-major drill: minor scale for 2 bars, major scale for the last 2 bars. Continue on through the next 2 lines, making the same application, pointing out that each line sounds good because you are changing the scales to fit the new keys. Then the form takes you back home again. As before, take the class through this procedure much as you did with the major application. Just keep checking that these notes sound "good" to the class and reinforcing why they do so. Review the paragraphs above regarding the major application - the minor and later applications will be a very similar process, but the phrases are now 2 bars (see ⊚ appendix 11.4, "Tonicizing 'Opportuneistic' with Minor/Major Scales," as well as ⊚ video 11.12, "Opportuneistic" with Minor/Major Scale Applications, and ⊚ play-along recording 11.12).

**Dominant-major scale applications.** Finally, replace the minor scale with the dominant scale, noting once again that what works for ii$^7$ also works for V7 and vice versa. Just as you did with the minor scale application, use the dominant scale in the first 2 bars and then resolve that to the major scale for the last 2 bars of each line (4-bar phrase, each key) (see ⊚ appendix 11.5, "Tonicizing 'Opportuneistic' with Dominant/Major Scales," as well as ⊚ video 11.13, "Opportuneistic" with Dominant/Major Scale Applications, and ⊚ play-along recording 11.13). As before, take the class through this procedure much as you did the major and minor applications. This is now the dominant/major drill. The process will always be similar in many ways, and the students will have a procedure that is reliable to build upon.

Of course, accomplished jazz musicians will have many applications that fit their style, technique, and sophistication. But to the beginning improvisor, these concrete ideas will ring true for their tonal beginnings. They will later appreciate that they can improvise over a tune in several ways, giving them several good choices. The sophistication of chord extension and alterations, as well as more colorful scales, will all be approached soon enough. Encourage students to mix and match these as well as any permutations that they might invent. Keep reinforcing that many mistakes are OK; they are part of the process of learning to improvise. The effective element here is that these, as well as many more variations to come, are idiomatic sounds in the melodic development of jazz. The more students practice them, the better their ear-to-hand coordination becomes.

## More Sophisticated Tunes

Just as applications were begun on "Opportuneistic," the same process will apply to "Bird Sounds" (see figure 11.2). (See ⊙ video 11.14, "Bird Sounds" by Mike Grace, and ⊙ play-along recording 11.14.) Begin by making sure that everyone knows the head, playing the tune several times through so everyone is reasonably comfortable with it. Initially, apply only major scales to the tune. It is important to note that "Bird Sounds" is not as textbook a tune as "Opportuneistic." It is not all 4-bar phrases; some are 2-bar phrases (2-bar keys) and some are 4-bar phrases (4-bar keys). Reinforce the idea that the more interesting the repertoire, the more variations in phrasing, more keys, variations in major and minor, etc. Refer to ⊙ figure 11.2 while you study the following analysis of the tune:

FIGURE 11.2 "Bird Sounds" by Mike Grace

- **Bars 1–4**: The first major scale will only last 2 bars—up and down only once. Stop to make sure that everyone understands this. Have the class answer the question of how they know; the answer is that the chords in the 3rd and 4th bars do not belong to the overall key of the piece as indicated by the key signature. They are part of a new ii$^7$-V$^7$-I movement. After you feel that the class understands this, move to bars 3 and 4. It will be very important to note that here there is only a II$^7$-V$^7$ progression. However, it implies that there is a major key, and the assignment is to play major scales throughout the piece. Remind the class that what works with tonic major (I) also works with the subdominant (ii$^7$) and dominant (V$^7$), just as when they played only a major scale in their very first drill on "Opportuneistic" across the ii$^7$-V$^7$-I of each line.
- **Bars 5–6**: Then the next 2 bars return to the original key again, using the major scale, which should be becoming more apparent at this point. The students will play the scale up and down only once, as it is 2 bars long. Keep asking the class how long each key lasts. Make them figure it out as they now have the ability to do so.
- **Bars 7–10**: The next key is a 4-bar phrase, and remember to have the class say how they know it: because it is a complete ii$^7$-V$^7$-I this time (the first complete one in the tune). Play the major scale in eighth notes up and down twice to fit the 4 bars.
- **Bars 11–12**: The next key is a 2-bar phrase, as it is a 4th new key by way of a ii$^7$-V$^7$ progression. Again, have the class answer how they know it is a new key. Stay with major scales all the way through the tune.
- **Bars 13–16**: The last key is *the* key of the piece, and make the point again that the tonality is back to home. You will now have "tonicized" this whole piece with only major scales (see ⊙ applications in figure 11.2).

Once students have played the tune, analyzed it, and understand how to apply appropriate scales to the progression, they are ready to begin practicing those applications. Just as students used scale applications with "Opportuneistic," have them make the same appropriate applications to "Bird Sounds."

**Major applications.** Have students play through the form with the correct major scales several times so that they can actually hear the keys/tonality change (see ⊙ video 11.15, "Bird Sounds" with Major Scale Applications, and ⊙ play-along recording 11.15).

**Major/minor applications.** Now proceed to the minor-major drill. Have the class play major scales on the major chords and minor scales on the ii$^7$s and V$^7$s, thus: 2 bars major, 2 bars minor, 2 bars major, 2 bars minor, 2 bars major, 2 bars minor, 2 bars minor, and 2 bars major (see ⊙ video 11.16, "Bird Sounds" with Major/Minor Scale Applications, and ⊙ play-along recording 11.16). That puts a new sound to the tune and is a deeper tonicization than just major. Now most students will begin to hear and sense the applications, all the while maintaining good style with the chords coming at the correct places; insist on this. Try some improvisation throughout the class with those who wish to do so. Still do not *make* anyone do it. That will come soon enough.

**Dominant/major applications.** As before, in "Opportuneistic," you can now make the dominant/major application, noting once again that what works for ii$^7$ also works for V7 and vice versa, thus: 2 bars major, 2 bars dominant, 2 bars major, 2 bars dominant, 2 bars major, 2 bars dominant, 2 bars dominant, and 2 bars major. Proceed just as you did with the minor/major application, this time having the students apply the minor/dominant application (see ▶ video 11.17, "Bird Sounds" with Dominant/Major Scale Applications, and ▶ play-along recording 11.17). Maintain eighth notes and stay in style. By now the rhythm section members should have a good idea of what they each have to do to furnish the style and the groove for which the horns can play over and sound like they are emulating good jazz style (see ▶ videos 11.18–11.21 for other relevant scale applications, as well as ▶ play-along recordings 11.18–11.21).

It is now time to try to some more improvisation, if in your judgment almost everyone understands the major, minor, and dominant applications. There will continue to be many mistakes. The horn players will probably have come through traditional music programs, being good readers but not really having much, if any, improvisation experience. And most certainly they did not think that there would be so much rigor in learning even this basic tonicization process. However, by now they should be seeing and hearing what the advantages are of knowing and making those applications.

# 12-Bar Blues Progression

It is now time to take a look at what is considered the most common form of popular music in the world: The blues. No study of jazz would be complete without an introduction to and an understanding of this most prevalent form of music. A blues means form to a jazz musician—specifically a 12-bar form, repeating the same chord progressions of the composition regardless of how many times one repeats the form. Take a look at a fine example of a blues by my colleague, Mike Titlebaum. "Blues for Ox" is a Bb blues with basic chord changes that would be played by not only jazz but also blues, R&B, country, and other musicians throughout most of the world.

There will be somewhat of a departure, compared to the previous tunes, in the applications for "Blues for Ox." Some previous examples will hold true and some will be momentarily abandoned, while adding new ones. Playing a blues requires a different approach than a $ii^7$-$V^7$-I tune. As we sort out the keys inside of the form and how to best tonicize those keys and other implied progressions, you will find that all the applications you have worked on can indeed be utilized. However, dominant scales and chords and bebop scales will give students the most idiomatic sounds of jazz when applied to a blues. It is best to stay in swing style in this example (see figure 11.3). (See ▶ video 11.22, "Blues for Ox" by Mike Titlebaum, and ▶ play-along recording 11.22.)

First, make sure that the class knows the melody and that the rhythm section has a good feel for the style. Then, just as students need to learn and practice appropriate scale applications for $ii^7$-$V^7$-I progressions, they need to do the same for 12-bar blues progressions. Start by having students play dominant scales over the $I^7$, $IV^7$, and $V^7$ chord changes, as illustrated in figure 11.4 (See ▶ video 11.23, "Blues for Ox" with Dominant Scale Applications, and ▶ play-along recording 11.23.) Once students are familiar with these changes and comfortable with the scales, other applications can be used, including dominant triads (see ▶ video 11.24, "Blues for Ox" with Triad Applications, and ▶ play-along recording 11.24, as

**FIGURE 11.3** "Blues for Ox" by Mike Titlebaum

**FIGURE 11.4** "Blues for Ox" with Dominant Scale Applications

well as ⊙ appendix 11.6, "'Blues for Ox' with Triad Applications"), dominant 7ths (see ⊙ video 11.25, "Blues for Ox" with Dominant 7th Chord Tones, and ⊙ play-along recording 11.25, as well as ⊙ appendix 11.7, "'Blues for Ox' with Dominant 7th Chord Tones"), and dominant 9ths (see ⊙ video 11.26, "Blues for Ox" with Dominant 9th Chord Tones, and ⊙ play-along recording 11.26, as well as ⊙ appendix 11.8, "'Blues for Ox' with Dominant 9th Chord Tones"). Note that these examples use the same "Basic Blues" chord changes. However, as previously mentioned, there are many possible variations of the chords in the blues form. The "head" will contain the composition chords, which should be played while introducing the melody; however, a variety of chord progressions during improvisation will surely be explored by most experienced improvisors (see ⊙ appendices 11.9–11.12, as well as ⊙ videos 11.27–11.30 and ⊙ play-along recordings 11.27–11.30, for different variations of blues progressions).

## Bebop Scales

Since the evolution of bebop (the architects of which were Charlie Parker, Dizzy Gillespie, Thelonious Monk, Charlie Christian, etc.), we may agree that improvisation has been harmonically generated for the most part. With the arrival of these "bop" musicians, and almost all who followed, an analysis of the way they improvised includes a small but very important melodic device called the bebop scale. It can be defined as primarily a descending mixolydian scale with a chromatic passing tone between the root and 7th, a nonaccented added major 7th, as you can see in figure 11.5.

I am using a "descending" scale, as jazz improvisors have always demonstrated a tendency to descend, creating an idiomatic phrase. Of course ascending can be just as effective. Here is where listening to a significant amount of recorded material by the masters becomes paramount in learning to play jazz. Emulation is a key element in understanding improvisation. This additional passing tone (the major 7th), when descending from the root of a mixolydian scale, allows for the chord tones to fall on the beat, expressing the chord in a more satisfactory manner. Of course these scales and a myriad of permutations can be played in an ascending manner as well. Start by having students play the appropriate descending bebop scales over each chord change in the progression (see figure 11.6). (See ⊙ video 11.31, Bebop Scales Applied to Blues Form, and ⊙ play-along recording 11.31.) Then have students learn and practice bebop scale permutations over just one chord (see figure 11.7). (See ⊙ video 11.32. Bebop Permutations Applied to Only the B♭ Dominant Chord, and ⊙ play-along recording 11.32.). Notice that in the last example the bebop scales continue throughout the 4-bar phrases. This application maintains a certain amount of "melodic tension," a characteristic that experienced improvisors prefer. Careful listening to exemplary recordings of some of the masters of jazz will demonstrate this principle. Tonality is maintained, and the tonicization process targets the chord changes with these "bop scales."

Note that once again many permutations can be created by adding additional notes, maintaining the key, before returning to the descending bop scale. Extending the bebop line becomes a continual process. Jazz musicians are always searching for melodic development in their improvisation. It can now be noted that almost all scale/chord tone applications

FIGURE 11.5 Descending B♭ Dominant and Bebop Scales

FIGURE 11.6 Bebop Scales for B♭ Blues

**FIGURE 11.7** Bebop Permutations

can be used to target any given chord within any given piece. Most likely the tempo and the style of the composition will govern just what permutations you will choose to apply. Familiarity with more and more permutations, melodic devices, material, etc., will give the improvisor increasing depth of application. Make bebop/major scale applications just as you did in the previous repertoire. For practice applying various bebop permutations, see ⊙ play-along recordings 11.32.2–11.32.9.

## Applying Bebop Permutations to ii⁷-V⁷-I Progressions

Bebop scales and permutations can be applied over 12-bar blues progressions as well as over ii⁷-V⁷-I progressions. For instance, figure 11.8 contains an example of how one might choose to tonicize the tune "Opportuneistic" using a combination of bebop scales and major scales. At some point, students will get the hang of this and will want to experiment with bebop scale permutations, as in figure 11.9. (See ⊙ video 11.33, "Opportuneistic" with Additional Bebop Permutations, and ⊙ play-along recording 11.33.) Finally, as students become more proficient and comfortable with applying bebop permutations to literature, have them try varying bebop permutations over chord changes (see figure 11.10). (See ⊙ video 11.34, "Opportuneistic" with Varying Bebop Permutations, and ⊙ play-along recording 11.34.)

And of course, all these applications can be used with "Bird Sounds" as well. As noted previously, some are 2-bar and some are 4-bar phrases. Choose the most appropriate permutation lengths per chord progression. Be sure to make all the bebop permutations that you can when you get to those applications. There are many combinations. Do not forget to also practice the chord tones on major, dominant, and minor phrases using triads, 7ths, and 9ths.

**FIGURE 11.8** Tonicizing "Opportuneistic" with Bebop/Major Scales

**FIGURE 11.9** Additional Bebop Applications Tonicizing "Opportuneistic"

**FIGURE 11.10** Varying Bebop Permutations

**FIGURE 11.11** "Bird Sounds" with Multiple Scale Applications

Then begin to make bebop applications and permutations similarly to how you did on the previous repertoire in this chapter (see figure 11.11).

## Conclusion

It takes a rather long time in one's musical career as a performing jazz musician to acquire enough of a repertoire to cover most playing engagements. However, it is of great advantage to begin learning some of the standards as soon as possible. This chapter focused on bebop jazz tunes, which are often composed primarily of the $ii^7$-$V^7$-I chord progression. However, these progressions often include chord extensions and alterations. These alterations provide color and often enhance the lyrics, which were an integral component of some of the early and most important composers of the "Great American Songbook." It would be difficult to imagine gifted writers such as Cole Porter, George Gershwin, E. Y. (Yip) Harburg, Irving Berlin, and Richard Rogers, to name just a few, being relegated to only the $ii^7$-$V^7$-I chord progression. With these thoughts in mind, please see ⊛ appendix 11.13, "Recommended Literature List," for a very abbreviated list of some of the most popular standards, with a few modern selections thrown in. I am using this particular list because it was the "Gig

Book" that I made for my advanced combos to use in their performances as emissaries of Community High School, the Ann Arbor Public School System, the State of Michigan, and the United States as we traveled and performed the world over. Of course these young, talented musicians performed an even larger repertoire of jazz tunes, especially at jazz festivals, concerts, and any other venues at which playing jazz was the order of the day. This requires extensive practice and attention to all music, as today's jazz draws from most of the world's great wealth of music. I hope that this chapter on jazz improvisation will assist in your appreciation that to play more than just the written page is the most creative endeavor of all!

## Questions for Discussion

1. Name two important aspects of jazz musicianship that a student needs to address.
2. How important is listening to the masters of jazz?
3. Discuss the importance of setting up a practice schedule and what it would consist of.
4. Discuss the importance of having performance ability in all keys, major and minor.
5. How will you find repertoire, idiomatic studies, and jazz material for your specific instrument?
6. Discuss the importance of hearing jazz performed live.
7. Understand what being musically literate means.
8. Discuss the importance of finding students of like interest to form a combo for rehearsing, learning repertoire, and bringing in an accomplished mentor.
9. Name other musical styles jazz has incorporated.
10. Discuss the importance of finding places for you and your friends to perform live music and how you find those places.

## Notes

1. In classical music theory, the term *tonicization* refers to the treatment of a pitch in a way that establishes a new and temporary key area. Use of this term in this chapter does not imply *establishing* a new key area, but simply *approaching* the ii⁷-V⁷-I as its own 3- to 4-bar key area.
2. Of course, each of these three chord categories has many alterations; however, playing these basic scales and chord tones is a good place to start. Guided by a teacher's careful implementation of appropriate applications, these will allow students the ear-to-hand facility to begin the process of tonicization.

# PART V

# Instrument-Specific Jazz Pedagogy

# 12

# Jazz Vocal

## Catherine Gale

**Style—You've Got to Taste It**

Bruce feels that the teaching of middle school jazz lies more in the understanding of jazz styles than in a deep understanding of the intricacies of the individual instruments—voice included:

> The orchestra teacher would probably do a better job teaching the rhythm section than I would because I don't know the first thing about bass. Well, I know the first thing about it, but not the second thing. And the choir guy would do a lot better job teaching the piano than I do. You just need to have a basic stylistic competence where you know what the style is of the music and you know how to teach that style.

Emily firmly believes that having students experience the style rather than being told how to produce the style is the best way for them to learn. She compares the learning of style to the sense of taste: "Do you read in a book about how things are supposed to taste? No, you've got to taste it":

> You hear it and you've got to do it. You've got to hear it and have that concept. You think about the difference between a Chet Baker sound or a Miles Davis sound. Some people like one and some people like another, but you have to decide what you like or what fits within the song you're playing or the group that you're playing with, or the audience that you're playing for.

The human voice was the first musical instrument and remains the most compelling one. The voice can convey joy and pain in ways that all other instruments seek to capture. Lyrics add another dimension of depth to any program because they help audiences connect strongly with music that includes vocals. Beyond the benefits to the audience, incorporating a vocalist as part of a large or small jazz group can add to the experience of the whole ensemble. Hearing and learning the words to a song adds to all musicians' understanding and interpretation of it while conveying a more complete story for both the band and the audience to enjoy.

This chapter contains a practical list of steps for preparing and performing a song in the jazz idiom. The first steps deal with personal preparation and the last are for rehearsals and performances. The order of these steps can be somewhat flexible depending on the circumstances that lead you or your students to a particular song. When working with a vocalist, you may want to consult the section on choosing a suitable key/vocal range first. Students may need your help to explore what their comfortable range is before choosing a song. This chapter covers initial preparation, learning jazz style, and rehearsal and performance.

# Initial Preparation
## Choosing a Song

The first step is for you or your students to choose a song. You may discover a song through listening to new or classic recordings, or find it in a book. The subject matter and content of the lyrics should be age appropriate for the performer, so make sure you evaluate the lyrics as well. There are many great tunes that work well for all ages of instrumentalists, but be aware that some lyrics may be inappropriate or awkward for the age or gender of the singer. For younger students, try to choose songs with a young perspective about love and/or more optimistic poetic themes. Some good examples are "Blue Skies," "My Romance," "Centerpiece," "'S Wonderful," and "I Got Rhythm." Depending on your group of students, you may pick an arrangement first and then choose a singer to perform it, or vice versa. Encouraging the strongest singers in your school to perform with the jazz band will give you more flexibility. There are many great songs that jazz vocalists should aim to be familiar with; see ⊙ appendix 12.1, "Suggested Listening List," for a selection of composers who have written many of the essential great songs that you and your students should have at least some familiarity with. A great introduction to many of these composers and some of their most popular songs is listening to the "Songbook" series that Ella Fitzgerald recorded in the 1950s and 1960s on the Verve label with the producer Norman Granz.

## Learning the Melody

When preparing songs from the "Great American Songbook," students should learn the melody from a primary source, preferably the original sheet music or songbook collection. Be sure they memorize every note and word. They should also become familiar with the song form and chord structure. It is impossible to overemphasize how important this step is. Learning the song's form and chords is the foundation of all students' further progress with jazz. For even more information, see the suggestions listed in chapter 21 in this volume.

## Listening

Listen to primary source recordings of the song (multiple versions). Listening to music is very important and enjoyable for us all. The best way to gain knowledge of jazz is to listen, to listen, to listen, to listen. When studying a new song, both students and teacher should listen to multiple recordings of it. There is rarely enough time to listen to all the music we want to, so make sure that you listen to primary sources first. In the case of jazz, a primary source performer would be a vocalist who was active when the song was first published or popularized, usually from the 1920s to the 1950s. I recommend recordings by these singers as essential primary source listening: Louis Armstrong, Ella Fitzgerald, Billie Holiday, Nat "King" Cole, Sarah Vaughn, Tony Bennett, Frank Sinatra, Peggy Lee, Dinah Washington, and Joe Williams. Two of my favorite current jazz singers to explore are Dianne Reeves and Dena DeRose.

It can be inspirational for a student to listen to a singer who is young and/or currently popular. More recent recordings can be great introductory or supplementary sources, but current pop singers or theater performers' recordings of standards should not be their only recorded reference. For example, when I was in high school a series of recordings was released by popular singers that fed a renewed interest in the big band era. Although the arrangements were good, and they were fine singers, they were not jazz singers. However, these recordings were a gateway that led me to explore earlier recordings of Nelson Riddle arrangements with singers like Ella Fitzgerald and Frank Sinatra in front of the band. It is also important to listen to "primary source" instrumental recordings of songs you are working on, especially in cases where lyrics were added as an afterthought. If Duke Ellington wrote the song your students are singing, make sure they listen to the Ellington band playing the song. It provides the best foundation for subsequent study. I recommend finding as much variety in listening as time allows!

## Choosing a Suitable Key/Vocal Range

Keep a comfortable range in mind and be open to alternative keys. Remember, the original key of a song may technically be within a student's range but may not be right for a jazz interpretation. Jazz singing is often more like speaking than singing and should make use of the warmest sound of a singer's most comfortable range. Many young singers are not used to using their lower range and are hesitant to explore it. At first, it might be harder for them to hear themselves as they sing lower, but as with all things, it will become easier with practice. Even if a singer is considered a soprano, it is still appropriate to perform a song in a lower key as long as none of the notes is completely beyond a singer's range. Tell them to think of speaking rather than singing the lowest notes. With practice and amplification, the students will grow more comfortable with the warmer, more conversational, and thus more authentic jazz sound (see ▶ video 12.1, Introduction).

There are thousands of "jazz band with vocal" arrangements commercially available for including a singer with your school's large jazz ensemble, and they usually list the range of the vocal part of the chart. Sometimes the same arrangement is available in two (or more) different keys. Your choice depends on the vocal range of your student(s) and/or the arrangements available to you. Female singers are likely to use the lower key, often a 3rd or

**FIGURE 12.1** Voice Ranges

4th lower than the original composition, in order to use their richest, fullest sound. Male singers may be comfortable with the higher (often original) key. There are a few reasons why this is so. Much of what is considered the standard jazz repertoire was originally written for Broadway shows or Hollywood movies. The keys were chosen to suit either the more classical sound that was common on Broadway through the 1950s or for a male voice. As jazz instrumentalists adjusted the feel and harmonies of popular music to suit the jazz idiom, jazz vocalists sang in keys that would highlight their interpretive strengths. To maintain the quality of conversational pitched speech, original (higher) keys are not well suited for a female jazz singer. If there was only one piece of advice I could give to teachers working with a (especially a female) jazz singer/student, it would be to lower the key of any piece they work with. If vocalists can avoid using mixed or head voice, they should do so. The more hollow or intense the sound of the upper range is, the less effective it is for the jazz style.

For a female singer, it is best to choose a key with the melody (approximately) in the range between G3 and B♭5. For a male singer that range is usually between B3 and D4 (see figure 12.1).

One of the best exercises for vocal students is to write their own lead sheets for the songs they are studying, in their preferred key. This exercise not only helps their own memorization process but is also especially important for small groups when no complete chart/arrangement is being used. Remind students to make copies for all band members and bring them to all rehearsals and performances. See chapters 20 and 22 in this volume for more discussion of selecting literature and arranging for your ensembles.

## Learning Jazz Style

Merely singing songs that are part of the jazz idiom is not singing jazz until the vocalist has taken some time to study jazz style. This is complicated somewhat by the fact that the field of jazz singing encompasses a variety of styles. The songs of Broadway and the American songbook may be the most famous part of the jazz repertoire, but blues, bebop, and Brazilian music are also important aspects of the idiom. Singing blues is different from interpreting standards of the American songbook or scatting bebop lines with a modern jazz ensemble. They are related to one another, but each features some unique aspects and approaches. Aspiring jazz singers need to listen to and study the same things that instrumental jazz musicians do, while also memorizing the words and finding a key that best suits their vocal range. You should find it useful to refer to parts of the instrumental chapters in this volume in your work with vocalists as well.

It is a frequent misconception that jazz singing is completely different from classical singing. Vocal techniques in the two idioms have more in common than is often presumed.

However, even experienced vocalists need to take time to study the aspects of jazz singing that make it unique. Jazz singing often creates the illusion of being effortless, but proper technique should always be used. Breath support is necessary even when singing in a conversational style. Though singers have unique sounds to their voices, there are some common characteristics that are desirable in achieving an authentic jazz sound.

## Vibrato/Timbre

One of the most obvious differences between vocal styles is the quality of vibrato and timbre. They may seem like entirely different aspects of music, but vibrato and timbre are closely related and difficult to completely separate. The vibrato used in solo jazz singing is quite different than in choral, classical, or Broadway styles. In choral singing, the goal is to blend with others and sound as one voice. Individual singers are encouraged to sing in a breathier, less forward sound and to match vibrato with those next to them. This approach is not effective for solo jazz singing. Many young students have sung exclusively in choral groups and need more solo singing experience. Classical singing generally features a consistent vibrato, which can often be pitch-variable, and also extensive use of the upper vocal range or "head voice." Broadway style was once closer to classical singing in its use of higher notes and vibrato, but in the later twentieth century a modern Broadway style developed that uses bright forward sound with a strong, often wide (often pitch-variable) vibrato. Sometimes the vibrato is so wide that the pitch is in question. In jazz, the intended note should never be in question.

Jazz singers seldom use pitch-variable vibrato or the "head voice." In terms of vocal placement and timbre, jazz (and pop) singing often has a brighter, more open "forward" sound than classical genres, yet not as strident as modern Broadway. Jazz singing commonly uses a warm, speech-like timbre with an essentially straight tone style and minimal vibrato (see ▶ video 12.2, Vibrato).

All musicians who play or sing have qualities that give them a unique sound. This is even more notable for vocalists, because they are both player and instrument. Many jazz singers, perhaps most notably Ella Fitzgerald, use this straight tone and then add a fast vibrato as they prepare to cut off the end of a phrase, also known as *terminal vibrato*. Sarah Vaughn had a wide vibrato that did not vary the pitch as much as make her sound shine. Her sound is probably the closest any authentic jazz singer has gotten to a classical sound; however, she usually kept her sound more forward and bright.

## Phrasing

Each song is its own story. The impact and meaning of a song is increased with effective phrasing. Phrasing should be guided by the words as well as the musical phrase. It is useful to read the lyrics as a poem and insert breath marks at the end of each phrase. I assign this exercise to students, and after doing it with a few songs they start to recognize the best place to breathe to tell the story and make music. A singer is like an actor playing a role, but in jazz the role is even more personal. Jazz singers interpret a song through their life experiences, thus making a song their own. Interpretations may (should) evolve as life experience grows through the years.

Because many modern pop singers breathe in the middle of musical phrases or even in the middle of words, the concept of effective phrasing can be unfamiliar to young students today. One excellent singer to study when analyzing effective phrasing is Frank Sinatra. He was famous for his study of phrasing and breath control in support of the musical phrase. Jazz can give singers the freedom to change up their phrasing, push ahead, lay back, or change tempos, to create a different feel. Sinatra did this when he sang, and he influenced such famous jazz instrumentalists as Miles Davis. Jazz critic Nat Hentoff recounts this story: "At his home in Queens, a borough of New York City, Lester Young, one of the most original tenor saxophonists in jazz history, was telling me he never played a ballad without first learning the lyrics. I asked him his source for the lyrics. Pointing to a stack of recordings near his chair he said, 'Frank Sinatra.' Later Miles Davis told me the same thing—he learned to get inside ballads from Frank Sinatra" (Liner notes, *Frank Sinatra: New York* box set, November 3, 2009 by reprise ).

If you direct a smaller jazz group or combo with a vocalist, encourage the vocalist to sing the melodies to instrumental jazz tunes as if the vocalist were a horn. As horns often emulate the human voice, singers should experiment with emulating horns as well. Encourage vocalists to blend in with and match the timbre, jazz feel, and articulation of your horn players, especially if your horn players already have more experience playing in a jazz style. Conversely, it can be an excellent pedagogical tool to have the instrumentalists learn the words and sing the melody. It can give everyone insight into the phrasing and emotion of a tune.

## Pronunciation/Diction

Following is a short list of some of the most common pitfalls and important pronunciations in the jazz style (see ⊙ video 12.3, Diction). English diction is markedly different in jazz and may be the quickest "tell" that someone is an inexperienced jazz singer. Vowels should carry the notes, and the consonants are gentle and just present enough to provide lyric clarity, which is also generally true in classical singing. Jazz diction is closer to natural casual speech. Most consonants should be underemphasized. It is desirable to sound relaxed, offhand, "hip," rather than using precise diction (see ⊙ video 12.4, Overpronouncing 1).

- A southern accent or New York slangy pronunciation can be used as shorthand to understand the pronunciation.
- "Ts" should be underpronounced, often closer to a "d" sound: little—liddle.
- Most "ing" endings should be pronounced as in'. Examples include words like *singin'* and *swingin'*.
- Vocalists should beware of stretching a diphthong; they need to hold the first vowel and only use the second as a brief "cutoff" to end a word. For example, die is Dah-yeh and sky is skaa-yih (see ⊙ video 12.5, Diphthongs).
- Word endings, especially at the ends of phrases, should be clear but understated.
- Vocalists need to look out for the letter "R." They should not roll "Rs" or hold them. They can sing the vowel, then slip "Rs" in right at the end of a note (see ⊙ video 12.6, R Endings).

- Scat syllables should also be pronounced gently. Precise diction on words like "doo bee bop shwee bop" can sound awkward and forced (see ⊙ video 12.7, Overpronouncing 2).

It is easy to let the words get in the way of singing a song. If a song is challenging, vocalists should step back and use a more instrumental approach. They can sing the whole song using just one vowel sound; "aah" and "eee" are the best ones to start with. This way, they can concentrate on an open full sound, their breathing, and the flow of the phrases. Using a single vowel sound is a good way to gain mastery of an especially challenging passage, or even an entire song. Singers can add the words back in when they are ready.

## Improvisation

Improvisation is an important part of jazz; however, vocal jazz improvisation encompasses more than just "scat" singing. There are many other ways to vary performance that are forms of improvisation. Among the great jazz singers, there is a wide difference in quantity of improvisation. Billie Holiday used a lot of inflection in her interpretations of songs, bending notes up and down to help tell a story. She never improvised with scat syllables, but chose new notes and rhythms to slip in with the existing lyrics in ways that are well worth studying. Both Ella Fitzgerald and Sarah Vaughn would scat sometimes, but often they would improvise by changing key notes in the melody, playing with the words and rhythms. Ella Fitzgerald would often scat in live performances, but seldom if ever on her studio albums. "How High the Moon" and "Flying Home" are two famous songs she improvised on that are essential listening. Louis Armstrong, often known as the first scat singer, crafted solos that were consistent in style and content between his voice and his trumpet. Vocalists can also learn a lot from listening to and emulating instrumentalists, especially horn players.

First, students should have learned and memorized any song they plan to improvise on. Performing a song essentially as written, with little or no melodic variation but varying the rhythms somewhat to establish a swing feel or emphasize important words, is a good place to start. Turning a ballad into a medium swing, waltz, up-tempo, or vice versa can help solidify understanding of the song and stimulate ideas for improvisation. Once your vocalists are comfortable with a song, they can try substituting a few notes to make the song seem more or less dramatic. Singing along with and transcribing classic recordings is an important part of studying jazz. A good exercise is to listen, analyze, and transcribe a favorite performance by a classic jazz singer, such as Ella, Billie, or Sarah. Which notes do they change? Are these notes attached to meaningful words? Compare the effect of the original melody notes to the changed notes. What part of the chord are the changed notes? Are the notes perhaps the 9th or major 7th? Encourage students to take these ideas and bring them to other songs.

## Intonation

Centered pitch (or good intonation) is especially important in jazz singing. If you have a tight harmony vocal group, centering pitch with little to no vibrato can be even more important. The piano, which is usually the tuning guide of a jazz group and plays the chords, can be the best frame of reference. Hearing and "feeling" the center of each note becomes especially important when melody or improvised variation notes are chordal extensions. The more vocalists practice, the easier it is to hear and actually feel where the note they are singing fits in the chord so that it sounds more intentional and thus more meaningful.

For example, if the students are singing a blue 3rd or 5th against a chord with a major 3rd, they need to feel confident in emphasizing the note and not backing off of it. I like to call this embracing the dissonance. These notes are often used with dramatic words like *love* or *pain*. Centering the pitch effectively and singing with intention helps to convey more love or more pain (see ⊙ video 12.8, Dissonance Blue Note).

## A Few Simple Exercises

In order to practice developing the centered pitch and bright timbre for jazz, I work with students on a progression of long tones and chromatic scale exercises. Students can progress even further once they are able to analyze their own sound. Recording practice sessions can help with this (see ⊙ video 12.9, Long Tones; and ⊙ video 12.10, Long Tone Exercises).

One of the best exercises for analyzing intonation, timbre, and vibrato is sustaining long tones. First practice long tones on different pitches in the most comfortable part of your student's vocal range. Play a reference note on the piano, direct your student to take a supportive breath, and sing "Nah." Both you and the student should listen. The student should try to produce the most open "ah" sound possible and the most centered pitch. It can help to use the N to propel the sound forward as if through the nose, and then open into the vowel ASAP. Hold for as long as the student can maintain a consistent quality of sound. Repeat until your student is able to instantly get to their most open and rich sound. Repeat this exercise on all other notes. Experiment with other vowel sounds, such as "noo," "nee," and "neh." Each time, try to keep the sound fully supported and more consistent. Hold notes longer each time if possible. When centering pitch on individual notes becomes a habit, move to a short chromatic line. You can use solfège if you like, but all you need is a piano or keyboard as a guide.

To explore your student's lower range, have the student take a supportive breath and sing "Nah," descending chromatically from a note in the middle of their range. Once again, use the consonant N to propel the sound forward as if through the nose, then open into the vowel ASAP. The student should send the sound forward, keep their mouth and nose open, and think "AH." Have the student take a breath after each phrase and cue the next phrase with a piano note (see figure 12.2) (See ⊙ video 12.11, Lower Tone Chromatics.)

**FIGURE 12.2** Exploring Your Lower Range, Exercise 1

Nah Nah Nah Nah Nah Nah Nah Nah Nah
Spoo - ky spi - der sca - ry spi - der ooh

**FIGURE 12.3** Exploring Your Lower Range, Exercise 2

Nah Nah Nah Nah Nah Nah Nah Nah Nah Nah Nah Nah Nah Nah Nah Nah

**FIGURE 12.4** Singing Up and Down a 5th

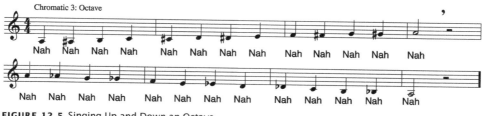

Nah Nah Nah Nah Nah Nah Nah Nah Nah Nah Nah Nah Nah

Nah Nah Nah Nah Nah Nah Nah Nah Nah Nah Nah Nah Nah

**FIGURE 12.5** Singing Up and Down an Octave

Start by ascending from middle C. Ascend and descend, using the syllable "nah" with each new note: C—C♯—D—D♯—E—E♭—D—D♭—C (see figure 12.3). As with long tones, the "ah" sound should be as open and forward as possible to help center the pitch. Some students remember pitches better with lyrics attached, so I sometimes give this exercise to them with these words: "Spook-y spi-der sca-ry spi-der ooh."

Once you are able to sing the chromatic line up and down a major 3rd, sing up and down a 5th from C to G (see figure 12.4). Finally, sing a full octave of the students' most comfortable range. Often for men that is (C3–C4), and for women it is (A4–A5) (see figure 12.5). (See ⊙ video 12.12, Chromatics.)

Another great exercise for achieving an open, forward sound is illustrated in figure 12.6. Take a supportive breath and sing with a "nyaah" to propel the sound forward. Think about keeping a consistent "ah" sound and an open nose to keep the forward sound more rounded than nasal. Repeat in ascending half steps.

The most important aspect of any musical study is regular practice. This develops muscle memory and facility. This is true across all instruments and idioms but bears repeating.

# Rehearsal and Performance
## Deciding on the Tempo and Feel

Before or during rehearsals, work with your students to decide on the tempo and rhythmic feel of each song (swing, bossa nova, ballad, or waltz, etc.). Often there is more than one way to perform a song. With many songs, the style can be changed to suit the mood or place in the program.

**FIGURE 12.6** Exercise for Achieving an Open Forward Sound

## Communicating with Band Members and the Count-off

Teach your students to do the count-off themselves. Before they count-off the band, they should communicate with the band members (or pianist). There should be a brief discussion about what is about to happen. Be sure they address questions such as: What is the song title, key, feel, and tempo? What is the form? What length of intro or ending do you want? Will there be solos?

When counting off, it often helps to audiate the most challenging or iconic passage in the song, so that they can find the most comfortable and compelling tempo. In rehearsals, have them do this aloud to be sure they're getting the tempo right.

## Recording Practice Sessions

After singers feel confident with the notes and lyrics of the tune, record them singing it a few times. Listen to the recording with them. What did they do well? Did they sing all of the melody correctly? Did they remember all of the words? Were the rhythms accurate? Did they have a consistent timbre and utilize the same vocal character throughout? Did they have any awkward (over-)pronunciations?

I want to emphasize how important it is for students to record any lessons and practice sessions so they can listen to and analyze their own progress. It is very difficult to examine what you are doing while you are doing it, so make sure your students have something to record with at lessons, rehearsals, and whenever they have some practice time. Over the years, I have used a small cassette recorder, then a small digital recording device, and now I just use my smartphone. Any computer can also work, but the beauty of using a smartphone is that you are likely to have it with you already everywhere you go. Singers should use any opportunity (especially near a piano) for singing tunes they are working on. I often listen to my recordings later while commuting or doing household tasks.

## The First Chorus

Encourage your students to always sing the first chorus essentially as written with no (or very few) variations. Even in jazz, the first chorus should belong to the composer, so make embellishment secondary. This is especially true if your vocalist will be scatting or singing two or more choruses in the performance.

## Amplification

In a concert, and often in rehearsal, jazz vocalists need to be amplified. Classical singing developed the way it did because of the need for voices to project past the increasing size of the orchestra. Jazz singing as we know it today developed alongside the advent of amplification and the advancement of recording techniques. As the technology was in its infancy, early blues singers such as Bessie Smith would deliver a song with a kind of declarative shout. As microphones improved in quality, they enabled the jazz singer to have more flexibility in both live performance and recordings. With proper amplification, a singer can be heard at a whisper and achieve a quality of intimacy and emotional impact even with a large ensemble.

It is important for a singer to have the opportunity to practice singing with amplification before a performance. It can be intimidating to hear one's voice amplified, so the more opportunities a singer has to develop microphone technique and sing with an amplification system before performing in front of an audience, the better. Make sure to have at least a few rehearsals at which singers are amplified so they can have practice hearing themselves in this very different way. It can be very useful to have an additional speaker as a monitor so that both the singer and the band can hear the vocal part. When the band can hear the vocalist, they can better adjust their performance to suit the mood of the piece. Even with a vocal monitor, it can be difficult to hear oneself when standing in front of a band, so try to reserve sufficient time for amplified rehearsal. If your band practices in the performance space, make sure to have a sound check so that singers have an idea of what they will be hearing during a performance. Someone (perhaps you) should go out into the auditorium and listen during the sound check to evaluate the balance.

Following are some additional factors for the vocalist to consider:

- Hold the microphone in your hand, rather than using a stand while you sing. This gives greater control over microphone placement.
- Sing directly into the microphone one to two inches away and adjust the distance for volume as needed.
- Never stand directly in front of a speaker or hold the microphone upside down; there is danger of feedback.
- Try to stand near the piano or guitar in case you need a little harmonic help.

I hope these ideas are helpful for you and your students in your exploration of jazz vocal style. And I strongly encourage you to use singers with your jazz ensemble.

# Questions for Discussion

1. Why do you think many school jazz ensembles do not use a vocal soloist?
2. What are the benefits to the instrumentalists of inviting a vocal soloist to sing with the band?
3. How is choosing a key different for jazz singing than for classical singing?
4. Why is it important to learn the original melody of a song?
5. Even though Billie Holiday and Ella Fitzgerald are both considered to be among the greatest jazz singers, they have very different styles. What makes their styles so different?

# 13

# Jazz Saxophone

## Mike Titlebaum

It's just music. It's playing clean and looking for the pretty notes.
—CHARLIE PARKER, 1954

## Articulation

Bruce finds that middle school students are often too heavy in their jazz articulation. He teaches articulation in jazz ensemble by having students "speak into the instrument" and physically apply different consonants to their tonguing, an idea that he got from Clark Terry when he gave a demonstration at Hope College years ago:

> I always tell them, "there are 21 consonants—is that right—21 consonants—that's 21 different ways to attack a note." We use T and D and L most of the time. You'd never want to use B or M, but think about how you would sing that and then play it the way you would sing it. But it's not slurred. I don't care—make it sound doo bah doo bah doo bah. Play it that way. Even in concert band when we are doing the Wagner—use an L there, don't use a T.

Emily talks about how in concert band the instrumentalists use different variations of articulations, but in swing style it is all about slurring. As a young professional, Emily was taught to swing using a very smooth and connected way of articulation, almost slurring the notes, and that is what she teaches her students. "We do a lot of tonguing on the same pitch. We'll take a scale, 'doo doo doo doo doo' to get that nice connection between notes." However, in jazz the accents are much more aggressive than in concert band music. Emily tells her students to end their notes by sticking their tongues right on the reed and using the syllable "dut"—a practice that is mostly avoided in concert band music. While Emily sometimes gives instructions about the physical motions behind producing the desired sound or style, she more often helps the students conceive of the sound or style that she wants them to produce and then gives them the responsibility and allows them the space to produce that sound:

> We were at Arturo's clinic in Chicago and some guy says, "what's the relationship of the opening of the aperture of the teeth and the" . . . and Arturo says, "I put it up and if it sounds bad I move it around." I think that's what it should be. I stay away from saying, "your tongue has to be here and your teeth have to be here." I'll say, "try this or try that," but that's not necessarily what is going to work for you. I think that you're going to hear it and then when you go home I want you to figure out what works inside to give you that. Now, I can tell you what works for me and I can tell you what I think is going to work for you, and I can make some suggestions to make it harder or softer or smoother or edgier, but in the end you have to do that yourself.

The saxophone is the most iconic instrument in jazz. Ask random people which instrument comes to mind when they think of jazz music, and it would surely be the saxophone. It is simply the symbol of jazz. In a big band, saxophones fill a niche similar to that of the strings in a symphony orchestra. Saxophones play throughout charts and are required to navigate a variety of textures and roles, including beautiful unison melodies, technical harmonized solis, chordal comping, and slow-moving background chords ("footballs"), as well as to fill out the body of the band during full ensemble tuttis.

One of the greatest compliments saxophonists can receive is that their playing sounds like a human voice. Like many great vocalists, the best jazz saxophonists are unique and immediately recognizable because they have a vocal quality to their playing. Many teachers assume that the tone is the most important aspect to this individuality. While tone color and timbre are hugely important to a saxophonist, stylistic traditions of articulation, phrasing, and vibrato are equally critical in defining a player's uniqueness. Listeners may hear great saxophonists and believe it is only their tone that is so compelling, but it is the combination of that tone along with style and phrasing that compel us. This chapter discusses teaching aspects of jazz saxophone playing that make it different from classical or symphonic band playing: articulation, vibrato, phrasing, blend, and tone.

# Articulation

Playing saxophone in jazz and popular styles requires a different approach to articulation than playing classical style. Four primary types of articulation are needed:

1. *Slur.* A note connected from the previous note, smoothly played without use of the tongue.
2. *Legato.* Tongued notes that are seamlessly connected together in a phrase.

**FIGURE 13.1** Legato Tonguing 1

3. *Staccato.* Tongued notes that are tongued and separated from the other notes in the phrase.
4. *Half-tonguing,* also known as doodle tonguing or "dud'n" tonguing; the technique for de-emphasizing or "ghosting" pitches.

Failing to adequately learn these techniques (half-tonguing in particular) can cause saxophonists to sound like "classical players trying to play jazz." To illustrate, imagine an American actor on a London stage using an incomplete British accent. A British theatergoer would notice this immediately. This is what jazz sounds like when "classical" saxophonists play it without stylish articulation. It's like they're using the wrong accent. Of course, when you teach jazz articulation, it is critical to remind students that while stylish for jazz, these articulations are inappropriate for most classical music and symphonic band settings.

**Slurs.** Smooth slurs are important to jazz phrasing (see ⊙ video 13.1, Introduction to Slurring). Students should practice slurring between two notes without using breath accents. Sometimes breath accents are entirely unintentional, and they might not even notice they are doing it. If you hear breath accents, one method to demonstrate this to them is to stand next to them while they play a single note and push a few keys down and up while they play, changing the notes for them, so they can't accidentally disrupt the airstream in tandem with the pitch changes you're making.

**Legato.** Listening to great jazz saxophonists playing smoothly might cause us to assume that they are slurring frequently. However, a closer examination of their articulation reveals that they are often tonguing legato (also called tenuto), even when playing long, sinewy lines of swinging eighth notes. For this reason, we should have our saxophone students practice legato tonguing, independently of songs or other exercises.

I encourage my students to begin the study of legato tonguing by repeating several measures of mid-register quarter notes (see figure 13.1 and ⊙ video 13.2, Legato) at a comfortable yet full volume, with the tip of the tongue articulating the rhythm on the tip of the reed/mouthpiece.

Students should blow a consistent amount of air throughout the exercise. They should not let their use of the tongue interfere with a strong, constant stream of air. The tongue's articulation shouldn't interrupt the tone; it should sound as if they are essentially playing one long pitch with the cleanest, briefest possible "T" or "D" sound. If their tongues linger too long on the reed, you will hear a significant interruption in the sound, which breaks up the phrase.

You can help students understand this concept with a visual representation. Writing artificially large legato articulations that almost connect with one another above the notes shows how the pitches should connect in a phrase (see figure 13.2). Students should repeat these exercises on various pitches, in high and low registers, and at loud and soft dynamics, to achieve consistent legato tonguing throughout the tessitura of the horn.

FIGURE 13.2 Legato Tonguing 2

FIGURE 13.3 Up/Down Tonguing Pattern

FIGURE 13.4 Staccato Tonguing

The most effective way to utilize legato articulation in jazz is by practicing a pattern of alternating tongued upbeats with slurred downbeat eighth notes, a technique commonly used by many jazz saxophonists. I refer to this as the "up/down" tonguing pattern (upbeat/downbeat) through the remainder of the chapter, but the technique is also called "slurring across the beat" in chapter 6 in this volume. One efficient way to get students started with this tonguing pattern is to ask them to play the first five notes of any major scale at a medium tempo, ascending then descending, with a swing feel, tonguing the upbeats, slurring into every subsequent downbeat, and then repeat it many times (see figure 13.3). (See ⊙ video 13.3, Up-Down Tonguing.)

The slur into the first note of figure 13.3 is parenthetic because the students should tie into the downbeat when they repeat it; they have to tongue the downbeat to start the exercise, but should slur into it for each subsequent iteration. Students should focus on keeping a solid stream of air, ensuring the sound isn't broken when they tongue. It's okay, and in some cases desirable, for the tongued notes to also be accented.

This "up/down" pattern of tonguing is only one part of jazz style, but it's a critical rudiment to master. As discussed in the section in this chapter on half-tonguing, saxophonists will often modify and personalize this pattern to allow notes other than the upbeats to be accented, which will emphasize pitches that are more important to the melodic line and harmony.

**Staccato.** In symphonic bands or orchestras, staccatos are often rounded and buoyant, articulated with something of a "tah" sound. Jazz phrasing is different because separated notes—indicated by a staccato or marcato accent—need to be actively stopped by the tongue. You will often hear jazz players demonstrate phrases in their singing by syllables such as "dot" or "daht," both of which show that they're audibly stopping the ends of the notes with their tongues by sounding a "t." To practice this technique, begin with the legato exercise from figure 13.2, then change every other quarter note into a tongue-stopped rest (see figure 13.4). (See ⊙ video 13.4, Staccato).

Even though there are rests written between each pitch, students should continue firmly pushing air through them. This may initially feel awkward because stopping the note with the tongue on the reed and mouthpiece will give 100 percent resistance to airflow. But

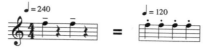

FIGURE 13.5 Tongue-Stopped Legato Notes

FIGURE 13.6 Half-Tonguing Notation

pushing air against this resistance is critical to the style. Listen to make sure students are actively tongue-stopping each note and pushing air though the rests. To confirm, ask them to leak a tiny amount of air from the corners of their mouths. Intentionally leaking air is not desirable on its own, but it is a way to help identify whether they are continuing to push air. If the leaking air stops or changes during the rests, they aren't successfully pushing air against the resistance of their tongues on the reed.

Once students have mastered this tongue-stopping technique, demonstrate to them that if you slow down the tempo but double the rhythmic values, playing separated legato notes would be the same process as playing stylish staccato notes with a jazz phrasing (see figure 13.5). I often do this exercise with an entire section, snapping or clapping at the faster tempo and counting out loud to emphasize the cutoffs. I then seamlessly change to snapping and counting a tempo that is exactly half as fast, which shows that the staccato notes are just like tongue-stopped legato notes. This equivalency implies that staccato notes are exactly 50 percent longer than full-length legato notes; however, in real musical situations this precision is not necessarily required. The length of the staccato notes can be quite flexible, depending on the style, tempo, and/or mood of the piece being played. However, the principle of tongue stopping staccato notes remains a constant throughout jazz style. It is critical to remind students that while tongue stopping staccato notes is stylistically appropriate for jazz, the technique is entirely inappropriate for classical music and symphonic bands.

**Half-tonguing.** Once tongue-stopped staccato has been mastered, students can begin learning the half-tonguing technique, which requires a previous facility with jazz legato and staccato articulation (see ⊚ video 13.5, Half-Tonguing).

Half-tonguing, sometimes called "ghosting" a note, is the most significant and ubiquitous articulation used by jazz saxophonists throughout the history of the music. Unfortunately, it is not typically taught. One reason for this may be that it is notated inconsistently or not at all. When the effect is notated, it may be seen as a parenthetic notehead or with an X replacing the notehead (see figure 13.6). (See ⊚ video 13.6, Half-Tongue Sample.) Half-tonguing is used to de-emphasize notes immediately preceding an accented one. Because the technique is not generally taught, many young jazz saxophonists try to approximate this effect by using less air to play the "ghosted" notes softer. This causes their phrasing to sound unnaturally broken because of the sudden changes in airflow, which is not how great saxophonists play.

Half-tonguing is similar to staccato, except that during the space between the notes (the "rest" in the exercise) the tongue touches the side of the reed, closer to the corner of the mouthpiece, instead of at its usual position in the middle of the reed tip. This tongue repositioning allows the reed to still vibrate but in dampened form while the tongue is still touching it. Young saxophonists often report that it tickles because they can feel the vibration of the reed directly on their tongues.

The effect creates something similar to an "N" or "L" vocal sound. When speaking or singing "N" or "L," the tongue is used at the roof of the mouth or on the teeth, dampening the tone. This may explain why some players refer to ghosting as "doodle" or "dud'n" tonguing.

Equally important to the sound of the dampened note is the accented note that follows it. The students should strive for an accent when they remove their tongues from the reed, because ghosting is used to accent the subsequent pitch. To practice this, have students start with the previous staccato exercise and gradually move the tongue over to the corner of the mouthpiece to allow the reed to continue vibrating while their tongues are still on it (see figure 13.7).

Once students have begun to achieve the ghosting effect, introduce a change in which the half-tongued notes will be different pitches, perhaps just a half step below the accented notes (see figure 13.8). This will allow them to focus on coordinating the accented release of their tongues with their fingers.

Once students can reliably half-tongue between two different notes, ghosting the lower note and accenting the upper note, introduce the up/down alternating tongue-slur pattern from exercise 2, with one critical modification: half-tonguing G, the note immediately prior to the highest pitch (see figure 13.9). This will place the accent on the following downbeat, beat 3 (see ⊙ video 13.7, Half-Tongue Gradual Speed Increase). Perfecting this modified up/down articulation with a single ghosted note begins to show a convincing jazz style. Have your saxophonists listen closely to great players who use this technique effectively, like Cannonball Adderley, Charlie Parker, and Sonny Rollins, to get the sound "in their ears."

**FIGURE 13.7** Half-Tonguing, Exercise 1

**FIGURE 13.8** Half-Tonguing, Exercise 2

**FIGURE 13.9** Half-Tonguing with Up/Down Tonguing

See ⊕ appendix 13.1, "Recommended Listening List," for a list of great jazz saxophonists to listen to.

# Vibrato

Use of vibrato varies greatly among great jazz saxophonists. Listening to the most influential saxophonists will show a few trends in their use of vibrato.

- Vibrato is often "terminal," meaning that it used more often at the ends of notes than at the beginnings.
- Vibrato is used more often at the ends of phrases than at the beginning or middle.
- Vibrato may be wider (with greater pitch variation in each vibration) and slower than in classical playing.
- Vibrato may vary in width and speed in a single song, phrase, or even pitch.
- In fast tempos, many notes will simply be too brief to use any vibrato, but many players will use vibrato on the somewhat longer notes even at faster tempos.

Some recent jazz players use vibrato less often. I believe this may be due to a perception that vibrato is "dated" or "uncool." But there may be another explanation. Vibrato connects directly to our humanity and conveys emotions like joy or love. Perhaps some jazz players desire a sense of cool, emotional detachment, so they use less vibrato or even none at all. Straight tone (the absence of vibrato) can be effectively used to achieve a "dry" sound, common to cool jazz and other styles. Expert saxophonists may choose to express their musicality without vibrato, but the study of jazz saxophone is entirely incomplete without an examination of it (see ⊕ video 13.8, Vibrato).

# Phrasing: Interpreting a Melodic Line

Even though great care is used by publishers to notate style, it is not uncommon for printed jazz ensemble music to have insufficient articulation. Players are often simply expected to interpret the style on their own. This is similar to string writing in orchestral music, in which the concertmaster is expected to make decisions about bowings and phrasing.

Professional players are experienced in interpretation, but students will need guidance using the various tonguing techniques to effectively convey the style. When studying a written line, some questions to ask are:

- Could the "up/down" pattern be used?
- Which notes could be brought out (accented) or de-emphasized (ghosted)?
- Any there any hemiola patterns (groups of three eighth notes) that could be highlighted?

Let's look at a sample alto saxophone part. The tune "All About That Rhythm" (composed for this book) contains a typical amount of stylistic detail for many published charts, as you can see in figure 13.10. Inevitably, this part requires additional exploration to effectively bring

**FIGURE 13.10** Melodic Line Example with Minimal Stylistic Notation

**FIGURE 13.11** Melodic Line Example Interpreted

out the subtlety and nuances of jazz phrasing. In ▸ video 13.9, Interpreting a Line, you can hear how plain a saxophone part might sound if the player did not add any interpretation.

Because the first two eighths begin on an upbeat, the up/down tonguing pattern would work well for the first two eighth notes. However, because the downbeat of measure 1 is accented, keeping the up/down pattern would be less desirable after the first two notes, because the pattern would cause the following downbeat to be slurred and therefore could not be accented with the tongue. The only other option at that point would be to use a breath accent, which could break up the phrase. To remedy this, the final eighth note of the pickup could be ghosted (half-tongued) to prepare the tongue accent on the downbeat of the measure 1 (see figure 13.11). (See ▸ video 13.10, Interpreting a Line, Pickups.)

This de-emphasis of the & of 4 can be justified in several other ways. The last eighth of the bar can be weak rhythmically, so de-emphasizing it is entirely acceptable. And because the pitch D has already been sounded earlier in the bar, it is probably less important melodically the second time it is heard.

Continuing through measure 1, beat 2 would need to be tongued, and then the up/down pattern can be used effectively afterward. The other aspect to consider in articulating measure 1 is that the final eighth note is staccato and therefore should be tongued clearly at the beginning of the note and tongue stopped at the end. (See figure 13.11 for how this could be revised, and also watch ▸ video 13.11, Interpreting a Line, Measure 1.)

The articulation written in measure 2 works well for the first 2 beats, but the slur over beats 3 and 4 should be reconsidered. Arrangers may write a slur over several notes, indicating a phrase marking rather than specific articulations because they want the line to *sound* smooth. However, in swing, legato tonguing will not break up smooth phrasing if done well. In addition, as long as the tempo is not too fast, a quarter note may be ample time to use vibrato; one or two vibrations can be plenty to convey a deep jazz feeling. (See ▸ figure 13.11 for how this could be revised, and also watch ▸ video 13.12, Interpreting a Line, Measure 2.)

Notice that the final pitch of measure 2 gets accented, even though it's on the weak & of 4 and it wasn't accented in the original part. Why? Because this is the highest note in the line so far and there is no pitch on the following downbeat, it is the most important pitch so far and therefore can be accented.

Measure 3 has no articulations written in the part. The up/down pattern can be used initially. However, a closer inspection reveals that the highest notes are in a hemiola grouping of three notes, a pattern found frequently in bebop. To emphasize this hemiola, accents should be added to each of the highest notes. The final note of measure 3 can be ghosted to complete the pattern (see ⏵ video 13.13, Interpreting a Line, Measures 3–4).

The last note in measure 4 should be tongued. Because it is presumably at the end of a phrase, a decrescendo and some vibrato would be a stylish way to wrap up that musical thought. Once all these artistic decisions have been made, the entire line—as might be interpreted by an experienced jazz player—would be as you hear in ⏵ video 13.14, Interpreting a Line, the Entire Phrase.

Looking at any single part may not always provide the complete picture. In a big band, it's entirely possible that this accent pattern could conflict with other rhythms going on in the brass section or rhythm section. These decisions do not have to be made in the void of just looking at a single part.

In a big band, the lead alto player has the right (perhaps the responsibility) to make these artistic decisions and communicate them to the rest of the section. The director can certainly help make these decisions, but I often work in conjunction with my lead alto players to help them make the right decision.

This type of analysis is not only effective in interpreting written parts. It can help teach your saxophonists the idiomatic "accent" of the jazz language, which they can utilize in their own improvisations. I often play recordings of my students' solos from concerts or rehearsals, help them transcribe some of the more interesting parts, then discuss strategies for how they might have interpreted them more effectively stylistically. I seek out "missed opportunities": moments that could have been improved by the use of more idiomatic phrasing.

# Blend

When playing in a section, saxophonists need to consider balance. To blend well, a section does not necessarily all need to have identical sounds. In fact, the most important jazz saxophone section of all time—Duke Ellington's—was comprised entirely of players who developed their own distinctive voices yet played together in a way that exposed the glory of the whole section and of Ellington's music. In many of their recordings, you can immediately identify the sounds of Johnny Hodges's lead alto and Harry Carney's baritone.

It is advisable to spend rehearsal time and/or sectional time balancing chords for purposes of intonation and blend. In sectionals, sit in a circle to maximize listening. Start with a stable chord at which each player is in a comfortable register. You can pull a chord out of a chart you're working on (even if it is written short, you can still use it for this purpose) or use your own. You can begin with the chord in concert key and transpose it for each member of the section (see figure 13.12).

You should all be able to hear the lead and baritone slightly more than the inner voices, but also be able to identify each inner voice. Have the students practice the chord loud and soft, and also while doing crescendo, decrescendo, and sforzando (or *fp*, "forte-piano") while keeping a consistent balance. Stop suddenly and ask the players if they think the balance was still good, or if an individual was either too soft or sticking out of the texture.

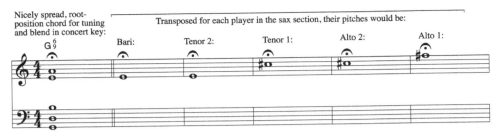

**FIGURE 13.12** Tuning and Blend, Exercise 1

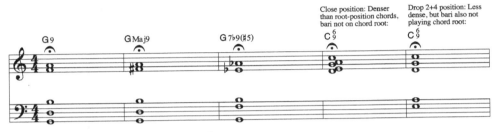

**FIGURE 13.13** Tuning and Blend, Exercise 2

Change the chord by moving it up or down by several half steps, by changing to a denser voicing, or by changing chord spacing or quality to something more colorful. For example, change the 6th to a major 7th or lowered 7th (for dominant chords) or add color tones (see figure 13.13).

Sometimes switch the assignment of the notes so each player gets the feeling of playing the 3rd of the chord at some point. Simultaneously remind the students that the major 3rd of a chord will inevitably need to be lowered slightly with the mouth or tongue placement, not by moving the mouthpiece, to play in tune. You might also ask: "Who is playing the 3rd of the chord now? Is it in tune?" Don't wait until a predetermined time to work on blend and intonation; you can improvise these kinds of exercises whenever the section needs it!

# Tone

The sound of every person's voice varies greatly. In jazz, saxophone timbre is likewise quite varied. Players such as Frankie Trumbauer, Lester Young, Johnny Hodges, and Paul Desmond preferred a light, pretty sound. Others such as Coleman Hawkins and Sonny Rollins expressed themselves with a huskier timbre, often coupling their tone with an articulation style that attacked the horn aggressively. In recent years, saxophonists have utilized brighter, edgier tone qualities in rock or jazz fusion styles.

A saxophonist's timbre is related to multiple factors: the mouthpiece (its manufacturer and the measurements or dimensions of the mouthpiece), reed brand and strength, the ligature, and of course the horn. However, the most important aspect of saxophonists' timbre is their own ears. They have to feel a desire to develop their sound, because that is what will drive them to find the right equipment. It is important that aspiring saxophonists conduct their own search for a sound, initially by listening to a lot of different players. Finding great players to admire can lead to the search for gear that will allow them to most easily express the sound that appeals to them, which will then ultimately represent themselves.

For this reason, it is important not to judge a young player's sound too quickly as being "bad," "thin," or too "bright" or "edgy." Some of the greatest saxophonists' tone qualities might be described these ways when comparing them to the ideal tone for classical saxophonists. Even if their tone sounds shrill, players' personal connection with sound conveys an immediate sense of their personality, wit, warmth, and charm. Therefore, uniqueness of tone should not be discounted as bad; it is a critical aspect of expressing oneself. The common elements among jazz saxophonists are personality and uniqueness.

Listen to recordings of the greats along with your students. Focus on selecting recordings of players with distinctive, compelling sounds, starting with those who can be identified from a single note, such as John Coltrane, Charlie Parker, and Sonny Rollins. Discuss with them why their tones are so immediately engrossing. The reasons are not always easy to put into words, but it is important to try.

Because of the complexities of tone and the individuality tied into it, I will not discuss brands of reeds, mouthpieces, or saxophones on the market. There are many blogs, websites, and Facebook groups devoted to these discussions. The search for this information itself provides the joy of discovery.

Finally, do not allow students to dwell too much on equipment. Playing jazz is about the quality of the player, not the gear. If great saxophonists were to pick up a student model saxophone equipped with a stock mouthpiece and an inexpensive reed, they would inevitably play great and still sound like themselves. Stories told by master saxophonist Phil Woods about meeting Charlie Parker (in addition to a large number of bootleg recordings made when Parker played with borrowed horns) prove this beyond a doubt.

I very much look forward to hearing the progress of your saxophonists!

# Questions for Discussion

1. What aspects of saxophone playing make it clear when a "classical" saxophonist is unsuccessfully playing the jazz style, and vice versa?
2. Why might jazz saxophone music contain insufficient articulation?
3. Why is it so difficult to recommend specific brands of mouthpieces or reeds to a jazz player?
4. What about their playing makes great jazz saxophonists instantly recognizable?

# 14

# Jazz Trumpet

Frank Gabriel Campos

## Just Flat Out Play Your Horn Better

Bruce's approach to teaching style in jazz ensemble is similar to that which he uses in concert band, although he wants to be sure that students develop the proper characteristic trumpet tone:

> The basic characteristic tone that I'm looking for—I don't want to deviate from that. There's a different language and a different style and a different treatment of the 8th note in jazz than there is in concert band. That we can agree on. But I don't want kids having a different idea of tone in jazz than they have in concert band.

While many professional jazz musicians use a variety of mouthpieces to suit different playing demands, Emily, like Bruce, wants her middle school students to use the same equipment in jazz ensemble that they use in concert band. This includes the brass players using standard cup mouthpieces and woodwind players playing "nonmetal" mouthpieces. Rather than on equipment, Emily focuses on developing students' musicianship by emphasizing that the principles that apply in concert band also apply in jazz band:

> My jazz kids get to festival and they say, "what do we have to do better?" And I say, "just flat out play your horn better. Play better in tune. Play with a better sound." Balance and blend and musicality are the same as in concert band.

Ensembles of all kinds call upon the trumpets for excitement and fireworks. The strength and quality of the trumpet section is a top concern for any jazz, pop, show, salsa, drum corps, and commercial music ensemble. A gifted lead or solo trumpeter is a jewel of any group, and a strong trumpet section can elevate a band to greatness. With the physical demands on trumpeters at an all-time high, care must be taken with young trumpet players to ensure they establish good habits from the beginning. The first part of this chapter discusses how to cultivate the daily habits that produce fine trumpet players. No matter what the type of music, the first step is to teach the students to flat out play their horns better.

# In the Wood Shed
## The Trumpet's Physical Nature

A major cause of poor trumpet playing is the difficulty of the trumpet itself. The trumpet is a very physical instrument, and playing it well, especially in the upper register, requires a robustly whole body approach. In addition, the shape of the lips, the shape of the teeth, and the exact placement of the mouthpiece are so important that they may ultimately determine whether or not an otherwise promising young musician will succeed on the trumpet.

Every band director wants strong trumpets with excellent range and endurance, but trumpet players always seem to have more than their fair share of physical problems. "Weak chops" is the usual reason given for an inability to play high, loud, or long, but this is not always applicable. In the vast majority of cases, the key to a stronger trumpet player is stronger wind power, not stronger lip power. Trumpet players typically ask the embouchure to do the job that should be done by the breath, but the embouchure is not built to carry the weight that the breath carries. Without the breath, the lips cannot make a sound. It is important to have a strong embouchure, but excellent range and endurance are not just a matter of making the embouchure stronger. The whole body is involved in trumpet performance, and the breath is the true source of power, not the lips.

The quickest way to improve the strength and range of the trumpet section is by the daily practice of breathing and other physical exercises. Playing high and loud takes great energy and stamina, particularly in the body's breathing muscles. When we strengthen the breathing muscles, some amazing things can happen, and playing the trumpet becomes easier and more fun.

In terms of a physical predisposition for the trumpet, individuals who can naturally produce a strong, pressurized airstream may be most successful initially. Producing and controlling a pressurized airstream is so critical to playing the trumpet successfully that everyone who wishes to master the trumpet must learn how to do it properly.

# Two Breathing Exercises

Following are instructions for two of the most effective breathing exercises I know for improving the physical ability to play the trumpet. If done every day, "Timed Panting" and

"Bud Brisbois's Favorite Exercise" will noticeably improve sound, range, control, endurance, and power. For demonstrations of both of these exercises, see ⊙ video 14.1, Building Strong Trumpeters.

## Timed Panting

This exercise is very simple. Pant like a dog through the mouth rapidly for as long as you can without stopping. Four "in and out" pants per second is a good average rate to work toward, but this is usually difficult at first. It is especially beneficial to hold your instrument as if playing it when doing this exercise. (Panting through the nostrils is even more effective, but it may be better to introduce this idea to more advanced players with secure technique.) Aim for 30 seconds of nearly continuous panting the first week and add a second or two each time you do it. When you can go for a minute, go for two, then for three minutes. Many advanced players can do six minutes or more of nearly continuous panting. Plan to have at least one session of panting each day. The best time is right before you play your instrument.

Timed panting is an unparalleled exercise to strengthen the muscles that suck the air in and blow it out as a highly pressurized airstream. Daily practice of this exercise puts more "sizzle" in the sound and "pop" in the attacks from the power of the compressed airstream. Air power is at the root of everything on the trumpet, so virtually every aspect of performance skill will improve with a stronger airstream. This works wonders for all wind and brass players.

## Bud Brisbois's Favorite Exercise

Bud Brisbois was one of the greatest lead trumpet players of all time. Here is his favorite exercise, in Bud's own words:

> The best breathing exercise I have ever known, and this works within a week. Stand in front of a mirror, without a shirt on. This takes one week, ten minutes a day. Put your hands high on your sides, and take a breath and try to push your hands out as far as you can. Then count slowly as you release your air, 1, 2, 3 . . . ." [Note: Bud is saying that when we inhale, expand the ribcage sideways as much as possible so that the hands on the sides are "pushed out."] As soon as you are completely out of air, take another huge breath. Make sure you are watching yourself in the mirror. The first day you may be able to get up to 15 or 16. By the end of the week, you're up to 25, 30, 35, 40, some up to 50 and 60. Repeat this for ten minutes a day.[1]

This exercise can be done while working at the computer or watching a movie. It seems very simple, but the results are extremely powerful. Ten minutes a day for at least one week brings about the feeling that the old-school players called "gripping the air." This wonderful feeling of strength and control cannot be explained, it must be felt in the body, and Bud's exercise is the quickest way to learn it. This exercise teaches the proper way to support the airstream while strengthening the most important muscles at the same time. Challenge your students to find out why this was the favorite exercise of one of the greatest lead players.

A lot of discussion is not needed when teaching these two exercises. Just establish with your students the necessity of doing the breathing drills every single day, and they will work their magic. The body learns what it needs to learn from simply doing the exercises, and the benefits come over time from steady and consistent daily work.

## Physical Exercise

In addition to breathing exercises, engaging in some kind of physical exercise on a regular schedule each week is highly recommended for every trumpeter. In addition to the usual jogging, swimming, walking, sports, or working out at the gym, students can check out the yoga routines called "The Salute to the Sun" and "The Five Tibetan Rites," or my favorite, the qigong "Eight Brocades." These three ancient and proven routines are each more than a thousand years old. They are made up of highly beneficial exercises that are practiced together in a single session. For something more modern, look at the Canadian Air Force Aerobic Fitness Program, a favorite of more than one world-class trumpeter.

## The Embouchure

It is commonly believed that one's success on the trumpet is determined largely by one's "chops." Whether one has weak chops or strong chops, good or bad chops, the main idea has been that the embouchure is the key factor. The embouchure is certainly one of the biggest determinants of a successful outcome on the trumpet, but the vast majority of mediocre players have embouchures that would work perfectly well if only they were used properly. The problem is not a weak or faulty embouchure; the problem is an embouchure that is starved for compressed air.

Of course, some players have embouchures that just do not work very well. The function of a trumpeter's embouchure is to vibrate freely, but to do this, certain factors must be just right. Most embouchure problems cannot be fixed quickly. It is best to leave embouchure changes to a private teacher, but there is nothing wrong with a student experimenting to find improvement. In order to do this, it is important to understand embouchure problems and their solutions.

## Dysfunctional Embouchures

The primary feature of a dysfunctional embouchure is an inability to produce a free and easy vibration. If the student consistently finds it difficult to make a clear buzz on the mouthpiece alone, for example, or simple tone production and response fluctuate radically from day to day, or the student always has an airy sound with poor flexibility, then the embouchure is likely at fault. Following is a discussion of common embouchure problems and suggested solutions. These brief sketches are only a field guide and not intended to replace an experienced trumpet teacher.

**Problem:** *Playing on the red* is when the mouthpiece is placed so low on the embouchure that the mark from the inner edge of the mouthpiece is inscribed into the red of the lip instead of the skin above the lip. In other words, the mouthpiece impression on the upper lip should not be inscribed into the red lip tissue; it should be inscribed into the skin, or at least on the border between lip and skin. It is extremely important that the inner edge of the mouthpiece be anchored on the skin surrounding the lip tissue, because this is where the primary embouchure muscle, the orbicularis oris, is located. The lips are composed of fatty tissue that cannot support trumpet playing. Setting the inner edge of the mouthpiece into the lip is a sure path to chronic restrictions in flexibility, range, endurance, and sound. Though some "on the red" players have the ability to play very high, it is often without endurance, flexibility, or control. There is no problem with setting the lower lip into the red as long as the upper lip is correctly placed.

**Fix:** An embouchure change is needed to move the mouthpiece higher so that the inner edge of the mouthpiece is off of the red tissue. Individuals who have overly thick, wide lips could try rolling both lips in, and others may find it necessary to move the placement of the mouthpiece to the left or right of center. This is not a problem as long as a free buzz is available at the new spot. From this point, it is a matter of reinforcing the new placement, which is discussed later in this section. Switching to low brass is oftentimes a good option here.

**Problem:** The upper lip has a point or a bulb in the center, known as a *Cupid's bow or dew drop upper lip*, making it almost impossible for the air to make a natural aperture at that spot. This is also true for scar tissue and any other lip anomaly that would cause a disruption inside the lip aperture. Unfortunately, even years of diligent practice will not change the day-to-day inconsistency that comes from building one's embouchure on so unstable a location.

**Fix:** Moving the mouthpiece to the left or right side of the point or bulb to locate a place that vibrates freely is a proven fix. It is not necessary to place the mouthpiece in the center of the embouchure. In fact, sometimes the center is the worst place of all. Have the student locate a new setting on the left or right side of the center that buzzes easily. Through trial and error, the student will find the best place. If the student nurses the new embouchure alongside the old embouchure over the weeks and months, with care and time it can become a fully functioning new embouchure.

**Problem:** *Extremely flat, sharp, or concave upper teeth* can cause performance problems that often go unrecognized and undiagnosed. The optimum teeth shape to play the trumpet is poorly understood. Ideally, there is a slight high point on the upper teeth that acts like a fret on a guitar. It allows lip flexibility and for blood to replenish the embouchure, but it is not sharp enough to hurt, bruise, or cut the lip. On the other end of the spectrum, a completely flat or concave teeth shape would be problematic. It is ironic that braces sometimes ruin the perfect teeth shape for trumpet playing. If the teeth are completely flat, then the embouchure can be easily pinned down between the teeth and the mouthpiece. This problem is worsened if the front teeth are concave. In such cases, playing may go well for a while, but when the player is fatigued and starts to force, the embouchure is immobilized by mouthpiece pressure, and tone production and flexibility are shut off.

**Fix:** As with the Cupid's bow or dew drop problem described previously, the student must, if possible, put the mouthpiece in a new spot that feels comfortable and allows an easy vibration when buzzing it. Developing a new embouchure is not a big deal if it is done slowly. We are not trying to change the old one, we are replacing it. The student should continue playing on the old embouchure while developing the new one on the side. At some point, the student must quit the old embouchure and fully adopt the new one. This process can take time. (For more on this topic, see my book *Trumpet Technique* [Oxford University Press, 2005].)

**Problem:** *Forcing the tone* is by far the most common embouchure problem, and the cause is a simple lack of air support. In these cases, the student is trying to get higher notes by jamming the mouthpiece harder and harder against the lips. Initially, the resulting compression from smashing the lip tissue can lead to a modest improvement in range, but it is temporary. Forcing is a downward spiral that can lead to an embouchure injury if left unchecked. Students who neglect a proper warm-up before strenuous playing are especially prone to forcing.

**Fix:** It does little good to suggest that the student try to play using less pressure. The student must develop and strengthen the breath using breathing exercises such as timed panting, along with traditional trumpet fundamentals like soft long tones, scales, lip slurs, and bent tones. A strong compressed airstream is the key. The student will gradually stop forcing the mouthpiece when the breath takes over more of the weight of playing.

## Range and Endurance Exercises for Trumpet Players

In addition to the breathing and physical exercises mentioned previously, have your students do the following simple yet effective exercises to build range and endurance.

**The 20-minute G:** Renowned Duke Ellington lead player Cat Anderson used to charge $200 to divulge his famous secret for playing in the high register, but here it is for free: play second line G on the staff "like a whisper" for 20 minutes every day. Long tones are tried and true, but in this version, play the G as softly as you can to the end of your breath, resting as necessary, and do it for 20 minutes. Long tones are a vital part of the daily routine of the world's finest players. At least a few minutes of soft long tones should be mandatory every day.

**Bent tones:** A bent tone is when you play any note with the fingering half a step higher. For example, play F natural (first valve), then go to the F♯ fingering (second valve), but keep F natural sounding. Alternatively, bend F♯ down to the F but keep the F♯ fingering. How do you actually bend the tone? Every player must figure that out through trial and error, and this is worth the trouble, because bent tones teach us the oral cavity shape and tongue position for playing in the extreme upper register. When you can play bent tones, especially higher on the staff, it means something important has changed for the better in your playing technique. To develop strength and range, play soft bent tones in sessions of five to ten minutes or more, and strive to play each tone to the end of your breath to get the most from them. This low resistance approach to range and endurance building is effective and easy, but the exercises need to be done daily over a relatively long period to get results.

**Scales and arpeggios:** Scales and arpeggios practice is fundamental to every musician, but most trumpet players do not realize that scales build range. Play major and minor scales slowly with a beautiful sound and a connected, legato approach, resting as necessary. Start them from the top of the scale for variety, and practice them with a swing feel.

**A thorough warm-up:** Trumpeters need to learn the importance of having a thorough warm-up to be ready to play at the downbeat. This is crucial to good range and endurance.

Warming-up the entire band will help everyone find a resonant, easy sound and good pitch. Similarly, a gentle warm-down, especially after a hard playing session, will help the next session immeasurably. If your jazz band rehearsals are before school, it is imperative to take the time to warm up, especially the trumpets.

# On Stage
## Playing in a Section

Although jazz music is based in the spirit of individual expression, when four or five jazz trumpet players play together, they must employ the same protocols that classical trumpet sections observe, such as starting and stopping together, good intonation, matching phrasing, matching time feel, matching dynamics, matching timbre, vibrato, and so on. All of this is just as important in a big band section as it is in a classical section. The place where trumpeters really learn to play as a unit is the trumpet sectional, when they rehearse together without the band.

**Lead players.** Lead players are very special creatures in jazz. Of the 100 trumpeters at the University of North Texas when I was there, it was said that only a handful were actually lead players, and the rest merely high note players. What makes a lead player? The ability to play high has the greatest value, but what makes one person just a high note player and another a lead player? The answer is the same three things that make a great classical player: sound, expression, and time. A lead player's sound and expression is highly unique. Bernie Glow and Conrad Gozzo, two of the greatest lead players in history, were not the ones with the most extreme range, but their fat, rich sound, time feel, and expressive sense of line set them apart. The lead player has to have a very clear conception of the music, combined with a bold physicality that puts the sound out there, loud and clear.

A lead player must have a great sense of time. Jim Hynes has been the busiest working trumpet player in New York City for decades. You've heard Jim dozens of times playing virtually all of the TV sports and news themes, hundreds of commercials, and platinum recordings with top artists. When asked what special ability or skill helped him in that competitive environment, he said: "My sense of time." Words cannot teach this. We must learn it from listening to the great players. See ⊛ appendix 14.1, "Partial List of Influential Lead Trumpet Players".

Because the literature for high school and college students is so demanding today, it is a good idea to have the students *split lead*, or divide the lead parts between two or more players. Many young trumpeters are incapable of playing parts that were written for big band or Broadway show trumpeters, but having another player to split the lead book will lessen the burden. It may be necessary to rewrite parts where the notes are simply too high, such as the final note of a chart. It is better to do this than have the students force their way through the music.

**Second trumpeters.** Second trumpeters are among the most versatile musicians on the bandstand. A jack of all trades, the second must completely support the first, making the lead player sound good, as well as occasionally assist by playing lead on selected passages or perhaps splitting lead on an entire chart or concert. In addition, the second chair is traditionally the jazz book, with featured solos and chord changes usually found here (or in the fourth book.)

**Third, fourth, or fifth players.** These players will fill out the section. The section players must always defer to the lead player, marking into their parts the various details of phrasing that are consistent with the lead player's interpretation. It is a cardinal sin to try to lead the band from a lower book, even if the lead player cannot play.

**The improvisor.** Many students are able to play by ear fairly easily with little need for chord changes, but they will go only so far before the difficulty of the chord changes rises above their natural ability. It is important for this kind of natural "ear" player to have some piano training and to learn to read chord changes. On the other hand, individuals who cannot play without notation or chord changes should be encouraged to get away from the music and spend more time playing by ear. To hear something in your head and have it come immediately out of the instrument (audiation) is the most important skill in jazz. It can be learned through practice. (See chapter 5 in this volume.)

## Jazz Trumpet Articulation

Articulation during an improvised solo is usually quite connected and legato. Although jazz trumpeters may firmly accent and severely shorten notes, especially on the "and" of the beat, the typical improvised line is mostly slurred with some notes tongued at the convenience of the soloist. When reading a big band chart, of course, the articulation should be played exactly as written on the page, or if in doubt, according to the lead player's interpretation. Young trumpeters who are new to the swing feel are inclined to play a dotted eighth and sixteenth rhythm in place of swing eighth notes, and they tend to articulate everything with a hard, short, and pecky "tut" attack. This "ricky-ticky" style is reminiscent of the 1920s and is inappropriate for nearly all jazz playing. Steering your young students away from hard dotted eighth notes and toward legato triplets is an important early task in teaching them jazz. Encourage young trumpeters to practice scales in swing eighths using a more connected, vocal style, as if scat singing the line. Instead of swing eighth notes played with a marcato "tut-ta-tut-ta-tut," they should play the scale with a legato "du-da-du-da-du." The important things about jazz articulation are to keep the air moving, legato tongue, and sing through the line. For a demonstration of this, see ▶ video 14.2, Articulation.

## Jazz Sound

There is no single jazz trumpet sound. Each of the great jazz trumpet soloists has such a unique and distinguishing sound and approach that a young player may well wonder whom to emulate. In jazz, our biggest influences are forever a part of the way we express ourselves, and that includes our sound. There is no need for students to go looking for their own unique sound; that will happen automatically after a lot of listening and playing. When we listen closely to the artists whom we wish to imitate, some part of them rubs off on us.

A jazz trumpet section would probably be described as having a sound that is "brighter" or "more brilliant" than that of an orchestral trumpet section. This is partly because of players' concepts, partly because of the needs of the music, and partly because of equipment. The single piece of equipment that makes the biggest impact on sound is not the type of trumpet, it is the mouthpiece.

## Mouthpieces

Some players chase after the perfect mouthpiece, but it does not exist. A reasonable compromise is all we can manage. The mouthpiece that gives us only good qualities and none of the bad is a myth. We can either find a mouthpiece that is successful for most of the things we do, or use different mouthpieces specifically designed for the job at hand. Mouthpiece makers today have models in their lines that are designed specifically for the upper register. These mouthpieces may have the same rim shape and cup diameter as the regular models, but the cup is shallower. A shallow-cup mouthpiece helps the upper register and emphasizes the upper partials of the overtone series. This can come across as overly bright or shrill in the wrong hands, but it helps lead players and those who work professionally in commercial music and shows. In general, lead players choose mouthpieces that are medium to small in diameter and considerably shallower than classical mouthpieces.

It is not a good idea for a young student to begin playing on a lead mouthpiece before a good concept of sound has been formed. I agree with Bruce and Emily that elementary and junior high school players should use standard mouthpieces for jazz. A high school or college student who is playing lead in a big band or a Broadway pit orchestra, however, would be advised to get a lead mouthpiece because it makes the job easier, and it produces the right sound for that idiom, just as an orchestral player would be advised to use a mouthpiece that produces a fuller spectrum of overtones and a greater volume of sound (see ◉ appendix 14.2, "Mouthpieces for Different Tasks").

## Mutes

Mutes are required equipment in a big band. Every player in the section should own a *straight, cup, plunger,* "*Harmon,*" and *practice mute.* Most mutes will tend to play slightly sharp with the exception of the cup, which can tend to play flat. Trumpeters must make an adjustment by pulling out the slide slightly or by lipping down, and then put the slide back in when they take the mute out. See ◉ appendix 14.3, "Mutes," for more specific information.

## The Flugelhorn

This warm-voiced sibling of the trumpet is requested in many jazz compositions today because it adds a rich, warm color to the composer's palette. The flugel is especially appropriate on ballads, and though it is played like a trumpet, it is not an instrument for the extreme upper register. Few high school trumpeters own flugelhorns, and a set of four is an expensive purchase, so when the chart calls for it, have the students play with the bell close to the stand, or use bucket mutes for a passable substitute.

# Closing Notes

The training of a young jazz trumpeter must take into account the very physical nature of trumpet playing. The implementation of the daily practice of breathing exercises and other fundamentals will make students physically stronger and lead them to better performance habits automatically. When we focus our attention on helping our students become better at playing their instruments, everything else will fall into place. Detailed information about many of the topics covered in this chapter can be found in my book *Trumpet Technique* [Oxford, 2005] and in my "Clinic" columns in the *International Trumpet Guild Journal*, available at the International Trumpet Guild website.

How fortunate we are to help young people find their own joy in the thrill of making music. My best wishes to you and your students!

# Questions for Discussion

1. What are some ways to build strong trumpet players?
2. Why are bent tones so helpful?
3. Would you recommend different equipment for your jazz trumpet section than for your concert band trumpet section?
4. My student seems to show the signs of a dysfunctional embouchure, but I am not sure. What should I do?

# Note

1. From a transcript by Kevin Seeley, found on Seeley's Bud Brisbois Facebook page, https://www.facebook.com/groups/91205462403/.

# 15

# Jazz Trombone

Christopher Buckholz

## Teaching Through Sound

Throughout his teaching in concert band as well as jazz ensemble, Bruce constantly models for students, whether orally or on an instrument. When he models on an instrument, he usually does so on trumpet because he feels that the timbre and register of trumpet is more accessible to middle school students than his primary instrument, trombone. "'It doesn't go doo doo doo doo doo...it goes, doo bah doo bah dot. Play that.' And then they'll play, 'dah dah dah dah dot.' And you say, 'no, doo bah doo bah dot.'

Emily also models for the students on her trombone every day. Playing for the students is one of the most effective ways for her to teach style, articulation, improvisation, and anything else that students must learn in jazz ensemble. When teaching, you can either tell the students how to do it, or you can play it for them. "Why wouldn't you play it? It's like the Navajo language, man, it gets passed down. You've got to play for the kids, man. You've got to play for the kids."

Emily's main goal here is to get students listening to professionals who play the same instrument. When students bring in their recordings this gives her the opportunity to introduce them to other players:

I always have something that I can add to the mix as necessary. "You like that? How about this? Oh, you like Gerry Mulligan? How about this? Did you know that guy plays piccolo? Let's listen to him play jazz piccolo." And then we can talk about style as a class. If you do it right then you get the kids passing them around and saying, "hey did you hear this guy, did you hear that guy."

As stated in the Bruce and Emily example above, listening and imitation are vital to young jazz musicians. They are especially crucial for young trombonists, because the trombone is a technically difficult instrument to master, and that cannot be done without good models. The embouchure is relatively easy to form and develop, but the slide takes far more work to play in tune and without glissando. More than any other wind instrument, the trombone requires a player with an excellent ear. With a little knowledge and forethought, the slide can be dealt with, and overall ensemble quality will be greatly improved. This chapter deals with the parts of the big band trombone section and its functions as a unit, followed by a discussion of the trombone's technical challenges in jazz (particularly with articulation), equipment, and important recordings. (See ⊙ appendix 15.1 for a list of influential jazz trombonists.)

# The Trombone Section

A big band trombone section is typically divided into four parts: lead (or 1st), 2nd, 3rd, and bass (or 4th). Each part has a specialized role. As a director, it is important that you understand the differences between parts so that you can assign chairs intelligently.

## Lead (or 1st) Trombone

The lead player needs to have a good high range, and more important, great endurance. The lead trombone part is usually voiced in a low trumpet range, which means that the lead player is playing in the upper-middle to high range most of the time. Lead trombone parts in typical school jazz band music do not usually venture into the extreme high register the way that lead trumpet parts do. However, they also do not have the amount of rest that a lead trumpet part would (or should). Lead trombone playing is primarily about endurance.

The lead trombone part is important stylistically, both to the section and the ensemble. Phrasing, inflections, articulation, style, and intonation in the trombone section all need to match the lead player's. Your lead trombonist has to set the example for the rest of the section. The lead trombonists have to match their interpretation with the lead alto saxophonist's and, most important, the lead trumpet player's. When the trombone section is playing independently, the lead trombonist has more stylistic latitude than when playing in tutti sections with the trumpets and/or saxophones. Finally, the lead trombone part is the one most likely to have an improvised solo written into it. The lead player should be a strong improvisor, especially if you are performing more advanced literature without written-out solos or chord changes in every part.

## 2nd and 3rd Trombone

The 2nd trombone part is often called the "jazz chair." This is a bit of a misnomer, because around half the improvised trombone solos are written into the lead trombone part. In my estimation, about 40 percent are written into the 2nd part, and about 10 percent are written into the 3rd or bass trombone part.

The 2nd and 3rd trombone players have to be able to follow the lead trombonist. They cannot impose their will on the section. They have to be able to listen well and have enough technique to match the lead trombonist. Usually, the 2nd trombonist will be playing with fewer inflections and less vibrato than the lead player. In many schools, there simply are not enough trombonists to have much choice in how you assign parts. If you do have the luxury to choose, you will want a good improvisor on 2nd trombone, but maybe not with the high range, endurance, sound, intonation, and style of the lead player.

The 3rd trombone part is a bridge between the upper two parts and the bass trombone. It is usually scored low enough that a large bore trombone with an f-attachment is a big help. The 3rd trombonist has to play with less inflection and vibrato than the 2nd player. Excellent intonation and the ability to blend with the 2nd and lead trombonists are strong attributes for a 3rd trombonist, along with a good middle to low register.

Of course, parts can be switched around between players. If your lead trombonist does not have the endurance to play all the lead parts, trading off parts with the 2nd or 3rd trombonist might be a good idea. However, the constant switching of styles and sounds between players can lead to inconsistencies in the section. Avoid switching around parts unless it is necessary.

# Bass Trombone

The bass trombone functions in a big band much the same way as the baritone saxophone. It can be the bottom end of the trombone section or the brass section as a whole. It can also be an independent solo voice or scored with the baritone saxophone and/or bass. Modern bass trombone parts can be very virtuosic in their use of register and technical demands. Older arrangements usually do not have a specific bass trombone part. Their 4th trombone parts (if there even is a 4th trombone part) are more like slightly lower 3rd trombone parts and may not require the use of an f-attachment (let alone the D/G♭ attachment) at all. So, the demands of bass trombone parts can vary widely depending upon the age of the arrangement.

The parts in your section should be set up as follows (as you are facing the band, from left to right): 2nd, lead, 3rd, 4th. Having a 5th trombone part is rare, and it usually only shows up in Stan Kenton charts written from 1958 to the 1970s.

If you don't have a full complement of four trombones, it can be difficult to decide which parts you want to cover. Following is a recommendation for part assignments:

One trombonist: cover 1st trombone
Two trombonists: cover 1st and 2nd trombone
Three trombonists: cover 1st, 2nd, and bass trombone. You might find some arrangements that sound better with the 3rd trombone part covered instead of bass trombone; do what works best for that particular arrangement.

# Technique

The principles of good trombone playing are really very simple. The slide has to be in the right spot—and stop moving—when the note is to be played. The embouchure has to buzz the exact pitch. Air has to get up to and move through the embouchure to make it buzz. The player's mind has to be able to conceive the correct pitch with good intonation and a good sound (see chapter 5 in this volume). Articulation has to be coordinated with the slide movement and timed correctly. This is true of any trombone playing in any situation, but these principles become highlighted in the jazz band because of the small ensemble size and range/endurance demands of the music.

## Slide Technique

The slide has to move quickly and smoothly (without jerking the entire horn) into the correct position. Students can facilitate this by holding the hand slide brace with their palms facing toward the torso. Most students hold the slide by placing it between the pad of their thumb and the side of their index finger. This eliminates the range of motion possible in the wrist and fingers and necessitates the slide being moved by the arm exclusively. By holding the hand slide brace between the pads of the index and middle fingers and the pad of the thumb, the wrist and fingers can be used to help move the slide (see ⓥ video 15.1, Slide Technique).

Most students have a poor understanding of where the fifth to seventh positions are. Positions can be marked off with a permanent marker on the inner slide tubes. They wear off in a week or two and do not interfere with the slide action. When the marks become faint, they can be redrawn. This may seem like a "crutch," but it is far better for the students to consistently go to the correct slide length.

Just as a sticky valve will create technical issues for a trumpet player, a sticky slide will create unnecessary intonation and technique problems for a trombonist. Students must have a slide with perfectly straight tubes, in proper alignment and free from dents. In addition, the slide must be properly lubricated and clean. A trombone slide cleaning rod, threaded with a cheesecloth (available at most grocery stores), is needed to keep the insides of the outer slide tubes clean. This should be used to swab out the outer slide tubes whenever the slide lubrication is changed, about every day or two. The trombone should be cleaned out with a flexible brush (or "snake") and soapy, warm water every month. Very few students are taught how to properly maintain and lubricate a slide. It should be obvious that a fast slide has the potential for better intonation and cleaner technique than a slow one (see ⓥ video 15.2, Caring for the Trombone).

## Breathing

Air is the motor force that makes an embouchure buzz. The more air we can get up to the embouchure and through it, the better it buzzes and the better the instrument will sound. Most students simply do not take in enough air to produce a good sound. The bonus is that the more air we can get up to our embouchures, the less tension they have to be under for a particular note. Also, it will be easier to get the air up to the embouchure with minimal effort. So to put it simply, taking in full lung capacity creates a better sound and makes it easier to play the trombone in any register.

When players inhale, they want to feel suction at the front part of the mouth (not the back of the throat), drop the lower jaw, take in air as relaxed and quietly as possible, and use their full lung capacity, allowing the entire torso to expand. This helps the bronchial tubes, throat/glottis, and tongue/oral cavity to stay open while playing.

Many "embouchure problems" are created by a lack of air getting up to it. The embouchure will develop around the air supply, making it vibrate. If the air is weak, the embouchure will over-tense and not vibrate well. It will still vibrate, but not well enough to produce a good sound or good ranges. Teaching your trombonists good breathing fundamentals from the beginning will save you a lot of work on sound and ranges, as well as the difficult task of retraining the embouchure once it has developed around an inadequate air supply. Given the physical challenge of playing in a jazz trombone section, particularly for the lead and bass trombonists, good basic breathing will improve your trombone section (see ▶ video 15.3, Breathing).

## Ranges

Many students do not have the range—either high or low—that they need to function in a jazz ensemble. The high range and endurance take years to develop fully. If the amount of air getting up to the embouchure is small (the result of not taking in very much air in the first place), the high and low ranges might not come at all. If ranges do happen to develop despite weak air conditions, they will have a very weak, pinched sound and be much more difficult to play. The foundation for range and endurance on a brass instrument is a good air supply.

Once a solid, consistent air supply is established, along with a good middle register sound, work can begin on expanding range. Students should be taught to think of expanding their middle range, rather than treating the high or low range as a separate entity. Drill forms like scales and arpeggios can be good for transferring the quality of the middle range up or down. Playing simple melodies in the middle register, then transposing them up or down by various intervals, can also be an excellent way to expand range. We do not want high or low notes without sound or intonation quality, which can be impressive to a young student but of little help to an ensemble. We want useable high and low ranges that sound just as good as the middle range.

# Articulation

Articulation is one of the weakest areas of trombone technique in students. This becomes particularly pronounced in the jazz ensemble. There are many more types of articulation required in a jazz trombone part than in a classical ensemble part. In general, they are harder in quality than in classical playing. As a consequence, the trombone section in a student jazz ensemble tends to have an uncharacteristic style and a weak sense of time. Developing jazz articulation in the young trombonist is a vital part of your ensemble's growth.

## Short Articulations

Short notes in jazz are attacked harder and are much more clipped than short notes in classical music. Most student jazz ensembles play short notes with the softer classical articulation and are surprised to learn how hard they have to articulate to play jazz correctly. On the trombone, this requires the tongue to be much farther forward in the mouth than in classical playing. The tip of the tongue when articulating in jazz trombone playing will be right on the top front teeth, or where the top front teeth meet the hard palate. Have your students say "dut" or "tut" multiple times. Then use the articulation while playing. Where the tip of the tongue lands when enunciating these words is where the tip of the tongue should land when playing short notes in jazz. If the tip of the tongue is landing on the upper lip, on both lips, or between the upper and lower teeth, it will create severe embouchure problems. If the tip of the tongue is farther back in the mouth, that is wonderful for classical playing but will not create the hard attack needed for separated notes in a jazz style. Figure 15.1 shows a typical jazz rhythm and notation.

Figure 15.2 shows how it would be articulated in jazz performance practice.

The other thing to note about articulating short notes in jazz is the fact that "dut" or "tut" puts a consonant at the beginning and end of the note. Ends of phrases and short notes will be stopped with the tongue—which you would almost never do in classical music. Even long notes in jazz will usually be stopped with the tongue, so that a firm cutoff point is created.

## Legato Articulation

Jazz legato articulation on the trombone is much more complicated. Most young students move the slide slowly and imprecisely. This creates glissando between notes and intonation problems—especially in legato playing—because the connection between notes means there is less time to move the slide. Moving the slide faster and more precisely will help your trombonists blend better with the trumpet section and create a better legato line. There are two ways that legato articulation can be created on the trombone: by crossing over a "partial" or "overtone" series, or by soft tonguing. Soft tonguing in jazz legato is best done with the syllable "du." This absolutely has to be done when playing a series of notes on the same partial series (see figure 15.3).

Using "alternate" positions can help your trombonists play cleaner and match the saxophones and trumpets better. One of the most common applications is to play D above the bass clef staff in fourth position in the keys of B♭ and E♭, instead of in first. This keeps the slide only one position away from C and E♭ in 3rd and uses natural slurs (or crossing over the overtone series of the trombone) to create the legato articulation. In general, trombonists

**FIGURE 15.1** Written Notation

**FIGURE 15.2** Played Notation

**FIGURE 15.3** Slurring

**FIGURE 15.4** Alternate Positions

A sharp sign means to play the position closer in than usual, and the flat sign means to play it farther out. The alternates are shown in parentheses.

**FIGURE 15.5** Using the Overtone Series

**FIGURE 15.6** Applied Articulation

should move the slide to the closest position possible. Figure 15.4 shows the "primary" and the most commonly used alternate positions for the upper octave of the trombone. The overtone series of the horn can do most of the work for us (see figure 15.5). The only tonguing needed in this example is on the first note. This is also made possible by the fact that the D is played in fourth position. If it were played in first, the D would be on the same partial series as the C before it and would have to be tongued. I would articulate like this for a modern, straight eighth-feel composition. In practice, this is how I would articulate the example if it was a swing rhythm, in order to emphasize the "and" of beat 2 (see figure 15.6).

Knowing and using the closest position possible has another advantage: getting rid of glissando. The farther you move the slide in legato playing (especially when playing notes on the same partial series), the more likely it is to get glissando between notes. Young players unconsciously clean this up by tonguing harder, thus allowing more time for the slide to move. But that means that their "legato" does not match the smoothness of the saxophones and trumpets. I have three slide position rules for legato playing:

1. Keep half steps on the same partial series.
2a. Use partial breaks whenever possible on intervals larger than half step.
2b. Move the slide to the closest position available.

Numbers 2a and 2b are related. If the players move the slide to the closest position available for a note, they will usually cross over a partial series and get a natural break. This may require the use of "alternate" positions (see figure 15.7).

The articulations that must be used for the positions given in figure 15.7 have been written in. In practice, students will normally tongue the whole thing. This is probably going to sound sloppy, with lots of glissando between the C and D, plus a rough bump and some

**FIGURE 15.7** Common Student Positions

**FIGURE 15.8** Better Position Choices

**FIGURE 15.9** Economy of Movement

gliss going from the D to the E♭. All this is eliminated if we play the D in fourth position (see figure 15.8).

When playing eighth note lines in jazz, I use a "du" syllable most of the time, with partial break articulation for notes that need to be de-emphasized, or ghosted. I also tongue the notes that need a slight accent. I use alternate positions to eliminate large back and forth movements of the slide and enable fast, clean playing (see figure 15.9).

## Multiple Tonguing

As you can see from the preceding discussion, trombonists have to articulate in more situations than saxophonists or trumpet players do. As the notes get faster, the players still have to tongue to create a clean front to the note and eliminate glissando. At a certain point, it becomes a necessity for trombonists to master multiple tonguing. There are three ways to multiple tongue on the trombone: double tonguing, reverse double tonguing, and doodle tonguing (see ⊙ video 15.4, Multiple Tonguing).

## Intonation

Good intonation on the trombone takes far more work than it does for valved instrument players. Practice with tuning drones—5ths in "pure" or "just" intonation—should be a part of every trombonist's daily routine. I recommend *The Tuning CD* by Richard Schwartz, as it plays pitches that are held for three minutes and gives students plenty of time to find the spot where the notes are in tune. The goal is to eliminate the "beats" that will be present if the note is out of tune. For any given key, I play major scales going up or down, then minor scales going the opposite direction. Do not move to the next note until the note you are on is perfectly in tune.

## Projection

Projection is the ability of a sound to get out into the audience. A bright sound projects better than a dark one, particularly when the ensemble is loud. Having a concept of where you want your sound to go is very helpful for projection. I usually imagine a spot in the middle of the back of the hall where I want my sound to end up.

The trombone is a directional instrument. The sound comes out the bell and will go wherever it is pointed. Most student trombonists point their bells down at the saxophonists in front of them while looking up at the music stand. As a result, and because of the use of large equipment, most trombone sections are underrepresented in the balance of the ensemble. Their bells should point out into the audience. Ask students to imagine the bell of the trombone as a flashlight and point it where they want the sound to go. Music stand placement is very important; it cannot block the bell. The slide should be on the player's left side of the stand, and students should get used to looking down at the music slightly. Some band directors have their trombonists turn their stands so that they are looking at the music at a 45-degree angle. I think it is better to simply get used to having the slide over the music stand and look down at the music, so that the bell has to point out, rather than trying to read the music at an angle. Looking at the music stand at an angle is a bad habit for solo playing and usually fails to get students to point their bells out toward the audience.

## Style

The way a Maria Schneider composition should be performed is vastly different from the way a Duke Ellington composition should be performed. Typically, student ensembles play every big band chart the same way. As your ensemble(s) grow in ability—beyond simply getting the notes and rhythms right—you should work on style (see ⓭ appendix 15.2, Resources, for a list of recommended recordings and texts). There are many variations, but the following styles can be generalized for the trombone section:

- Count Basie. This includes the vast library of big band standards that were written for the Count Basie Orchestra or are in that style. It uses lots of fast, wide jaw vibrato (see the section on vibrato in this chapter), usually from the lead player only, and short notes that are played extra short. There can be some intentional laying back, but generally the time is very slightly behind the beat. The typical fault is to play so far in back of the time that it drags.
- Duke Ellington. This includes very heavy vibrato from the entire section. Short articulations are longer than in Count Basie style. Time is on top of the beat.
- Stan Kenton. Vibrato is from the lead player only. Inflections come from the lead player and may be continued down the section. Some trombone solis are played without vibrato.
- Commercial big bands of the 1930s–1960s. This includes heavy use of slide vibrato by the entire section, very short notes, and bright sounds.

- Modern, straight eighth (typified by the Maria Schneider Orchestra). This involves no vibrato, little inflection, and dark sounds. (See ⏵ video 15.5, Style.)

# Recommended Trombone Equipment

Just like every other instrumentalist, trombonists have a variety of instrument and mouthpiece choices. There are two basic sizes of trombone: small bore and large bore. The small bore instruments take a "small shank" mouthpiece, and the large bore instruments/bass trombones take a "large shank." This is because of the great variety of bore sizes available in trombones; one size of mouthpiece shank does not work well for all the different bores.

## Jazz Trombones and Mouthpieces

Most high school students invest in a large bore tenor trombone with an f-attachment as a step-up instrument. This equipment is fine for classical ensembles, but it is too large to be effective in a big band. Not only is the sound too dark to blend well with the trumpets, but it also does not articulate or project as well. The size and depth of the mouthpiece means that young trombonists often do not have the range and endurance needed to play lead and 2nd trombone parts (and if they do, they are working too hard and developing bad habits to get the notes out).

The solution is to play on smaller equipment. There are hundreds of excellent used, professional-grade small bore trombones available online at any given time. Many of these instruments are 40 to 70 years old but in excellent condition. Another option is to have students play on their "beginner" horns, which have a smaller bore/bell size and take a small shank mouthpiece. If no other option is available, a 6½ AL or 6½ AM large shank mouthpiece, or a small shank trombone mouthpiece with a large shank adapter, is a good choice for playing on a large bore trombone (see equipment recommendations in this section).

A good used jazz trombone can be purchased for under $1,000, and there are many excellent instruments available. It should have a bore size between .485 and .525 inch and a bell size of 8 inches or less. These are the models I recommend:

- Bach Stradivarius Models 6, 8, 12, 16, 16M, 36.
- Conn 4H, 6H, 12H (Good vintage horns are marked Elkhart, Ind, or Conn, USA, with scroll engraving and a three-marching-men logo. The upper end of the bottom outer slide tube will be stamped with the model number.)
- King 2B, 2B+, 3B, 3B+
- Yamaha 891Z, 897Z

Good jazz trombone mouthpieces include Bach 12C, 12, 11C, 11, 7C, 6¾ C, 6½ A, 6½ AM, 6½ AL, Schilke 46, 47, 47B, 48, Wick 10CS and 7CS.

## Trombone Mutes

The most commonly used mutes in a big band trombone section are cup, plunger, and bucket. Most beginner level arrangements will not require the use of mutes at all. Older big band arrangements use straight mutes more often than contemporary ones. Duke Ellington compositions often require a straight mute/plunger combination for Tricky Sam Nanton (or his successors) solos in the 2nd trombone part (discussed later in this section).

At a minimum, young trombonists should own straight, cup, and plunger mutes, as they will be used most often in their jazz and classical ensembles. Advanced students should add the following:

- Harmon mute
- Bucket mute, preferably one that fits inside the bell rather than clipping on the bell rim
- Tom Crown copy of a Magosy-Buscher Non Pareil trumpet straight mute, with extra mute corks glued on and shaved to fit inside a trombone bell. This is for the Duke Ellington/Tricky Sam Nanton solos mentioned previously. The corks should be thick enough so that the bottom of the mute is flush with the edge of the bell.

## Questions for Discussion

1. What are the reasons it is helpful to model for students?
2. Who were some of your jazz influences? How did they influence your playing?
3. Why is articulation problematic for the jazz trombonist, and how would you teach it?
4. Why would watching videos of the great jazz trombonists be important?
5. Why is knowledge of ensemble/historical styles important to the entire jazz ensemble?
6. What are the most common technical problems young trombonists have, and how do you correct them?

# 16

# Jazz Guitar

Bob Sneider

## Guitarists and Their Megadeth Stickers

While piano players find the group dynamic a difficult transition from solo playing, guitar players are often used to playing in ensembles, usually small rock bands, and their transition to group playing is not as difficult. However, like young piano players, guitar players often have difficulty reading jazz ensemble notation. Bruce describes how guitar players are often used to reading chord changes (or tablature) but are often not used to playing in the keys in which most school jazz ensemble music is written:

> When [guitar players] come to jazz band for the first time and they figure out that they have to be able to play in B♭ and F and everything is not G, D, and C, and they go, "Oh, I can't do this." OK—I'll find someone who can, because I can't teach you.

While Bruce will allow guitar players into his middle school jazz ensemble, he does not actively recruit them:

> You ask the kids, "anybody know someone who can play guitar?" And they say, "yeah, sure, so and so can play guitar" and then of course they come and they have their Megadeath stickers on their guitar and they don't know anything other than to play really loudly and out of tune in G, C, and D. At [the high school] level it's different because it is a class here and we rehearse four hours a week. But at the middle school, I don't find them—they either come to me or we don't have them.

# Instrumental Technique

Throughout the history of jazz, the guitar (predated by the banjo) has been an omnipresent voice as a rhythm section instrument and a solo voice. Having a strong guitarist in any jazz ensemble is a benefit and significantly increases the breadth of material that an ensemble can effectively perform (Dixieland, swing, bebop, fusion, funk). The techniques described in this chapter are based on my 20 years of experience mentoring collegiate, high school, and middle school students at the Eastman School of Music and Eastman Community School. I teach students ranging from novice jazz guitar players (middle and high school) to graduate students and professionals. Taking a student with limited notational staff reading and chord vocabulary on the journey toward being a well-functioning guitarist in a jazz ensemble is no small feat! The single most important piece of advice that I give to educators is to find a respectable and experienced jazz guitar teacher who is able to help a student progress. The goal of this chapter is to address the technical possibilities/limitations of the guitar, diagnose the needs and strengths of a young guitarist, recommend best practices, and provide a hands-on demonstration of learning through notated melodic and chordal examples.

Beginning with finding a qualified teacher, always consult colleagues who have had great experiences with referring guitarists to a community music school or college teacher (or graduate assistant). Since there is an abundance of rock and folk guitar teachers, it is especially important to find a teacher who is versed in the jazz guitar idiom. Guitarists who become members of school jazz ensembles usually get their start as rock, pop, folk, and occasionally classical guitarists. Since guitar is not typically a primary band or orchestra instrument, ensemble playing, notational reading, and phrasing are underdeveloped compared to students who have played in band/orchestra since around the fourth grade. The world of guitar education for young people can be a bit inconsistent. Many students get their information from YouTube or music store teachers who only teach the latest popular songs and classic rock through tablature notation.

Fear not, even with little guitar playing experience in methods classes or having not taken jazz pedagogy courses in college, you can help your budding jazz guitarist progress. By understanding how the guitar *functions* in jazz, *educational practices in guitar study* (good and not so good), and *chordal* and *melodic technique* best practices, and by learning from solid teachers with specialties in traditional band instruments, you can have a positive impact on young guitarists.

## Guitar Mechanics

The guitar is an amazing instrument, with tens of thousands of chord combinations and limitless melodic possibilities in three plus octaves, and the player can also play pianistically (chords + melody + inner moving voices). The guitar is tuned to open 4ths and one major 3rd (lowest string E-A-D-G-B-E). Wire frets chromatically separate each string. For a right-handed guitarist, moving from left to right along the frets of a string raises the pitch by one-half step.

The guitar is a concert-pitched instrument that actually sounds an octave lower than written. Guitarists read primarily in treble clef, even though many of the pitches that they produce are significantly below middle C on the piano. Figure 16.1 shows how the first few measures of "All About That Rhythm" sounds, and figure 16.2 shows that this would be notated an octave higher than it sounds.

## Posture

Proper sitting and standing posture of guitarists is very important. The guitar neck should never be angled down toward the floor. Achieving a slight angle—20 to 45 degrees—even when sitting provides a more ergonomic approach to left-hand technique. Among other qualities of solid technique, thumb placement should be behind the neck (not draped over the top of the fretboard), the palm should be away from the neck, and fretting fingers should be properly arched to allow the upper tips of the fingers to press the frets down. Proper angling of the neck makes it possible to play with greater facility for chording and melodic playing (see figure 16.3).

**FIGURE 16.1** Sounding

**FIGURE 16.2** Notated

**FIGURE 16.3** Proper Angling

## Playing with the Pick

The attack of notes is done with a plectrum, aka a pick. A pick is a plastic teardrop- or triangular-shaped piece of plastic that varies in thickness. Always confirm that your guitarist is attacking the strings in a more or less perpendicular manner (see figure 16.4).

Early training on the guitar involves mostly downstrokes with the pick. Later on, upstrokes are added. Pay attention to see whether your guitarist is predominantly using up- or downstrokes. Employing all downstrokes is ideal for swing chord comping. For melodic passages of eighth notes, triplets, and sixteenth notes, alternate picking is preferred. With appropriate pick technique, guitarists can play passages at the same rate as horn players. Alternate picking makes it possible to have a more rounded swing feel as well. The markings for picking are akin to bow markings for a string player (see figure 16.5). Picking notations have been added to excerpts of "All About That Rhythm" and "Blues for Ox" in figures 16.6 and 16.7. (See ⊚ video 16.1, Alt Picking B♭ Scale.)

## Slurs

The other way that guitarists can sound out notes is by slurring (see ⊚ video 16.2, Legato Technique). Slurs can happen through *hammer-ons/pull-offs and slides* (single fret chromatic move or glissando) (see ⊚ video 16.3, Hammer-Ons; and ⊚ video 16.4, Pull-Offs). Arpeggiated runs can be executed with a pseudo-slur called *sweep picking*, which involves consecutive downstrokes (ascending) or consecutive upstrokes (descending) (see ⊚ video

**FIGURE 16.4** Picking

Downstroke    Upstroke

**FIGURE 16.5** Picking Notations

16.5, Sweep Picking 1; and ⊙ video 16.6, Sweep Picking 2). If ensemble parts for the guitar sound a bit strange and muddy, they usually need to be transposed up one octave. In the notated guitar parts for "All About That Rhythm" and "Blues for Ox," fingerings, fretboard positions, and occasional slurs have been added to make the guitar sound stylistically appropriate (see figures 16.6 and 16.7). The manner in which young guitar players learn the

FIGURE 16.6 "All About That Rhythm" Notated

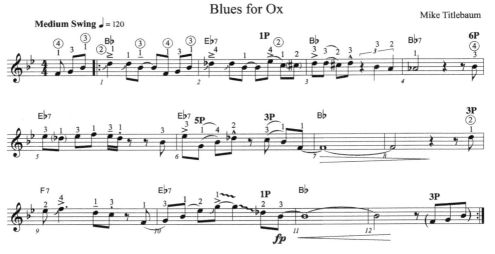

FIGURE 16.7 "Blues for Ox" Notated

FIGURE 16.8 Chord Shapes

guitar is from the open position or folk strumming area. This means that lots of open strings are being played and mid-low register notes predominate. Open position is not ideal for phrasing jazz melody lines or for playing chords. It is rare that a guitarist is a strong reader at a young age in higher fretboard positions, even though it is a very simple task of finding notes due to the chromatic setup of the frets and strings (see ⊕ video 16.7, "All About That Rhythm"; and ⊕ video 16.8, "Blues for Ox" 3].

## Chords and More Chords

The most immediate need for young jazz guitar players is to develop a working use of chords in order to survive even the simplest of jazz ensemble charts. I remember that when I was a youth, my teacher would notate my parts with pictures of chord types until I memorized them and developed the ability to transpose the chord shapes with ease. Eventually I could get through jazz band parts without the chord pictures. Music is an aural art form, but visual learning and shape memorization really help speed things up. Chord shapes are the placement of the left-hand fingers forming the chord (see figure 16.8). I utilize this technique with my younger jazz guitar students, with great success. This comes in very handy when students lack the jazz theory skills to voice out simple or complex chords. Many of the recently published jazz ensemble charts for school-aged students include suggested chord fingerings.

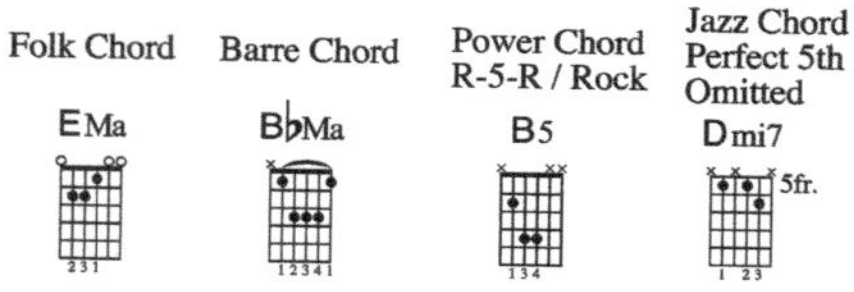

**FIGURE 16.9** Folk, Barre, Rock, and Jazz Chords

## Chord Varieties

A truly innovative step that non-guitar-playing jazz ensemble directors should take is diagnosing what kinds of chords the guitarist is utilizing. Guitarists use four chord varieties: folk, barre, rock, and jazz (see figure 16.9). *Folk* chords are rarely used in jazz ensembles due to open strings' ringing out not being ideal in the rhythm section. Folk chords are located in the region of the guitar closest to the headstock. Most folk chords contain multiple open strings, which allows for easy fingering and strumming. Folk chords are not movable shapes (transposable by moving the entire shape to a higher or lower fret).

*Barre* chords are not widely used in the jazz ensemble because they often produce doubled or tripled roots and 5ths, which are not idiomatic in jazz styles. A telltale sign of barre chords is a flattened index finger across all six strings. If you notice your guitarist favoring folk and barre chords, have a discreet conversation about better choices. Barre chords are movable shapes because the array of intervals stays the same when moving the shape from fret to fret. Some *jazz* chord voicings or shapes will have a half barre or a couple of notes covered by one finger. Do not be alarmed—it is the big six note chords with the doubled 5th and root that are problematic. Jazz chords are movable shapes that do not double any part of the chord (root-3rd-5th-7th). Movable chord shapes are defined by a uniform construction of chord intervals (not containing any open strings). Hence, a shape for $Cm^7$ can be moved up in pitch by two frets (half steps), and the resulting chord is now a $Dm^7$. Similarly, moving down by one fret or half step will result in $Bm^7$. Once a student learns a few varieties of chord shapes for each symbol, encourage strategies to not leapfrog all over the fret board in order to grab chords. Finding chords in closer proximity usually leads to better voice leading. Another possibility to trim down any chord is to skip the 5th unless a flatted 5th or augmented 5th is indicated in the chord symbol (see ⊚ video 16.9, Troubleshooting).

## Freddie Green

Even though jazz big band repertoire has expanded into many genres (Latin, pop, and funk), the most important skill for jazz guitarists to master is Freddie Green–style comping on swing tunes. Green was the rhythmic driving force of the Count Basie Orchestra's classic rhythm section. Playing exclusively quarter note chords was his primary role, and he was in lockstep with Walter Page's grooving bass lines and Papa Joe Jones's time feel on drums. The Basie rhythm section sound was completed with Freddie Green's crisp attack on every beat. One of the great misconceptions in jazz education is that to achieve the Freddie Green sound, students are taught to pound beats 2 and 4 with heavy accents—similar to a backbeat.

In order to achieve the Freddie Green swing style, encourage guitarists to use two- or three-note chords (see ⊚ video 16.10, Freddie Green Style on "All About That Rhythm"; and ⊚ video 16.11, Freddie Green Style on "Blues for Ox"). Guide tones (scale degrees 3 and 7) make great choices. The right hand smoothly and percussively cuts across the strings with equal emphasis on every beat, while the left hand pulsates lightly in sync with each beat. The right hand always plays downstrokes. The pulsation of the left hand dampens the strings in order to avoid needless sustain. Achieving a sweet chord delivery on the point of each beat is the goal. Freddie Green played unamplified throughout his career; nonetheless his presence was always heard and felt. To help achieve that effect, encourage guitarists to turn down their volume a bit so they can "dig" into the quarter notes. Obviously, if a student is playing a solid body guitar, it will be impossible to be heard without amplification. Even if your guitarist does not play an archtop guitar, it is possible to achieve a Freddie Green sound (see figure 16.10). Note that all chord shapes are moveable. Moving up a string by one fret raises the chord by a half step. Conversely, moving down one fret lowers the chord by a half step.

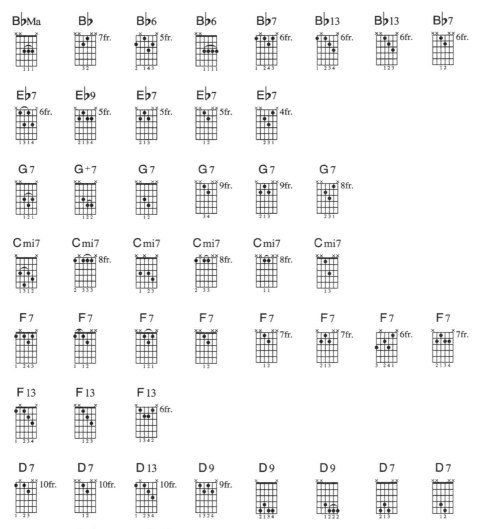

**FIGURE 16.10** Rhythm Guitar Chords

## Notational Reading and Technique

Notational reading for the young guitarist in a jazz ensemble can be quite challenging when the fretboard knowledge beyond the open position is a mystery. As mentioned previously, a high percentage of guitar teachers do not teach reading or possess the jazz skills to effectively help young jazz guitarists. In fact, many do not read standard musical notation or know their notes beyond the open position. The guitar can be a fun and satisfying instrument to strum favorite pop and rock songs without actually learning the notes one is pressing down. Many novice learners get started with a simple method book such as *Alfred Basic Guitar Method (3rd edition; Copyright 1966, 1990, 2007; By Alfred Music Publishing Co, Inc, USA)*. Once students learn a few basics, many teachers switch to tune learning by tablature and ear.

Since the guitar is not a traditional school band instrument, no traditional ensemble opportunities exist for guitarists at the elementary school level. The reading skills and ensemble experiences developed in grades 4–6 by orchestral and band students lead to better phrasing and *rhythmic acuity*. By the time most kids begin middle school jazz bands, reading has developed to the point that tougher syncopated rhythms become more approachable. Conversely, for the young guitarist, subdivisions beyond quarter and eighth notes are completely underdeveloped. The beginner method books of the guitar world do not help much with jazz rhythms. The combination of incomplete fretboard knowledge, lack of rhythmic vocabulary, and technical limitations makes reading on the guitar very difficult for young players. I have noticed a trend in which my best student readers started out on other instruments like piano or violin. Without expecting doom and gloom from guitar player reading, ask students what they are working on with their private teachers (see ⊙ appendix 16.1, Recommended Resources).

## Phrasing

There is no tried and true approach to phrasing jazz on the guitar, because many melodies are not written for it. Developing a strong sense of legato playing, slurs, a relaxed jazz eighth-note feel, and a sixth sense of articulation and accenting is critical. Because the guitar is a non-wind instrument, dynamic phrasing goes a long way in assisting swing. An aural sense of how jazz should sound is critical, because a player's fingertips and a plastic pick cannot alone produce magic from a steel-stringed wooden box. Listening to jazz is critical. Use group lesson time and ensemble rehearsals to introduce students to examples of swing and improvisation. I have found that two methods work best for fostering an intuitive sense of swing and authentic jazz phrasing:

1. Encourage students to sing along with Basie, Ellington, vocalists (Nat King Cole, Sinatra, Ella Fitzgerald), bebop heads, and solos (Charlie Parker, Dizzy Gillespie, Clifford Brown, Sonny Rollins, Art Blakey and The Jazz Messengers, Horace Silver Quintet, and others). See chapter 12 in this volume for ideas on other singers to listen to.

2. Have students play along with written melodies or transcriptions with the master recording. With today's technology, it is easy to slow down tracks to make even the fastest bop heads approachable. In lessons, I often record myself phrasing ensemble parts and bebop heads for my students.

## Jazz Theory and Chord Shapes

Along with the logistical and rhythmic reading challenges of melodies, the harmonic language of jazz exceeds the normal applied theory understanding of middle school and many high school students. There is a steep learning curve when guitarists who are more akin to deciphering basic major and minor chords try to realize complex or challenging chords with extensions on the fret board. In my experience of doing workshops and clinics, some ensemble directors do not have the chord nomenclature and jazz theory acumen to meaningfully help guitarists with chords. When guitarists are presented with large chords like a 13(♯11, ♭9), choices need to be made. Otherwise, you have a seven-note structure and six strings with which to play it. Many jazz ensemble guitar parts simply spit out each and every alteration and extension that exists in the chart. In reality, a better solution is to simply voice out the guide tones (3rd/7th) and add one other note. In the case of 13(♯11, ♭9), simply playing the 7th/3rd/13th is plenty. You could easily add the ♭9th if desired. The guitar's intervallic layout does not allow for arpeggiated orders of notes. A qualified teacher can help simplify guitar parts and keep the emphasis on rhythmic accuracy.

Other dilemmas for less-experienced guitarists in jazz ensemble charts are slash chords, polytonal chords, voicing chords with a particular melody note, written out piano-style chords (with intervals too tight to execute), and the dreaded rhythmic comping while moving chords. False root chords or inversions, also known as *slash chords*, are triads with a particular bass note (e.g., B♭/D or A♭/G♭, etc.). Always advise your guitarist to skip the lower note unless it is easy to execute, because the bass notes will be covered by the bass, piano, bari sax, or bass trombone. Polytonal chords are the combination of two triads. They will look like mathematical fractions. In this instance, advise playing the higher pitched triad (numerator). Playing chords with a particular melody note on top requires advanced fretboard harmony skills. Start the student guitarist out by playing the melody notes with proper rhythms, then retrofit in easy-to-grab chords. Cherry-picking a few choice notes that are reachable is best. In my experience, contorting your fingers in order to be accurate makes the rhythm suffer and will make your hands hurt! Moreover, discourage independent addition of extensions to simple chords. If a guitarist decides to substitute a dominant 9th chord shape for every written dominant 7th chord, clashes can occur if a ♭9th is in the horn parts. During improvisation sections without backgrounds, pianists and guitarists have more freedom to add extensions or alterations.

Listening to jazz is clearly the best way to get the language of jazz on an instinctive level. Young players who listen to rock know how it sounds, so that makes it easier to emulate. If students gravitate toward the innovative and legendary voices on their instruments, they will have a much better shot at understanding their role in a rhythm section and as a soloist. In addition to the great jazz guitarists listed in ⦿ appendix 16.2, it is important for guitarists to check out the great innovators on other instruments.

# Amplification

## Amplifier Settings

For jazz ensemble conductors trained primarily in woodwind, brass, and percussion, comprehending the guitar and amplifier gear world can be a bit overwhelming. Dynamics and tone can be an issue for guitarists who do not have an awareness of how the guitar functions in jazz. Many young guitarists play with too much reverb and either too much treble or bass, so advise more neutral amplifier settings on swing and bebop charts. Funk tunes can involve occasional use of effect stomp boxes (wah-wah, or overdrive). Keeping guitar volume and intonation in check will ensure a better blend in the rhythm section and when the guitar is in unison with other instruments.

Seat placement within the ensemble and amplifier location can have a dramatic impact on the effectiveness of the guitarist in the big band. Ideally, place your guitarist in the crook of the piano just in front of the bass and drums and close to your lead tenor. For unison melodies or linear backgrounds, this seating places the guitar in line with all of the lead instruments. In addition, having the guitarists in the heart of the rhythm section ensure that they are hearing the bass, piano, and drums. Keeping the rhythm section seated tightly keeps everyone on the same tempo. Hearing the piano helps to make it possible to phrase rhythmic chordal big band hits together and avoid harmonic clashes when both instruments might be comping at the same time.

To change up the colors behind soloists, experiment with switching off chord comping: one solo the guitar comps and piano comps on the next. Too much activity in chord accompaniment behind soloists can make it tricky for the soloists to navigate the chord changes. Guitar and piano can function well together as chord accompanists as long as they are listening to one another. Funk, Latin jazz, and other straight eighth-note-feel grooves allow for greater collaborative chord comping.

Amplifier placement is the wild card that can nullify a guitarist's diligent work in all other facets of big band playing. The amplifier should be placed a few feet behind the guitarist, preferably on a chair. If the amplifier is too close, the guitarist has a false sense of high volume and may play too weakly, especially on solos. The human body is a natural sound barrier and will absorb the volume. Placing the amplifier on a chair ensures that low frequencies do not spread on the floor's surface. Another benefit to raising the amplifier is volume control. If the guitarists' sound is at their feet, they have no way to really judge how their volume relates to the ensemble as a whole. With the amplifier raised up and your guitarists situated between the rhythm section (with the amplifier behind a few feet), they will be able to balance the sound in relation to the horns and rhythm section. These simple adjustments can have a dramatic impact on your ensemble.

## Guitars, Amps, and Maintenance

The most traditional jazz guitar tone can be achieved by playing an archtop jazz guitar. There are lots of affordable brands. A jazz guitar with a solid carved top will have the most acoustic resonance. Some guitarists prefer a semi-hollow guitar—sometimes described as 335 style—made famous by the Gibson ES-335. It allows for the rich and warm jazz tones, while offering the flexibility to play with more of an electric tone in order to cover a variety of styles. Solid body guitars can produce clean and perfectly acceptable jazz tones for big band performance. One of the most prolific big band guitarists of all time is Ed Bickert. He played a Fender Telecaster in Rob McConnell's Boss Brass. Encourage your young guitarists to learn the basics on whatever instruments they own.

Many ensemble conductors are pressed into duty to diagnose maintenance issues. Brass and woodwinds have their quirks and occasional simple fixes. If a guitarist sounds horribly out of tune even after tuning by ear to A = 440 or with a digital tuner, two simple questions can lead to improved intonation:

1.  When was the last time you changed your strings?
2.  When was the last time your guitar was set up?

The latter question deals with the natural harmonic and scale of each string. Since each fret represents a half step, the twelfth-fretted note is exactly one octave above the corresponding open string. The fretted note should match the harmonic at the twelfth fret. It is best to have the student bring the instrument to a qualified luthier to make the proper adjustments. A choked sound or fret buzz will also warrant a trip to a repair shop.

At the risk of turning this section into a guitar periodical or online blog post, I want to note that amplifier settings can make the difference between your guitarist sounding like a punk rocker and a true jazz guitarist. Most often the guitar sound in the jazz idiom is clean. That means the guitar is achieving its purest tone. Many amplifiers today have digital modeling that can over-color the sound of the guitar. Any effect that uses pitch modulation, like a stereo chorus, can make the guitar sound out of tune compared to the other instruments even if the guitar is in tune! With the exception of modern jazz arrangements that call for it, be sure your guitarist is not overdoing reverb and not using a digital delay (this will impact ensemble blend and phrasing). Following are a few amplifier basics to consider to optimize a clean jazz tone:

1.  Never set the gain knob at a higher level than the master volume (this causes overdrive). However, for a John Scofield-ish sound or edgy jazz-rock tune, this could be what you are looking for.
2.  Keep the reverb at a maximum of 2 or 3 on the dial. Chords and melodies will lose definition.
3.  Set treble, middle, and bass frequency knobs in neutral positions. Too much treble makes the guitar sound crackly or twangy. If the bass is turned up too hot, the sound gets muddy and lacks definition. The middle knob, if the amp has one, should never go above 50 percent. Any variety of gain, presence, and bass boost buttons should be avoided.

It cannot be overstated: sculpting a pleasant and appropriate jazz tone is a significant obstacle for guitarists when many of their influences are coming from the world of rock and roll. Listening to the pioneers and innovators of jazz guitar can certainly aid in developing an aural picture of what jazz sounds like on the guitar. In my experience as an educator and guest clinician, fixing the sound at the electronic and logistical levels truly helps. However, it does not make up for or substitute for having a sound technique and a solid conception of jazz colors: attack, slurs, and rhythmic approach.

It is impossible to replace the weekly private lesson's reinforcement of the technical and stylistic facets of jazz guitar performance used in a large jazz ensemble. However, an awareness of the guitar's technical, historical, harmonic (jazz theory/fretboard harmony), melodic, postural, and geographical placement in the rhythm section and the audio possibilities of your student guitarist enhances the student/director relationship. In addition, the quality of your rhythm section and entire ensemble improves when your guitarist is a true contributor.

## Questions for Discussion

1. Do you think that Bruce's approach to recruiting guitar players is representative of many other band directors? Have you had success with any other approaches to recruiting guitar players?

2. What are the benefits and challenges of having guitar players in the school jazz ensemble? How are those challenges the same as or different from challenges with the other rhythm section instruments?

# 17

# Jazz Piano

Russell A. Schmidt

## Pianists Are Free Agents

Recruiting piano players has been difficult for Bruce. When he does get pianists to join jazz ensemble, he finds they often get intimidated and quit because the skill set for playing jazz is usually very different from the way they have been taught:

> I can't get piano players to play in jazz band. I don't know why. Well, I do know why—because they are intimidated. They are all playing Chopin and stuff like that and then you put a jazz chart in front of them and they don't know what to do. They know how to take a [classical] piece home to practice and play it. But if you hand them a jazz chart, they look at it and say, "but there's no notes, what do I do?" And you say, "well, these are chords," and you sit down to show them what the chords are and how they can do it. But they don't know what to do. They get intimidated and they quit.

Further, Bruce notes his experience has been that middle school pianists, often having played only by themselves, find it difficult to operate within a group setting, in which the rehearsal may progress at a pace different from that which the student would follow if practicing alone:

> They're not used to it. We don't have time to stop and let you figure this out. We're going on now. A lot of them are perfectionists and I keep telling them, "it's OK, you're going to play a lot of wrong notes and get lost—we're all lost—that's the way it is." Well, they never come back.

Emily recruits her pianists by word of mouth. Often students within her concert band play piano in addition to their wind instruments. She finds that this situation provides

> a good opportunity for students who might play a nontraditional jazz instrument in concert band to participate in jazz ensemble. Her pianists usually come to her having taken private lessons and never having played in a group setting. She finds that this inexperience playing in a group often means they have an underdeveloped sense of steady time:
>
> > [Prior to jazz ensemble], the piano players have been free agents. They play their piano piece and they're probably the only one playing it, so if they drag a little bit or if they rush a little bit, they're happy. They don't mind that at all.
>
> Consequently, Emily's most immediate goal for pianists who are new to jazz is to develop their comfort and confidence playing in a group so that they can endure the steep learning curve that they will experience.

Performing as a pianist in a jazz ensemble can be very rewarding. But to ensure participation is satisfying for both the individual and the group, requisite skill sets for performance must be learned, and musical responsibilities to fellow performers must be understood. The first portion of this chapter presents useful harmonic theory and practical exercises to help developing jazz pianists build a strong foundation. In the latter portion, a general philosophy regarding the role of the piano within the jazz ensemble is offered.

## The Importance of Learning Chord Symbols

Notational approaches found in jazz ensemble piano parts can run the gamut from fully notated music (found in some educational market repertoire) to scarcely there parts providing only chord symbols and slashes. This latter format typically presents the greatest challenge to developing jazz pianists, which aligns with the difficulties experienced by Bruce in student recruitment and retention. So what is the first skill that needs to be developed to successfully read parts that show only chords with slash notation? Jazz pianists need to achieve a mastery of chord symbol nomenclature, as they will never be able to read such parts without it.

To offer a meaningful comparison, I often tell students that one cannot be a successful chemist without memorizing important details found on the periodic table. For instance, one has to memorize that the symbol for the chemical element sodium is Na. Similarly, one cannot be an effective jazz pianist without memorizing that the notes found in the symbol $E^7$ are E, G♯, B, and D. In both settings, an abbreviated symbol is used to represent a valuable (and more substantial) piece of information. For a budding jazz pianist, there is simply no way to work around the requisite memorization of chord symbols. (Further consideration of chord symbol nomenclature is found in chapter 2 in this volume.)

# Harmonic Theory and Practical Exercises for Developing Jazz Pianists

**Voicing selection.** After learning the rules of chord symbol nomenclature, one must decide exactly how to voice jazz harmonies. I encourage developing jazz pianists to focus on two-hand, four-note voicings in drop 2 format. Drop 2 chords were commonly used by Bill Evans (as well as many other great jazz pianists). These voicings sound quite stable, having an outer interval of a 10th much of the time, and are also used by guitarists and arrangers. The term "drop 2" comes from the method by which these voicings are created: After placing the notes to be used in close position (spanning less than an octave), one *drops* the second note from the top down an octave (see chapter 22 in this volume for a writer's perspective on voicing options).

**Harmonic equivalence.** After settling upon a voicing option to practice, some chord theory can be useful in maximizing one's harmonic technique. Specifically, understanding how different varieties of chord symbols may be related is most helpful. This knowledge can allow pianists to take voicings they already know for one chord symbol and effectively redeploy them for other harmonies, as opposed to having to learn new sets of voicings for every chord symbol presented. Harmonic equivalence (explored here using three very common 7th chord types) can highlight interrelationships between different chords.

*Applied to major 7th chords.* In searching for such interrelationships, we find that some structures can be reused to represent multiple chord symbols. In figure 17.1, voicings for CMaj⁷ are also shown to work well as Am⁹ and D¹³sus voicings.

How can they function like this? In part they assume the presence of a bassist. Later in the chapter I explain why I recommend that jazz ensemble pianists avoid the tendency to play the root at the bottom of their voicings. But it is instructive here to note that the latter two chords in the first grand staff of figure 17.1 are represented only by their upper structures (3rd, 5th, 7th, 9th for Am⁹; sus⁴, 7th, 9th, 13th for D¹³sus). This leaves the root to the bassist who, in a sense, recontextualizes the harmony played by the pianist.

*Applied to minor 7th chords.* In examining the harmonic possibilities connected to Cm⁷, one finds the same voicings can convincingly represent E♭⁶, A♭ AMaj⁹, and F⁹sus (see figure 17.2). Cm⁷ and E♭⁶ contain the exact same four notes; the only real difference between how we hear those harmonies depends on what we perceive as the lowest note. But for A♭Maj⁹

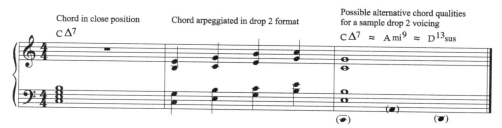

**FIGURE 17.1** Harmonic Equivalence in Major, Four-Note, Drop 2

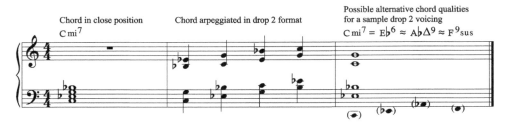

**FIGURE 17.2** Harmonic Equivalence in Minor

**FIGURE 17.3** Harmonic Equivalence Half Diminished

and $F^9$sus, we again play only the upper structure in the piano voicing (3rd or sus⁴th, 5th, 7th, 9th), leaving the root to the bassist.

**Applied to half-diminished 7th chords.** One additional 7th chord option to consider, $C\emptyset^7$, yields four possible partners: E♭mi⁶, A♭⁹, D⁷alt, and F⁷($♭9$)sus (see figure 17.3). Once again, $C\emptyset^7$ and E♭mi⁶ contain the same four notes. For A♭⁹, D⁷alt, and F⁷($♭9$)sus, the voicings once again include only upper structure tones (3rd or sus⁴, 5th, 7th, 9th).

How is this information useful? If pianists are aware of the relationships between these harmonies and has practiced voicings for major 7th, minor 7th, and half-diminished 7th chords in all 12 keys, they will have actually practiced *12 different types of common chord symbols* in all 12 keys. The fingers will have already practiced the voicings, so no additional muscle memory is required. Instead, a level of mental acuity is necessary to remember that Cm7 ≈ $F^9$sus, and so forth. The more pianists learn about the relationships between these harmonies, the quicker they will realize that complex chords can be voiced convincingly without every single note actually being present. A solid long-term goal should be the ability to accurately remember these harmonic equivalence relationships as one needs them in real time. See ⊙ video 17.1, Jazz Harmony and Piano Voicings for a demonstration of these concepts. Also, see ⊙ appendix 17.1, "Harmonic Equivalence 1"; ⊙ appendix 17.2, "Harmonic Equivalence 2"; and ⊙ appendix 17.3, "Harmonic Equivalence 3" for complete harmonic equivalence charts, providing examples in all 12 keys.

**Drop 2 chords in a functional progression.** Figure 17.4 shows a form of harmonic exercise, using these drop 2 voicings in a common ii⁷-V⁷-I progression. In these progressions, voicings from the three basic 7th chord types shown previously are now used to represent more expressive harmonies: major 7th chords as the upper structure for minor 9th chords, half-diminished 7th chords as the upper structure for dominant 9th chords, and minor 7th

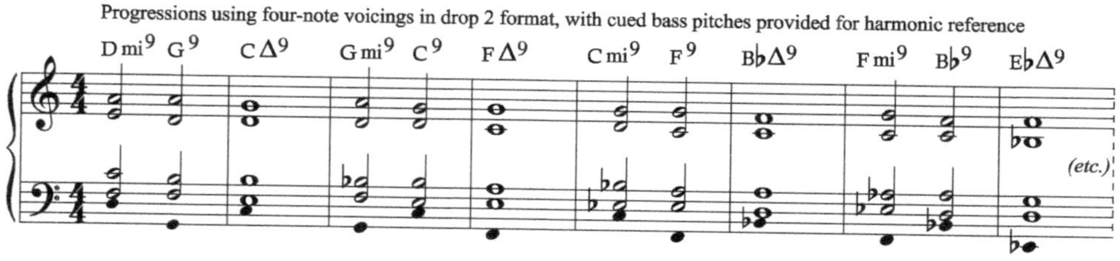

Progressions using four-note voicings in drop 2 format, with cued bass pitches provided for harmonic reference

**FIGURE 17.4** Drop 2 Chords in a Functional Progression

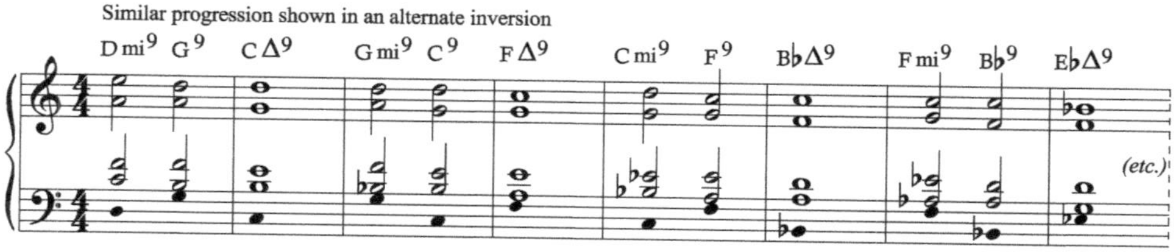

Similar progression shown in an alternate inversion

**FIGURE 17.5** Placing Key Chord Tones in the Left Hand

chords as the upper structure for major 9th chords. Harmonic equivalence theory is fully evident in figure 17.4. Refer again to ⓥ video 17.1 for a demonstration of these progressions.

Note that bass pitches are cued in the figure, but the four-note, drop 2 voicings are intended to be played with two notes in each hand. I often encourage students to sing the bass pitch while playing the other four notes as a way of aurally internalizing harmonic equivalence. (Some students may need to move voicings up an octave in order to sing the bass pitch *beneath* what they play.)

**Placing key chord tones in the left hand.** Figure 17.5 shows the second of four possible inversions for these voicings. In both Figures 17.4 and 17.5, emphasis has been given to voicings that—for *these* harmonies, at least—have the chords' 3rds and 7ths in the left hand; the two inversions not shown place the 3rds and 7ths in the *right* hand. Keeping basic, critical chord tones (3rd and 7th, $^7$sus$^4$, or 3rd and 6th) in the left hand should be of particular import to younger jazz pianists. Those necessary, foundational chord tones will be part of most three- and four-note, left-hand voicings to be studied subsequently as one's jazz keyboard skills continue to grow.

# The Role of the Piano in the Jazz Ensemble

Nearly 20 years ago, I served on the faculty of the Birch Creek Summer Jazz Academy (Egg Harbor, WI). In addition to various high school student ensembles, the program featured a big band comprised of jazz faculty and college-aged assistants. A special aspect of that program was that when big bands performed, the piano would be situated at the very edge of the stage, allowing two or three jazz piano students to sit just a couple of feet away during faculty concerts. At that proximity, from just offstage, they were able to see the notation as well as watch my hands as I performed. Inevitably, after these events I would have students ask me about musical decisions made on various charts. Those inquiries led me to codify more consciously what I had observed in others and learned myself when playing in jazz ensembles over the years. In my experience, these are perhaps the most critical issues upon which developing pianists should focus: style-based performance practices, partnerships in the rhythm section, and making positive contributions to the music.

## Performance Practices of Various Styles

The style of repertoire performed can greatly influence the content of what a pianist contributes to the music. The performance practices in different styles of jazz may dictate how active or sparse pianists are with their comping, whether they should play a repeated pattern (as an ostinato) or be more free with their rhythmic approach, how much they should use the sustain pedal, and so forth. Given these possibilities, how can an ensemble director guide a pianist toward a better understanding of traditional practices for playing different types of jazz repertoire?

**Directed listening.** The first step should be to listen to musical examples in various styles by historically significant jazz artists. With music streaming services and videos online, it has never been easier for students to gain access to important jazz recordings. But they need to make certain they are *actively* listening to the music, not having it on in the background while they multitask, lest the subtleties of stylistic difference escape their notice. (If those listening examples feature frequently performed compositions, so much the better. See chapter 21 in this volume for an examination of the value of learning common repertoire.) After the requisite listening, one is in a position to make better-informed musical decisions in the ensemble (see ⊕ appendix 17.4, Directed Listening List).

**Comping considerations.** When presented with big band music that is new to the pianist, an early focus should be determining how to comp effectively. Again, the performance practices of the style will play a large part in determining the pianist's contributions. Swing and Afro-Cuban charts typically call for crisp, incisive playing with little use of the sustain pedal. Funk pieces also require less use of sustain pedal and, commonly, more aggressive comping. Conversely, ballads are treated more gently, with comping chords occasionally arpeggiated and more liberal use of the sustain pedal, providing the music with a greater sense of horizontal connection.

Another performance aspect to consider is that certain styles of jazz call for more ostinato-based playing. In certain Afro-Cuban and Afro-Brazilian jazz styles, recurring 2- or 4-bar rhythmic patterns may be preferable to comping with a freer, improvised-sounding rhythm. The same may hold true with jazz ensemble charts that fuse jazz with contemporary grooves such as funk or hip-hop. In such cases, holding to a rhythmic ostinato in the comping may be the best choice to make, even though that approach would be less successful on many swing charts.

However, even in swing-based music, it can be useful for a developing jazz pianist to learn some basic, idiomatic comping rhythms such as the Charleston rhythm (emphasizing beat one and the & of 2) or playing in a manner closely associated with Red Garland (comping on the & of 2 and the & of 4). Growing comfortable executing these sorts of rhythms will help the pianist build a rhythmic vocabulary for comping.

**Harmonic anticipation.** One final performance consideration related to the style of music chosen is that some types of jazz require an anticipatory approach to outlining the harmony. (This critical stylistic detail receives too little attention.) In medium and up-tempo swing pieces, comping instruments can generate a beneficial—and idiomatic—sense of forward momentum by playing new harmonies an eighth note earlier than shown in the printed music.

Consider a piece like "Autumn Leaves," in which there is a different chord symbol at the beginning of most measures. Harmonic anticipation does not *require* pianists to play something on the & of 4 in every bar. But if they *do* play something on the & of 4 when playing this tune in a swing style, they should play the harmony of the upcoming measure. See ⏵ video 17.2, Harmonic Anticipation for Comping Instruments, for a demonstration. Also, those with a particular interest in arranging for school jazz ensembles (see chapter 22 in this volume) should take note of this performance practice in their writing.

Students seeking a performance role model of how to convincingly execute harmonic anticipation would do well to listen to some mid-1950s recordings by the Miles Davis Quintet with the aforementioned Red Garland at the piano. For instance, Garland's playing on "All of You" from '*Round About Midnight* (recorded in 1955–1956) is a textbook example of how to execute this technique in a way that sounds effortless.

Admittedly, there are many subtle factors that can influence a young jazz pianist's musical choices. But instead of trying to memorize a seemingly endless list of factors, it is worth reiterating that the most valuable way to study these performance practices is to listen to recordings featuring acknowledged masters of the genre (and to see them live, whenever possible).

## Understanding Rhythm Section Partnerships

It is very important for rhythm section members to understand their interlocking roles. When working with younger groups, I often find they have little awareness of their fundamental responsibilities to rhythm section mates. Emily characterized her pianists as "free agents." But developing pianists *must* work on these musical relationships to become effective partners with bassists, drummers, and guitarists.

**Critical role shared by piano and bass.** Pianists share with bassists the responsibility of outlining a piece's harmonic structure, of maintaining the chord progression. That seems simple, yet it is not uncommon for a developing pianist or bassist to unintentionally shift the harmonic structure a bit. Once this happens, the performer in question might continue playing in the wrong place for a long time (ahead of or behind the group by some number of beats or measures), apparently unable to self-correct. Many jazz educators have heard this from their rhythm sections. But why does this happen?

Commonly, younger musicians' eyes become so buried in their parts that they only hear others at a superficial level, perhaps just enough to maintain the same tempo. Here then is another example in which active listening can be of great use to developing players. If the pianist is out of harmonic sync with the bassist, then a foundational responsibility to the rhythm section is going unmet. So the pianist must actively listen to the bassist at all times to ensure that a harmonic unity is being maintained.

**Critical role shared by piano and drums.** Pianists and drummers also share a role within the rhythm section, one that is subtly complex: comping. The rhythmic manner in which a pianist outlines harmonies is clearly comping. But drummers also comp, often in the form of the commentary played by the left hand on the snare drum. With some grooves or feels, such as swing, the left hand may be contributing the least ostinato-based element of the entire kit, and that component is a form of comping.

It is important for pianists to know that they share a comping role with drummers. Such knowledge can help these musicians work together to shape the music's intensity at any given point. For instance, pianists might be able to help horn players shape the dramatic architecture of an improvised solo by manipulating the density and intensity of their comping. Or on a jazz ballad, the rhythmic vitality of the comping may be the element that convincingly transitions the music into a double-time feel.

**Overlapping responsibilities shared by piano and guitar.** In considering how piano and guitar can work together effectively in the rhythm section, I have found great success when the two musicians are not duplicating functions. More specifically, they should not freely, actively comp together simultaneously. When one of the two is actively comping, the other should seek out an alternate, complementary role. For instance, the pianist might comp freely if the guitarist has committed to a Freddie Green–style, "rhythm guitar" approach (playing quarter notes). But if the guitarist is comping more freely, the pianist might instead contribute a simpler guide tone element, perhaps playing a slow-moving line in both hands, two octaves apart.

These are creative choices that can enhance the overall effect of the rhythm section's contribution to the ensemble. When a more novice rhythm section is playing, it might be understandable and appropriate for the director to want everyone participating and contributing as much as possible. But in most other cases, options regarding what pianists and guitarists can (simultaneously) contribute should be discussed openly to ensure the music is best served. See chapter 16 in this volume for additional perspectives on rhythm section comping.

## Making Positive Contributions

Pianists have tremendous latitude in the musical choices they may make, particularly if their parts provide only chord symbols and slash notation. However, one must learn to make positive, effective contributions to the music on a consistent basis. Various factors should impact the choices made.

**Fulfill obligations unique to each ensemble.** When working with jazz ensembles, I have had occasion to discourage younger pianists from overemphasizing the bass pitch. They tend to play the root of the chord at the bottom of their voicings too often. This choice, using only "root position" voicings, ignores voice-leading concerns. Perhaps more important, it can muddle the bassist's contributions. Such playing often leads to murky, ponderous sounds in the lower register, diminishing the clarity of the entire rhythm section. (See chapters 7 and 10 in this volume for more information about the role of the pianist within a developing rhythm section.)

But an ensemble director may have legitimate reasons to ask a pianist to duplicate bass function in a big band. It could be that bassists are struggling to play their part. The director may want additional harmonic support from the pianist, who could choose voicings that feature the root of the harmony as the lowest note. Or harmonic support might come from duplicating a bass line on the piano, though this approach typically works better for ostinato-based parts on certain Afro-Brazilian, Afro-Cuban, or funk pieces than for an extended walking bass line (on a swing chart). In all cases, it is incumbent on the pianist to try to fulfill the unique needs of each ensemble.

**Respond to what you hear when comping.** My primary goal when performing as a big band pianist is to think like an orchestrator. I actively listen to each chart and determine what I can add that will enhance the music. There's a hint of that creative philosophy evident in the previous section, too (examining how piano and guitar might play together). Ultimately, I never play something just because the part indicates I should. When I play something, my intention is to make a meaningful contribution to the music.

Returning to my experiences with the faculty big band at the Birch Creek Summer Jazz Academy, I was often asked by students why I played so little on certain pieces. I explained that with some jazz ensemble repertoire, dense writing between horn sections often leaves no room for additional input. There are sometimes extended segments featuring a near-breathless call and response between an active sax section and incisive brass parts. What can a pianist hope to contribute to this type of music?

*Silence as a viable option.* When music is very densely scored, there may be nothing I can add from the piano that will enhance the music. I can try to shoehorn in some un-necessary comping, but that won't make the music sound better. It will just add clutter. Silence often works best in such moments, even when chord symbols are present in the piano part.

A willingness to play nothing even when the part indicates one should play *something* reveals a pianist who is thinking orchestrationally and making musical choices through active listening. Such decisions cannot be arbitrary or capricious; they need to be informed by listening to various factors, including the general musical context, the density of the orchestration, and the architectural trajectory of the chart. The ensemble director should encourage the pianist to shape musical contributions by listening and responding, understanding that there are many times when pianists should make choices based on what their ears (not their eyes) tell them.

Of course, there is latitude available to pianists that generally does not exist in the same way for bassists and drummers. For example, a bassist cannot look at chord symbols and slash notation in a *shout chorus* and choose to play nothing because the horns are densely scored. And what a director *needs* from a particular ensemble's pianist (discussed previously) is also an important consideration.

**Respond to what you hear when soloing.** Although the discussion has focused thus far on a pianist's contributions as a comping instrument, the same orchestrational approach should be applied to improvised solos as well. In many big band charts, the beginning of a piano solo may be supported by just bass and drums. After a while, horn backgrounds typically enter. These backgrounds may grow more dense or loud over time until the solo concludes. But if the chart's backgrounds become too active, too competitive, the pianist may disappear, swallowed up by the ensemble texture before finishing the solo.

When I have an improvised solo in a jazz ensemble chart, I continually assess the musical environment supporting the solo. And I change the content or presentation of the solo to fit that evolving environment. If it is indeed just piano, bass, and drums at the beginning of my solo, I will work to interact, to have a musical dialogue with my rhythm section collaborators. As backgrounds enter and grow, I usually have to change my focus. Perhaps I can attempt to interact with background elements. But I may also have to change my orchestrational approach to the keyboard or the register in which I play in order to cut through a competitive background and be heard as the soloist (see ⊙ video 17.3, Soloing as a Pianist in a Jazz Ensemble).

Even when improvising, I try to think like an orchestrator in order to make the best choices in my approach to the keyboard. By actively listening to the musical surroundings, then responding appropriately, I can find an orchestrational option that serves the ensemble well. And savvy directors will encourage *their* pianists to explore a similarly engaged, discerning approach as they make their contributions to the jazz ensemble.

## Questions for Discussion

1. Bruce cites a big challenge many pianists face when joining jazz band: an inability to read chord symbols. How might a director help young pianists successfully transition into jazz ensemble, especially given limited rehearsal time?

2. A pianist's role would be easier to fill if jazz ensemble charts were always published with notated piano voicings, but some would argue against that practice. Is the tradition of reading chord changes so ingrained that music educators would be reluctant to use charts that include completely notated piano parts?

3. In addition to stylistic role modeling, what other benefits might pianists gain from directed listening sessions?

4. How might understanding rhythm section partnerships positively impact the contributions a pianist makes to the ensemble?

5. Though learning harmonic equivalence concepts can afford clear benefits to a developing jazz pianist, are there ways to make these harmonic interrelationships any more intuitive?

# 18

# Jazz Bass

Nicholas Walker

## Bass Players: Happy to Be Needed

Sometimes in middle school jazz ensemble, Bruce will use a keyboard player to play the bass line when he cannot recruit a bass player to play with the group. This year he has a bass player whom he recruited from the orchestra class, who takes private bass lessons, and "she knows what she's doing, which is good because all I can say to the bass player is this is the sound that I want. I can't tell them how to do it, though. I never have been able to." Bruce usually has little difficulty recruiting bass players because "you just go to the orchestra and say, 'I need a bass player in jazz band.' And they're just so happy to see that somebody needs them."

Emily has not had much success recruiting bass players from the strings class at her school. Part of the problem is that students only get to take two electives, and she finds that it has been a tough sell to get strings students to fill their second elective with jazz ensemble. These students are used to playing with multiple bass players in the strings class, and when she has been able to recruit them, Emily has found that they often struggle with the independence of being the only bass player in jazz ensemble. If she is able to recruit a bass player, the student must know the instrument before joining the group. "I just tell them, I'll teach you style, but I'm not going to sit there and move your fingers on the strings. You've got to know your fingerboard. You've got to know how scales work."

Instead, Emily often recruits piano players to play the bass line on a synthesizer using the bass setting and refers to that person as the "bass player." Emily feels that the bass player is the most important person in the rhythm section and the entire ensemble:

When it comes to bass I tell the kids, "you're driving the bus, running the show." You don't have to have a drummer but you have to have a bass player. That's the deal. You have to have a bass player. So, whoever is playing bass you just tell

> them, "you're driving the bus. You are responsible for time." It's like a march in
> a band. If you have a bass drummer you just tell them that "you're it. If our time
> is good in this march it's because you were right." You just tell your bass player
> right off the bat, "if you're playing bass, you are the most important person in the
> ensemble."

This chapter is designed to introduce a double bassist to jazz playing. The chapter begins with fundamental information about bass setup, posture, and technical approaches that allow for full expression unhindered by physical pain and injury. Subsequently I introduce approaches to learning bass lines by ear and present a progressive sequence of skills that allow a bassist to embellish simple traditional bass lines creatively and personally.

# Setup

Setup of the instrument is an often-overlooked aspect of pedagogy, one that can have the greatest impact on student success. If the instrument is set up with strings that are too heavy, too tight, or too high from the fingerboard, the instrument will be too difficult and painful to play with joyful enthusiasm. As a general rule, ensure that the G string is not higher than about 7 mm measured at the end of the fingerboard; 4 to 5 mm ought to be just fine in most cases. The height of the strings at the nut (where the strings leave the peg box) need only be about the thickness of a business card. When the fingerboard is properly planed, these measurements will allow the student to "dig in" with the right hand, without buzzing and without developing repetitive stress playing injuries.[1]

One practical suggestion for setting up a double bass for younger players or beginners that is both affordable and practical is to string the bass with a set of Thomastik Spirocore solo strings. "Solo strings" are designed to be tuned a whole step higher than normal tuning, but when they are tuned down to normal tuning, they hold far less tension and are relatively easy on the hands, while still providing a round, sustaining jazz sound. An instrument set up in this way will also work quite well with the bow in an orchestra, wind ensemble, chamber music, solo playing, etc. One of the best ways to develop a warm, bouncing swing feel is to play on some authentic gear, so if your program has a dedicated double bass and you do not anticipate much bowing work for that instrument, you might consider stringing it with pure gut strings or a simulated, synthetic gut string, such as the perlon core strings manufactured by Pirastro.[2]

# Playing the Bass
## Technique

In-depth specifics about pure double bass technique are essential for serious learners but too extensive to cover in this chapter. (See the following website for more technique-specific information on double bass playing: http://isbconnect.org/an-introduction-to-arm-weight-application). Whenever possible, seek out a great teacher, someone who sounds great and also looks comfortable and easeful in action: injury free, joyful, reverent of the art, and kind-hearted to others.

The double bass requires a fair amount of force to create a beautiful, swinging, resonant sound. There have been powerful men who have attained this force through brute strength, but the use of natural body weight is almost always preferable, both for the health and wellness of the player and for the tone and feel of the music. The great masters have found a correlation between a balanced body posture derived from natural skeletal alignment, allowing the use of natural arm weight, and the fundamental quality of sound and rhythmic feel.

## Exercises in Applying Weight in Time

This first exercise is helpful in calibrating movement, space, and time for the desired rhythmic feel, while also fostering the desirable physical comportment and rich, resonant natural tone. To help them build a strong internal sense of time, have students practice this exercise with the metronome at various tempos and experiment with having the metronome on all 4 beats, only on beats 2 and 4, and only on beat 4 (see figure 18.1).

Whereas the preceding exercise of descending pitches primarily involves pulling the arm to the right, or *toward* the body, the next exercise requires recovery movements in order to pluck the next higher string (the string that is farther away from the string that was just plucked). These recovery movements should be slightly circular in the arm and be prepared in the manner previously described. As in the previous exercise, have students practice this one with the metronome on all 4 beats, 2 and 4, and only on beat 4. They will observe that the lowest string responds noticeably slower than does the highest string, and that considerably more preparation is required when moving from low strings to high strings than in descending (see figure 18.2).

Students should improvise and experiment with this manner of approach, inventing personalized grooves and syncopated subdivisions to their delight. It goes without saying that others can collaborate and join in, quickly turning this right-hand-only exercise into a fun, real-time jam or even an original composition.

I've never met a double bass player who did not at some point develop blisters on the plucking fingers. I suppose it is possible to build calluses through consistent incremental increase in playing time day to day, and thus avoid creating any blisters. But nearly all of us have so much fun playing as beginners that we push our uncallused fingertips to the point of blistering. Avoiding any unsanctioned medical advice, which surely I am unqualified to offer, I will share only that in my experience, my blisters have healed more quickly when I popped

**FIGURE 18.1** Applying Weight and Time, Exercise 1

**FIGURE 18.2** Applying Weight and Time, Exercise 2

them than when I left them full of pus or blood. Eventually the hands build up tougher skin that is callused enough to withstand regular playing. To the teacher/mentor I say that the process of building calluses is a kind of rite of passage, and a blister can be a badge of honor, so to speak. There may be a day when your new bass player really needs to sit out of a rehearsal. My advice is to honor this as a moment of "coming-of-age." On the practical level, double bass players should avoid intensive plucking just after washing their hands, when they are softer and less resilient. For additional demonstrations of bass technique and exercises, including body movement, weight application, plucking, root movement fingerings, and hammer-ons and pull-offs, see ⓥ video 18.1, Hammer-Ons and Pull-Offs 1; ⓥ video 18.2, Hammer-Ons and Pull-Offs 2; and ⓥ video 18.3, Hammer-Ons and Pull-Offs 3).

## Playing Music

A note about the musical examples in this chapter: it is important to stress that the musical examples in this chapter are meant only to be an entry point for understanding how it all works, meaning how bass lines can be learned and understood simultaneously through the ear, body, intellect, and eyes (looking at notes on the instrument and on paper). Think of these written examples as stock phrases in a tourist guide designed to enable a visitor to begin to communicate and interact with others in a basic way.

The goal for a serious learner is to develop fluency in the language to enable spontaneous, meaningful communication with others. This is learned through immersion in the culture: listening to, observing, and imitating others, and endeavoring to express oneself without any inhibition.

Music is a language. As in speech, one naturally begins with simple words and direct concepts to communicate about essential thoughts and feelings. We develop fluency over time and subsequently hear and articulate our ideas with more complexity and subtlety, usually with the ears comprehending more than the tongue can articulate. The simplest utterances of a child (or an adult learning a new language) are not to be invalidated, even when they are mispronounced or misunderstood. A child does not have the feeling of waiting to become a unique human being worthy of participating in meaningful communication with others; the child is born that way.

So it is with music. Each of us is unique and has the right to make music from the very beginning. Tell your students to be the bassists you dream to be from the start. Sure, maybe they won't play all the notes they hear, and maybe the sound will not be what they know it can be (get used to it; this part never changes as we progress), but music is more than the notes, just as verbal communication is more than the words. From the beginning, they should play with the feeling and the spirit that moves them and do so without shame, pretense, or hesitation. We all have a natural DNA for communicating in this way; they should trust themselves to develop fluency naturally over time.

Now let's make some music. The first note in each measure of figure 18.3 can be used to create a simple D-blues accompaniment line using only open strings. This could be played on all 4 beats of the measure even by someone who has never touched a double bass before. Have students simply follow the form of the blues, where the second string

## D Blues - Playing While Saying "Oh, Four, One, Four"

FIGURE 18.3 "Oh, Four, One, Four"

(D string, labeled II in figure 18.3, because it is the second string down) is the tonic or "one chord," the top string (G string, labeled I) is the "4 chord," and the third string (A string, labeled III) is the 5 chord.

Now let's make it more musical. In figure 18.3, D Blues Playing While Saying "Oh, Four, One, Four" begin by saying the words "Oh, Four, One, Four" for each measure, where 0 represents the open string, 4 the pinky, and 1 the index finger (see ⊙ video 18.4, D Blues).

I have used this exercise in clinics and conferences to get people up and running in a matter of minutes. The trick is to put the left thumb in the crook of the neck, a position often referred to as "block position." In most cases, without modifying/adjusting the natural skeletal shape of the left hand at rest, the player can find this position by playing the harmonic underneath the first finger. The natural spacing between the first and fourth fingers lends itself to a whole step (e.g., from D to E on the top string).

The next step is to play the piece with more embellishments. In ⊙ video 18.5, D Blues Variation, I have included one simple, intuitive/ergonomic/stylistic example by adding the two pitches that fall under the same fingers (1 and 4) on the adjacent string, but a player can simply "noodle around" with fingers 1 and 4 in block position across any of the strings while maintaining the form and feel of the blues, striking the open strings on the downbeats.

One ideal aspect of this pedagogical introduction is that many people naturally hear the form of the blues and can begin to intuitively sense when the harmony will change. Someone with more experience may need to call out the name of the open string the first few times through the form, but soon beginners will be up and running independently.

Note that several bass players can play this D Blues at the same time. This progressive pedagogy (beginning with one simple note and adding embellishments as one is both able and inspired) adapts naturally to multiple levels simultaneously, wherein some folks can play improvised variations while others sound only the open strings in sequence and in time. Because the double bass has so much resonance, the key to making it work with more than one bassist playing at a time is to cultivate a keen awareness of sound and feel; manage resonance so that the feel is buoyant, but not too boomy; and strive to hear all participants at once, even while following one's own ideas.

## Hearing Bass Lines

Every bass player needs to learn the specialized skill of hearing bass lines. The bass lines of familiar songs have scalar and triadic diatonic structures that are rather different than those of melodies we learn to sing from a young age. One of my favorite approaches to developing the skill of hearing bass lines is to sing the lyrics of a well-known tune and simply replace the normal melody of the song with the bass-line movement instead. After singing the melody of a well-known tune, I sing the bass line with the very same lyrics.

## Constructing Bass Lines

Let's turn our attention to the construction of bass lines. There's an old joke about what it takes to be a professional gigging bass player that goes something like this. A student decides to learn the bass; the first five notes on the E string are taught at the first lesson; the next week the first five on the A string; and at the third lesson the first five notes on the D string are taught. In the fourth week, the student cannot make it to the lesson because the student has a gig!

The message here, of course, is that it does not take much to be a hire-able, desirable collaborator as a bass player; one just needs good time, a good feel, and only a few notes—usually the lowest ones. Of course, learning five chromatic pitches one at a time, string by string, is not a very good pedagogy. But it is also true that much can be accomplished with just a few pitches played the right way at the right time.

Indeed, all sophisticated bass lines can be broken down to the simple, essential harmonic rhythm (the moments in musical time when the chords change). For this reason, it can be an effective pedagogy to learn the role of the double bass by beginning with one simple note per chord (as we did with the D Blues). After this is internalized, players can add bass line embellishments until walking lines and more stylistic grooves emerge out of this fundamental understanding. Students can develop fluency with added embellishments that mirror the distinct stylistic development of the jazz art form, beginning with New Orleans tailgating tuba lines (first on one pitch, then including the 5th) and gradually adding distinctive connective walking tissue, or scalar approaching bass lines from one chord to another. Eventually one develops this fluency to a point where walking lines can be spontaneously composed through an entire song form for many choruses in dialogue with the other musicians.

Figure 18.4 is an example of this progressive approach using a blues form, this time in the key of B♭. (These lines can be used alongside Mike Titlebaum's composition "Blues for Ox," found in other chapters of this volume.) (See ⦿ video 18.6, B♭ Blues Bass Line 1 for a complete chorus using this approach.)

Note that sometimes bass line construction looks more complicated on paper (or at the piano or horn) than it is at the bass, which is tuned symmetrically in 4ths. The preceding example falls quite naturally under the hand for the bassist. Have students try the previous

**FIGURE 18.4** B♭ Blues Bass Line

FIGURE 18.5 B♭ Bass Line Using Root, 5th, and 6th

FIGURE 18.6 B♭ Bass Line Walking, Root, 5th, and 6th

FIGURE 18.7 Down a 5th

example up a whole step, in C, or up a minor 3rd in D♭. They will notice how the kinesthetic feeling of moving the first or fourth finger to each of the primary root locations persists. Soon a player's kinesthetic sense works in tandem with the ear to guide the construction of lines. Students should keep this in mind (and in their muscle memory) as the complexity increases in the following embellished examples.

The second example uses the root, 5th, and 6th of each chord, with a distinctive and stylistic jazz rhythm (see figure 18.5). (See ▶ video 18.7, B♭ Blues Bass Line 2, 5th and 6th Added for a complete chorus using this approach.)

For the third example, let's add a few iconic walking figures when the chords change (see figure 18.6). (See ▶ video 18.8, B♭ Blues Bass Line 3, 5th, 6th, and Walking, for a complete chorus using this approach.)

**Hearing and understanding circle of 4ths/5ths chord progression.** Sound, kinesthetic feel, and theoretical function can, and should, be learned in tandem. This approach can also be used in a progressive way. Let's begin with a simple dominant to tonic relationship, the fundamental harmonic movement in Western music. This chord progression can be broken down into two simple shapes: from the pinky to the index finger one string lower (down the 5th), or the same finger up a string (up a 4th).

*Down a 5th*: Let's take the key of A, for example. Placing the thumb in the crook of the neck as we did with the D Blues, the student puts the first finger on the A♮ (located a 5th above the open D string). Notice that the pinky finger naturally falls over the E♮ located a 6th above the open G string. A beginner can play and hear V-I, from the fourth finger E to the first finger A (see figure 18.7).

*Up a 4th*: The other approach is to play the E one string below the A, also with the first finger. In this case the movement is up a 4th, from E to A (see figure 18.8). (As the player's technique improves, it will become possible and more efficient to bar across both strings at the same time with the first, second, or fourth finger.)

FIGURE 18.8 Up a 4th

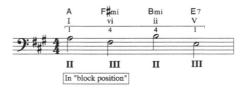

FIGURE 18.9 Turnaround Progression

Notice that simply placing the first finger on the tonic pitch (A♮) puts the E above and the E below within reach. The same is true for any other pitch on the middle two strings. The student should practice playing V to I in all 12 keys, beginning with the first finger on each tonic pitch, descending chromatically from the A in the preceding exercise down to the B-flat one half step above the open A string. In this way, fingering, sound, and harmonic function are all learned together.

Because the most common movement of bass lines in nearly all styles of music is the circle of 4ths/5ths, a bass player will do well to internalize the complete sequence through all 12 pitches, both ascending and descending. Soon the player will begin to recognize the sound of moving a 4th or 5th away in association with the visual and tactile shapes under the hand. These, along with a learned understanding of the sequence of pitches, will help a player exceedingly in the creation of improvised bass lines (see ▶ video 18.9, Circle of 5ths).

Perhaps you already have an idea about how simple it would be to add the 4th to the dominant and tonic hand setting used previously. The 4th is located directly across from the root, one string higher; or one whole step below the 5th. With I, IV, V chord progression in the bag, a bass player has everything needed to be ready to take on most bluegrass gigs once the feel and song forms are internalized.

**Hearing and understanding a ii⁷-V⁷-I progression.** However, it is the ii⁷-V⁷-I chord progression that is perhaps the single most prevalent chord progression in the jazz idiom. Notice that the root of the ii⁷ chord is located one whole-step above the tonic and a 4th below the dominant.

**Hearing and understanding a "turnaround" progression.** Let us conclude this section with a standard turnaround sequence, I-vi-ii-V. Have the student place the first finger on a tonic pitch, A♮, located in block position on the D string, and the root movement for all four of these chords will fall neatly under the hand (see figure 18.9). This works just as well in first position on the G string, or down a half step in the key of A♭, in half position, up a whole step in the key of B♭, or just about anywhere on the bass. Have the student play this sequence in all 12 keys, speaking the words, "one, six, two, five, one."

**FIGURE 18.10** Turnaround Progression with Nonchord Tones

Using this hand setting, the second finger can be easily deployed to connect one chord to another with nonchord tones. See ▶ video 18.10, Turnaround Progression, All Four and Walking, for examples of these exercises. Notice also how this turnaround pattern falls neatly into one hand setting. Figure 18.10 shows it in the key of B♭. When a player begins to associate harmonic function with the geographic relationship to the tonic, the fingering, the function, and the sound are all learned together.

## Conclusion

To conclude this chapter, let's apply this progressive learning approach to Michael Titlebaum's "rhythm changes" head, "All About that Rhythm." With a song such as this, in which the harmonic rhythm moves largely by half notes, an excellent beginning point for a bass line is simply to play quarter- notes on each of the bass tone pitches in succession. (In this example I use this method in each of the first two A sections.) At this level, it is not even necessary to know the quality or the function of the chords one is playing in order to compose this line. Again, a beginner need not wait for complete theoretical understanding to join in the fun. Thumping away on the roots with a good sound and a swinging feel just might land someone a gig, as in the joke above. Notice that in the B section I use some roots and 5ths, and in the last A section, I use a more diatonic, sequential approach (see ▶ video 18.11, B♭ Rhythm Changes; and ▶ appendix 18.1, "All About That Rhythm"). Remember that the creative possibilities for playing bass lines are endless, and so are sources for inspiration. Study and imitate the masters, and do not hesitate to get involved before you feel completely ready. I hope this chapter helps you get up and running.

## Questions for Discussion

1. Sometimes in middle school jazz ensemble, both Bruce and Emily will use a keyboard player to play the bass line when they cannot recruit a bass player to play with the group. What do you think about this approach? What are its benefits and challenges?
2. What is Bruce talking about when he says that bass players are "so happy to see that somebody needs them?"
3. Emily talks about bass players struggling with part independence. Why is this the case, and how can this be alleviated with limited rehearsal time?
4. Why does Emily describe the bass player as the "most important person in the rhythm section and the entire ensemble?" Do you agree with her? If you had to pick the most important role in the ensemble, what would you choose, and why?

# Notes

1. There are urban legends about great bassists who have had their strings much higher, but typically these were gut strings, which are far lower in load and tension and much easier to depress. I have played on the instruments of Ray Brown, Milt Hinton, Arvell Shaw, Percy Heath, John Clayton, George Duvivier, Ron Carter, Gary Peacock, and Marc Johnson, and they are as described here.
2. Pure gut strings are fantastic for learning sound and feel (both *arco* and *pizz*), but can be prohibitively expensive and can also be much less stable and durable than synthetic strings.

# 19

# Jazz Drums

## Gregory Evans

### Drummers Are Mine

The bass, piano, and guitar players in Bruce's jazz ensemble typically come from choir, orchestra, or an ensemble outside of school. However, the drummers typically are percussionists within the concert band; thus Bruce has some background with these students that they do not with the other members of the rhythm section. Many of these students who have learned concert band percussion instruments often also have drum sets at home.

Bruce takes a sort of "hands-off" approach to teaching drum set:

We have a set—it's not very good. Sit down and play around with it. If they're a good percussionist, chances are that they'll be able to pick it up. I might say, "here's the name of a teacher or talk to that kid and find out who their teacher is," but I don't sit down and teach them drum set. I don't know anything about it and it is another instrument that I don't really like, anyway, so I don't teach it because I don't know it. I can't do everything.

Piano players typically enter Emily's jazz ensemble having played piano and taken private lessons, and Emily teaches them to read chord changes, voice the chords, and comp rhythmic patterns. However, the drummers are usually percussionists within their concert bands who enter never having played drum set. Consequently, "you have to show them how to do it." Emily begins by selecting a tune from the radio that they like and having them keep time with it on the hi-hat. As drummers become increasingly comfortable keeping time on the hi-hat on 2 and 4, Emily has them add quarter notes on the ride cymbal. Emily emphasizes to her drummers that they have to read the music. Playing drums in jazz ensemble is more than just keeping time; drummers have

> to know what the horns have and how to complement those parts with setups and fills. Emily encourages her drummers to listen to and imitate the professionals:
>
> > So, you tell the kids, "this is some cat in his late 20s, early 30s, 40s, how do they play it? You like it? Good. Do it. Go home and learn it."

It is no secret that music educators are faced with unique challenges when engaging young musicians who play drum sets. Often these challenges are confusing to address because educators are not aware of the many roles the drum set, in an ensemble setting, is responsible for. Many educators aren't drummers themselves, so the language of the drums can feel quite foreign. Just as it does for Bruce, this can create some fear and uncertainty and ultimately lead educators to avoid, rather than embrace, the wonderful and exciting world of jazz percussion. Without a basic understanding of the drum set, the teacher can find it difficult to help the drummer musically contribute to the ensemble.

This chapter discusses conceptual and technical approaches to understanding the role each component of the drum set contributes to the ensemble, as well as the role of the drum set in its entirety. This chapter also touches on how dynamics can change the function and style of a groove, as well as creative ways to encourage your students to move beyond pattern playing.

# Function(s) of the Drummer

## Misconceptions

There is a common misconception that the drummer is *responsible* for "time," and that the rest of the ensemble plays *to* the drummer. This is wrong on two fronts: within an ensemble, the drummer is not responsible for the time; rather, all the musicians in the ensemble are responsible for the time. When we tell drummers that they are responsible for the time, that gives the ensemble permission to not subdivide, and when the drummer falters in timekeeping (all drummers do, as no musician is perfect), the ensemble loses their only rhythmic anchor.

When looking at the drummer through the lens of the rhythm section, it is the bass player who establishes the time. Swing music's groove is quarter note oriented, and the instrument that plays the most obvious quarter note is the bass player. It is for this reason and this reason alone that the timekeeping element of the rhythm section comes from the bass. You can have a swinging rhythm section without a drummer, à la the Oscar Peterson Trio, but something can feel awkward when a rhythm section doesn't have a bass feel.

## Roles

If time doesn't come from the drummer, then what does the drummer do? First and foremost, the drummer establishes the style or what is commonly referred to as the groove: swing, R&B, $\frac{12}{8}$ blues, boogaloo, bossa nova, mambo, songo, fat back, waltz, shuffle, etc. It is through the drums that style is dictated. For examples of all these styles, see ⊕ video 19.1, Swing; ⊕ video 19.2, R&B; ⊕ video 19.3, ¹²⁄₈ Blues; ⊕ video 19.4, Boogaloo; ⊕ video 19.5, Bossa Nova; ⊕ video 19.6, Mambo; ⊕ video 19.7, Songo; ⊕ video 19.8, Fat Back; ⊕ video 19.9, Waltz; and ⊕ video 19.10, Shuffle.

The ensemble (large or small) also gets its formal cues from the drums. For example, when the ensemble arrives at the top of the formal structure, it is the drummer's responsibility to punctuate the musical arrival point. The drums should also highlight the following with either a fill or a change in groove texture: solo sections, changes in soloists (beginnings of choruses), transitions into the "B" section or bridge of the tune, and transitions from intro to melodies and from melodies to outros or tags.

Before drummers begin to experiment with improvising using rhythmic content, they can start by using textural changes as a vehicle for improvisation (see ⊕ appendix 19.1, Improvisation). A drummer can be asked to describe how the energy of the music changes when moving the swing pattern from the ride cymbal to the hi-hat. The rhythmic content is the same, but the sound is profoundly different. Drummers can be encouraged to categorize how different sonic relationships can affect the music. Let's assume the drummer has a four-piece drum set, two cymbals, and a hi-hat. (For a few examples of some textural variations related to energy intensity, see figure 19.1 and ⊕ video 19.11, Low- and High-Energy Swing.)

Drummers can then use their custom-made categories to help them begin to shape a piece. In a small group setting, the drummer can use the textures from the "low energy" column in figure 19.1 for the A sections and then use the textures from the "high energy" column when the band arrives at the bridge of the tune. These are just examples. It's up to the musicians and the teacher to determine these textures for themselves. In a big band, the drummer can use the "low energy" items to shape the melody and the "high energy" items to shape the shout chorus.

The drummer also helps to establish dynamic changes in the music. When there is a change in dynamics, the first place that it should be musically represented is in the drums. The rest of the ensemble can play a static dynamic level, and if the drums get soft, the music will sound soft. The opposite is also true. However, ensembles that are taught to listen and respond to the other sections in the bands will also react to what the drummer plays. If the drums begin to play soft/loud, instinctively, the other members in the ensemble will react to the dynamic level they are experiencing from the drummer. This is also true for shaping crescendos and diminuendos. This approach could be a great complement for Emily's student who is working on refining reading skills.

| Low energy | High energy |
| --- | --- |
| Time on closed hi-hat | Time on ride cymbal |
| Cross stick on snare | Snare drum on head |
| No bass drum | Feathered bass drum |
| Fills on toms | Fills on snare drum |
| No crash cymbals | Crash cymbals |

**FIGURE 19.1** Low- and High-Energy Swing

# Configuration

Often, some of the challenges drummers present us with can be easily managed by addressing their setup. When a drummer is playing something that is sonically inappropriate, a solution can be found by making adjustments to the setup. Inappropriate sounds can sometimes be a manifestation of the drummer's body trying to compensate for being uncomfortable behind the drums.

## Feet

Your drummers should sit on the throne with the space of about a 45 degree angle between their legs. You can ask them to sit down on the seat with both feet on the ground as if they are about to eat a meal; that usually produces the desired physical position. Then you want to look at each leg individually. There should be a space between the calf muscle and hamstring of a bit more than 90 degrees for each leg. This will give them the largest potential range of motion in their ankle joint. This ideal range of motion for their ankles will allow them to get the appropriate sound and control on the hi-hat and bass drum pedals.

Because we often work with musicians whose bodies aren't fully developed, young drummers will often get as close to the drums as possible. This will force them to play the pedals with their toes. I'm sure we've all experienced in our bands or have heard bands of young musicians in which the bass drum is too loud; this is why. The drummer is physically forced to play the bass drum with the entire leg instead of the ankle. Because jazz music requires some finesse on the bass drum, the drummer is now creating a stylistically inappropriate sound. We plead with drummers to play the bass drum softer, yet no matter how many times we ask, the bass drum is too loud. It's not that they aren't listening to you or understanding what feathering (playing barely audible quarter notes) the bass drum means. They physically can't control the bass drum beater. Drummers are trying to move the bass drum beater inches using extremely large muscle groups. To get the appropriate sound, they need to engage smaller muscle groups. If you have drummers who play the bass drum "too loud," look at their legs. Chances are the space between the calf and hamstring muscles is less than 90 degrees. With the feet in the proper position, the pedals will go right under the feet and the rest of the drum kit can be set up around the drummers' comfortable foot position.

## Hands

The snare drum should be sitting between the drummers' legs and not touching the sides of their legs. The angle of the drum should be at a position where the drummers' forearms and biceps create a 90 degree angle, as if they are holding a glass of water. If your drummers are short and the snare drum stand is at its lowest setting, you will have to then angle the drum toward them. If your drummers are taller, they will have to use a combination of raising the drum and changing the angle of the drum to what is comfortable to play either on the head or with a cross stick sound.

The position of the toms and cymbals should be such that the drummer doesn't have to reach for them. To reach the toms, drummers should only have to move their arms up a few inches to reach the rack tom or over a few inches to reach the floor tom. This movement will come from extending the bicep muscles. The shoulders should stay relaxed, and the stroke should still come from the wrist. The same is true for the position of the cymbals, which should be just a few inches further in arm extension than the toms. The angle of the cymbals should be in a position such that the bead of the stick strikes the ride portion of the cymbal with a natural stick stroke. To get around the entirety of the drum set, drummers should not have to move their arms more than 6 to 12 inches in any direction.

## Position of the Drum Set

With your drummer comfortable behind the kit, you also need to be aware of how the kit should be set up in relation to the rest of the ensemble. There is no absolute when it comes to setting up your rhythm section, but the most important things should be that each player in the rhythm section is able to hear *and* see the others. Generally, in jazz rhythm sections the bass player and the ride cymbal should be in extreme, but comfortable, proximity to one another. This approach can be used in both small and large ensembles because the bass and ride cymbal are almost always in rhythmic unison when playing swing music. If the bass player is using an amp, then the amp should be behind both the drummer and the bass player. You want your drummer to be playing with the bass, not with the amp.

In large ensembles, the drums should be next to the trombone section. Sometimes the drummer is closer to the sax section, sometimes closer to the trumpet section. This can be left to personal preference. When I am playing in a big band, I like to be almost parallel to the trumpet section. This allows the rest of the rhythm section to be closer to the band and will help the band listen to the drummer. Often educators set up the drums, and therefore the rhythm section, too far from the band. This makes it difficult for drummers to fulfill their role, as the band will have trouble hearing the nuances in their playing.

# Functions of the Sound Sources

One of the contributing factors to the uniqueness of the drum set is that it can play four different sounds in unison. In addition, drummers have other sounds available in their sound palette. Because of the abundance of sounds drummers have at their disposal, it is easy to lose sight of how specific sound sources contribute to the groove.

## Ride Cymbal

In swing music, specifically that of the bebop era and beyond, it is the ride cymbal that establishes the groove. The strong presence of the ride cymbal is one of the factors that defines what a swing groove is. The moment the sound of the ride cymbal becomes overpowered by another sound source in the drums, the swing groove ceases to exist. There are other elements that can contribute to a swing groove, but it is the ride cymbal that defines it.

There is a misconception that the "spang-a-lang" ride pattern is the definitive motif that the ride cymbal plays; it is not. If a drummer in a rhythm section stops playing "spang-a-lang" and begins to play only quarter notes, the groove still sounds like a swing groove. This demonstrates that the "spang-a-lang" is not what defines the groove, but rather is a variation on the groove. The quintessential ride groove is *even, constantly articulated and phrased quarter notes* on the ride cymbal. Like Emily, if you have an inexperienced drummer whom you are trying to have function in a jazz setting, start by having the drummer only play quarter notes in the ride cymbal, but without the hi-hat. The same method can be used when trying to help an experienced drummer navigate the nuances of playing swing.

The ride cymbal is also used to complement or contrast soloists. Usually a drummer will have two different ride cymbals. One cymbal will have a long sustain, and the other cymbal will have a fast decay. One cymbal will have bright overtones, and the other cymbal will have dark and low overtones. One will have a strong stick definition, and the other will have a muted stick definition. These contrasts of cymbal qualities will complement or contrast the timbre of various instruments as well as give the drummer the option to exploit the many different sounds available at the drum set.

The ride cymbal doesn't exist in a vacuum. The swing groove established in the ride cymbal has a profound relationship with the bass; the ride and the bass are sonic complements. The ride cymbal gives the bass an elongated sustain, and the bass gives the ride cymbal a bottom end that is not inherent to its sonic spectrum. Because of this strong sonic relationship, the bass player and the drummer should always strive to play their quarter notes together.

An effective exercise is to have a bass player walk changes and the drummer only play the ride cymbal. Both musicians are not to deviate from the quarter note—no embellishments. What will be revealed to the bassist and drummer is that most of their quarter notes are not together. Before any rhythmic variations are played by the drummer and bassist, they should practice hearing and playing with each other's quarter notes. They can practice this alone or, since what they are playing is the essence of the swing groove, it can also be practiced in an ensemble setting. When the drummer and bassist begin to achieve a consistent execution of their respective and collective quarter notes, then they can begin to slowly embellish their quarter notes: begin to play the "spang-a-lang" ride pattern. This will take some time.

## Bass Drum

The bass drum is unique in that it is used both for establishing the groove and for embellishments. The bass drum's function is similar to that of the ride cymbal: it contributes to the quarter note swing groove. The bass drum has a unique relationship with the bass. It is used to supplement the attack of the bass articulation, which can often get covered up when played with a band. The bass drum essentially replaces the lost attack. This can become a bit more complicated when the bass is being supported by amplification. Generally, the bass drum is played dynamically under the bass.

In a big band setting, the bass drum can be treated as a complement to the saxophone and/or trombone section. When rhythmic figures in these sections need to be supported by either rhythmic unisons or complementary rhythmic figures, the bass drum sound is a great complement. It blends well with the smooth tone of the saxophone and sits in the same sonic register as the trombone.

## Hi-Hat

The hi-hat is used to accompany the swing groove that is played in the ride cymbal. It is also used to accentuate the weak beats in a phrase of $\frac{4}{4}$. In music that has a strong backbeat, like rock music, there is a clear representation of the strong and weak beats—the strong beats being beats 1 and 3 in the bass drum and the weak beets being beats 2 and 4 (usually played on the snare drum). In swing music, the relationship of strong and weak beats becomes obscured by the ride cymbal being played even on all quarter notes. The hi-hat brings some clarity to where the strong and the weak beats fall. In swing music, the hi-hat is played on beats 2 and 4. The sound of the hi-hat is unobtrusive, as it complements the sound of the ride cymbal. Because of this complementary timbre of the hi-hat, there is a presence of strong and weak beats, but they are not felt as strongly as in rock music. This is what contributes to the cyclical nature of swing groove.

## Snare Drum

The snare drum is used in a variety of ways. In a small ensemble, it is used to communicate with both the soloist and the other "comping" instruments. During a solo, a pianist/guitarist will accompany the soloist with rhythmic figures. These rhythmic figures can exist in three ways relative to the soloist: (1) as reinforcement—the figures can be played in rhythmic unison with the soloist to strengthen the musical meaning of the figure; (2) responsively—the figure can be played in the silence left by the soloist; and (3) contrasting—the figure can be played opposite the soloist. For example, the soloist plays a flurry of notes, and the comping musicians plays something rhythmically simple. The snare drum is used in the ways mentioned relative to the soloist. Simultaneously, it is also used in the same manner relative to other comping musicians.

The snare drum is also used to accentuate the weak beats (2 and 4) when there needs to be a more obvious representation of the strong and weak beats. Grooves that might need this stronger representation of the strong and weak beats could be labeled funk, shuffle, blues, or jazz-funk. This would be accomplished by playing the snare drum on beats 2 and 4 or some variation on 2 and 4. In the swing style, this backbeat would still be underneath the ride cymbal dynamically so as not to obscure the swing groove.

# Bottom-Up Approach

## Foundation

When it comes to keeping time, or playing a groove, everything that a drummer plays fits on top of the feet. If the bass drum gives us the strong beats and the hi-hat gives us the weak beats, it is the hands that phrase the space between the strong and weak beats. Take a simple rock beat: it's not what the feet are doing that make the groove, it's what the hands are playing. To allow the hands to play correctly, the feet must play strong and rhythmically steady. This will not only give the drummer a strong physical foundation behind the drum set, but also give the music a strong foundation.

## Heel-Toe

Heel-toe refers to a method of playing the hi-hat. This method can be a bit awkward at first. It requires that the drummer move a total of four times per measure; however, only two sounds will be made per measure. The way to think about this is that drummers are articulating four times, but only two of those articulations are audible, on beats 2 and 4. The first movements have drummers rocked up on their toes to have the hi-hat in the closed position. The second movement has them drummer rocking back on their heels to open the hi-hat. This continues in the pulse of quarter notes. Essentially the drummer is playing beats 1 and 3 with the heel and beats 2 and 4 with the toes. Everything the drummer plays from this point can be related to the heel or the toe. For example, if the drummer is playing on all up-beats, the drummer should think "Heel-and, Toe-and, Heel-and, Toe-and" (see ⏵ video 19.12, Heel-Toe).

Not only does this give drummers mental subdivision, it also gives them a physical subdivision. Jazz music can obscure beat 1, and musicians have difficulty feeling music when there isn't an obvious beat 1. By dropping the heel on beat 1, even though drummers are not hearing the beat, they are feeling physically and conceptualizing beat 1. By using the heel-toe hi-hat method, the drummer, when playing swing time, now has all four limbs participating in the quarter note.

## Adding the Bass Drum and Other Limbs

When drummers become familiar and comfortable with using heel-toe, they can add the bass drum to the process. The bass drum will be played on all four quarter notes, a sound that should be familiar to them. This sound exists in march music that they may have played in concert bands, and it is a sound that has existed in pop music for decades. Because drummers are familiar with that sound, integrating the bass drum into the heel-toe method shouldn't be difficult.

Step 1: Have drummers play quarter notes on the bass drum. Have them alternate, counting out loud the following: "Heel-toe-heel-toe One-two-three-four." This is an easy 2-bar phrase for them to latch onto. Step 2: Have the drummer look at the hi-hat foot while playing the bass drum and counting out loud: "Heel-toe-heel-toe One-two-three-four." This will help the drummer play the bass drum while not looking at it and focusing on the left foot. Step 3: Have the drummer begin to use the left foot while looking at the left foot and counting out loud: "Heel-toe-heel-toe One-two-three-four." Step 4: Have the drummer repeat this process with the hands individually, then try to have all four limbs play quarter notes in unison (see ⏵ video 19.13, Adding Limbs to Heel-Toe).

# How to Get Your Drummer to Function in an Ensemble

## Groove Hierarchy of Dynamics

When your drummers are able to function by themselves, the next step is to get them to work within an ensemble. We've all listened to inexperienced drummers play, and while the content they are playing is correct, something just sounds "wrong." Nothing is in fact wrong; what is happening is that the drummers may be familiar with the rhythmic

Key: 1=loudest, 2=softest

| Swing | Rock | Bossa | Afro-Cuban |
|---|---|---|---|
| 1: Ride cymbal | 1: Bass drum | 1: Hi-hat | 1: Clave (snare) |
| 2: Hi-hat | 2: Snare drum | 2: Bass drum | 2: Hi-hat or ride cymbals |
| 3: Snare drum | 3: Hi-hat/ride cymbal | 3: Snare drum | 3: Bass drum |
| 4: Bass drum | | | |

**FIGURE 19.2** Groove Hierarchy of Dynamics

content, but their execution is flawed. Young drummers are often exposed to content from method books. This is their main source for learning to play jazz, funk, bossa nova, and Afro-Cuban grooves. What many of these books fail to address is that there is a dynamic scheme associated with these grooves. Figure 19.2 describes the dynamic spectrum of each limb related to a specific groove. Generally, when students are playing this groove, they should adhere to this hierarchy of dynamics. These dynamics are specific to how the limbs relate to each other. It is then the drummer's responsibility to relate the sum of all it parts to the ensemble.

These dynamic hierarchies are not absolute, but they will give the drummer somewhere to grow from. We've heard inexperienced drummers critiqued as "talented but plays jazz like a rock drummer." That actually doesn't communicate to the students what they need to know to make adjustments. This may be an area in which Bruce is finding it difficult to communicate to drummers. What the student needs to know is that when playing swing, the ride cymbal needs to be the texture at the top of the drum set dynamic spectrum. That is a more tangible idea for the student to grasp (see ▶ video 19.14, Groove Hierarchy of Dynamics).

An effective exercise is to have students draw their own "groove hierarchies of dynamics." Have them listen to three to five tunes in a similar style: bebop, funk, rock, big band, disco, etc. They will begin to hear how the dynamics of each limb fundamentally affect how the groove feels, and that understanding will begin to show up in their playing (see ▶ appendix 19.2, Influential Drummers).

# Basic Elements of Common Syncopated Grooves

## What Makes a Groove?

It is important to understand what sounds help to make a groove work. Most styles have one or two sounds or rhythms that define a particular groove. These elements are important to know, as they can help you engage very inexperienced players and still allow them to participate in the ensemble when they get their technique together. When teaching your students about building a functional groove, the groove hierarchy of dynamics may be out of their technical reach. Perhaps they don't yet possess enough technical independence/interdependence to control their limbs. Maybe they're just starting on the drum set, or maybe their bodies haven't yet caught up with their conceptual understanding of the groove. If your drummers don't yet have the independence, they can begin by playing the most dominant sonic characteristic of the style (e.g., just playing the ride cymbal in swing) and gradually add others beneath it as they acquire more limb independence. This way, they can still provide the simplest function of the drum set in your band.

**Bossa nova.** When getting inexperienced students to play a bossa nova groove, the first place to start is the hi-hat. You will want them to play an even eighth-note pattern on a closed hi-hat texture. This will be the most functional part of the pattern that they can play. This will also allow you to have another percussionist play a pair of claves along with your drummer if they are unable to coordinate two limbs. The next limb that you want to get your students to incorporate is the bass drum. Often in a bossa nova, drummers will play in unison with the bass player's quarter note/two eighths, quarter note/two eighths pattern. If your students are struggling with this coordination, have them play half notes on beats 1 and 3. Even if your students are technically proficient, this half note pattern can still be quite effective for creating a solid groove in your rhythm section. The next limb to add would be the snare drum limb. Drummers can often use a 3-2 or 2-3 son clave pattern to help round out the sound of a functional bossa nova (see ⦿ video 19.15, Elements of Syncopated Groove, Bossa Nova).

**Afro-Cuban.** To get your drummer started on playing a functional Afro-Cuban groove, the first place to start is the clave rhythm. No matter what your drummer is capable of playing on the drum set, it is this rhythm that the rest of the ensemble will lock into. If your drummers are only capable of playing this rhythm, if might be more appropriate to have them play this rhythm on a pair of claves and forget the drum set altogether. However, if your student is capable of playing the clave rhythm and beat 2 and 4 using "heel-toe" on the hi-hat, this would be ideal. Once the left hand and left foot are working well, the next limb to add would be the right foot. The best rhythm to use to engage your student is a dotted quarter/eighth, and a quarter note on beat 4—the 3 side of the clave. This rhythm is great because your student will have two limbs playing in unison: the left hand and the right foot. It may be difficult for a student to grasp this cross-body coordination, so if you need a functional drummer, the next best thing is to have your student play half notes on beats 1 and 3 while getting this syncopation together. Afro-Cuban rhythms can be very syncopated, and traditionally, the right hand would play a rhythm called "Cascara." If your drummers don't take to syncopation too well, you can have them start with half notes on beats 1 and 3 on the bell of the ride cymbal to mimic a cowbell sound. This would give the student the same rhythm as the less-syncopated bass drum previously mentioned. This way, the right hand and right foot are in unison (whole right side of the body), and the left-hand clave is the only true syncopation being played. This is all of course being related to the "heel-toe" motion (see ⦿ video 19.16, Elements of Syncopated Groove, Afro-Cuban).

**Rock/funk.** Students are not only eager to play, but often more suited to, this style because these grooves are more accessible in their everyday musical engagement. However, drum set players will often interpret rock/funk to mean overly syncopated. A great place to start with students to make this groove functional is to have them play eighth notes on a closed hi-hat, "4 on the floor," and a backbeat on the snare drum on 2 and 4. If the groove is still feeling a bit "off," try to have them play quarter notes on the hi-hat to take some of the syncopation out of the groove. This will allow all of their limbs to be working in unison and produce a tighter sounding groove (see ⏵ video 19.17, Elements of Syncopated Groove, Rock).

# Final Thoughts

Make sure that your students understand that drumming is a lifelong journey. Each musical doorway that they walk through will lead them to another doorway. That's what I find fun and exciting about this instrument: the endless possibilities. When we analyze groove-based music, we are trying to quantify something that isn't meant to be quantified: musical feeling. That process is challenging and takes consistent engagement. Stay positive and encourage your students to embrace the challenge, not to be defeated by it. It's supposed to be hard; it's unfamiliar territory. Together, you and your students will begin to understand this instrument and the joy it will bring to your musical lives.

# Questions for Discussion

1. While pianists, bass players, and guitar players come to Bruce from outside of concert band, the drummers in the jazz ensemble are typically also the drummers in his concert band. How could teaching students who have these different musical backgrounds influence the classroom dynamics?
2. Bruce admits that he does not know anything about playing or teaching drum set. Instead, he tries to recruit students who have already taught themselves how to play it. He notes, "I can't do everything." Do you think that his approach is typical of many band directors, or should we only teach instruments that we are proficient on?
3. Emily notes that bass players and piano players come to jazz ensemble with some prior experience on their instruments, but that drummers come with generally no prior experience on drum set. Would you rather have students come to you having played concert band percussion and teach them drum set, or would you rather they come to you having already taught themselves to play drum set and try to "beat the rock band out of them?"
4. Drum set is one of the most ubiquitous instruments. How can Bruce quantify what his students may already be sonically familiar with to help engage the instrument?

# PART VI

# Jazz Literature

# 20

# Choosing Jazz Literature

Daniel Fabricius

## This Isn't Jazz at Lincoln Center

Bruce chooses music for his middle school jazz ensemble based mainly on two things: what the students want to play and what is already in the music library. "This year we did "Spiderman" because Kevin Wright said, 'can we play Spiderman?' And I said, 'sure.' If the kids ask me if we can play a tune, I'll almost always try at least to get it because it's there for them." Bruce chooses literature that is simple and follows the rule that "if they can't read it, it's too hard." Consequently, he does not do many ballads with the group. Instead, he usually programs a Latin tune, a pop tune, and a swing tune. "And of course at Christmas time you have to do 'Frosty the Snowman.'"

When choosing literature for her middle school jazz ensemble, Emily tries to find a blend between pop tunes and jazz tunes:

They're kids—this isn't jazz at Lincoln Center. You know, these are kids, man. So, you've gotta find the blend. So, when it comes to picking literature, it's like anything, you've got to balance learning new styles with some motivational stuff that they understand. Occasionally, we'll get a real dog of a tune that the kids [have to play]. An attractive young performer is singing it or Coldplay is playing it and so you spend some money and you're only going to play it once. But on the whole, you want to give the kids the real meat and potatoes of what jazz is about.

One of the things that impressed me most about Emily's middle school jazz ensemble was the number of tunes that they have (and play) in their folders. Students have 30 to 40 different charts in their folders that they might pull out at any time and rehearse or perform. Whereas some middle school jazz ensembles might rehearse only the same three to five tunes that they are working on for their upcoming performance, Emily's group had a much wider selection of literature to play and perform:

> What if you and I played the same 30 or 40 tunes forever? If you're a little kid and you have three or four or five tunes, well, that's no fun. Plus, you don't get a chance to do as many different styles. We could do that—we could have five gargantuan tunes that are just really hard and you got to woodshed them forever—who wants to do that? You want to play this style, get a chance to blow, and move on to the next tune.

Think for a moment about *why* you decided to pursue a career in music education. I believe that music educators were first drawn to the sound of great music. Each of us can probably recall several moments as young musicians when we realized that we had just played or heard an amazing composition. We felt enjoyment through the experience of making music, chose to spend our time mastering a musical instrument, and eventually developed the need to share our passion for music with others. Our experiences with artistic compositions awakened us to the power of music and essentially directed our lives toward a career in music education.

As educators, we *must* recall how playing amazing music affected us as young musicians and then seek to provide the same experiences for our students. As we search for literature, we will consider many variables and will sometimes find that our literature choices are not always based on artistic merit alone. However, I think that a vital element in our work is selecting music that fits our educational criteria *and* will often evoke the feeling that "*this* is really great music" in our students.

Readers should find helpful information regarding many facets of literature selection in this chapter. It discusses narrowing the literature search, using resources to research possible selections, and how to realistically evaluate your teaching situation. You will read about selecting music to "match" your band by determining the appropriate level of difficulty and by examining instrumentation options. And you will learn to select repertoire that addresses issues such as presenting a variety of styles. This chapter is comprised of five main sections: (a) finding common resources, (b) evaluating your situation, (c) instrumentation and doubling considerations, (d) stylistic programming considerations, and (e) budget considerations.

# Finding Common Resources

There are many resources available to assist in the search for appropriate music. A simple internet search for "recommended" jazz ensemble literature will produce quick results. State music lists, such as *The NYSSMA Manual* in New York, are another valuable resource. These state lists of compositions have been deemed suitable for state evaluation festivals and are generally divided into various levels of difficulty. Once you have an initial list of pieces that are "recommended," it is important to discover *why* someone thought they were good. There must be something about these pieces that makes them suitable, so devote plenty of time to perusing scores and listening to recordings. This can be a time-consuming task, but it is absolutely necessary for you to make informed decisions about literature. It can also be an easy task because many music publishers and retailers host web pages that commonly provide descriptions of compositions, PDF files of scores, and links to recordings. A substantial list of web pages for major jazz ensemble music publishers, distributors, and vendors is included in ⊚ appendix 20.1, Resources for Choosing Literature.

The most valuable resource may be someone who has some experience with the music you are considering, so definitely seek the advice of colleagues. You can discuss your search by using social media to communicate with colleagues from anywhere in the world. Also, go to concerts to hear the music selections that comparable school groups are performing. The real challenge in choosing literature is to use the available information to make *informed* decisions that will best serve your students.

Eventually all music teachers will develop their own "core repertoire": pieces that they consider to be the best choices for various teaching and performance situations. These pieces should also represent various styles, instructional topics, and historical periods. These are the pieces that you "love" and that you feel you can teach most effectively. See appendixes 20.1–20.5 for documents to further assist you with concert planning and literature selection.

## Evaluating Your Situation

I suggest that you review various aspects of your teaching situation before getting too far along with evaluating the music and planning concerts. First, consider these questions:

- Do you have a philosophy of programming?
- Will any of your music selections be used only as sight-reading material?
- How much rehearsal time do you have to prepare for each concert or unit?
- What are the performance details, and how will the type of performance affect your music choices?
- How much music will be needed for each performance?
- What is the anticipated difficulty level of the music for the group?
- Are there any instrumentation variables for the group?
- Is there a theme for any of the concerts?
- Will there be a guest artist performing with the group?
- Do you want to feature any specific student musicians?
- Are you inclined to program music that covers a variety of jazz styles?
- Do you "know" all of the pieces currently in your school library?
- What is your budget to acquire new music for the group?
- Do you have access to music that can be borrowed?

## How Many Pieces Do You Need?

Teachers in most subject areas divide their classes into units of instruction. They also devise ways to evaluate the progress of their students and their understanding of the subject. Most would consider music performances a culminating evaluation activity for *their* units in the jazz ensemble class. Although there are probably some school jazz bands that do not perform, it is much more common for students to actually rehearse and prepare musical selections for public performances.

Most schools plan their concerts many months in advance so that dates are already reserved before to the opening day of school each year. Yes, it is possible to add extra performances later, but I suggest starting the year knowing when major school performances will occur. The task of planning literature for the entire school year starts with this list of performances (see ⊚ appendix 20.2, Jazz Ensemble Performance Calendar Planning Worksheet). List every known performance, such as concerts for the public, the school open house night, an appearance at the local shopping mall to highlight Music in Our Schools Month, evaluation festivals, the annual nursing home gig, and any other event at which the group will play for an audience.

Once the performance dates are in place, look at a calendar and come up with a good estimate of the amount of rehearsal time needed for each performance. You will also need to consider the overall length of each program. For example, suppose that these scenarios applied to your situation:

- We need to play three selections for our performance at an evaluation festival.
- We are sharing the concert with four other groups, and each group can be on the stage for a total of only 16 minutes.
- Our performance is a full concert (including an intermission) with a guest artist.

I suggest that you also ask yourself how long the audience might be willing to sit still for a concert.

## Selecting Literature at an Appropriate Level of Difficulty

Music teachers should always make a thoughtful, educated guess about the appropriate level of difficulty before the first rehearsal. Obviously, they need to *know* their students. It can be a dreadful error when any ensemble performs music that is too easy or too difficult for the group. Yes, students need to be challenged, but they should not be crushed when they enter the rehearsal room. Students should also never feel bored with the music. Part of the *learning* process is for students to experience at least *some* individual or ensemble challenges during the rehearsal process. Since groups are always evolving, it may be best to settle on a portion of the program and then finalize the remaining selections after hearing the group play a few rehearsals.

We need to be concerned with matching our *possible* choices to the *actual* group that will play the music. Publishers and vendors usually assign a difficulty level to all of the pieces in their catalogs, and larger publishers also tend to assign pieces to an appropriate series (see ⊚ appendix 20.3, Jazz Chart Classification).

It should be easy for teachers to avoid selection errors if they carefully study the various resources. For example, while it is fairly common for advanced groups to play professional-level music, there are many "difficult" pieces that have been arranged for developing bands.

A great example of this practice is the composition "Shiny Stockings," originally written by Frank Foster. The Count Basie Orchestra played a beautiful version of this song arranged by Sammy Nestico. However, Nestico eventually wrote a simplified version that captures the spirit of the original piece but is intended for intermediate groups. Both versions have the same title and the same arranger and are distributed by the same publisher.

## Matching Music to the Band

The task of matching music to the band must include evaluating the potential of the ensemble (see ⊙ appendix 20.4, Jazz Band Profile Worksheet). A major part of the research for filling the performance selections list is to review charts. You need to listen to recordings and examine scores. These activities will help you find selections that are a good "match" for the band. Consider the following specific factors:

- rhythmic vocabulary of the players
- comfortable range of the brass players
- stylistic capabilities of the players
- notation reading capabilities of the players (key, accidentals, etc.)
- tempo
- instrumentation variables with the group
- harmonic progression that matches the improvisation skills of the players

## Instrumentation Configurations

The jazz ensemble has evolved into what is considered a standardized instrumentation made up of four sections: saxophones (or reeds), trumpets, trombones, and rhythm instruments. The specific instrumentation consists of five saxophones (two altos, two tenors, and one baritone), four trumpets, four trombones, piano, guitar, bass, and drums.

While nearly all professional-level pieces conform to this standard instrumentation, there may be a few variables. Some of the earlier professional jazz bands (such as the Duke Ellington band) sometimes used fewer players. There are also plenty of examples of professional bands using more than the standard instrumentation (such as the Stan Kenton Orchestra). Please also note that it is common for jazz musicians to "double" on additional instruments. The following instrumentation variables are based on artistic decisions by the composers and arrangers:

- soprano sax replacing 1st alto sax
- any of the saxophone players doubling on other woodwind instruments, such as flute, piccolo, clarinet, or bass clarinet
- addition of a 5th trumpet part
- addition of a 5th trombone part (often a bass trombone)
- trumpet players doubling on flugelhorn
- use of various mutes to present a variety of timbres in the brass section
- addition of an electronic keyboard or synthesizer effects
- use of effects on electric guitar

- specified usage of either electric bass or acoustic bass
- addition of vibraphone
- addition of a percussionist to play auxiliary instruments
- use of a featured vocalist

# Instrumentation and Doubling Considerations

The 4th or 5th trombone part is often designated as bass trombone in more advanced charts. While a standard tenor trombone will usually "work" for these parts, it is often easier for players to use a real bass trombone in order to play more comfortably in the lowest register. The addition of a 5th trumpet and/or trombone often creates a fuller sound and also allows composers and arrangers to present more colorful harmonies in the brass section.

Composers and arrangers commonly require jazz ensemble brass players to utilize a variety of mutes. Most trumpet and trombone players have experience playing with a standard straight mute. However, in jazz charts arrangers often use a wide variety of mutes, such as cups, Harmons, buckets, hats, and plungers. These mutes all create effects that add much to the orchestration possibilities and also create timbres unique to the jazz style.

For many teachers, it almost seems unfair to only have one drummer in a school jazz ensemble, especially if there are several student musicians available who are nearly equal in interest and ability. I suppose this is why many school groups utilize "extra" percussion players, who can participate by playing vibraphone or any number of other percussion accessory instruments. The addition of these instruments can have a positive effect on the tonal colors of the band and also adds to the rhythmic interest.

It is common for jazz composers to write pieces that reflect the known talents of the musicians who will play their music. Duke Ellington is an early example, writing specifically for the individuals in his bands. Ellington wrote some great parts for his players who doubled on clarinet, not considered a current standard instrument in the jazz ensemble. It is now common that contemporary jazz musicians are expected to play several of the reed instruments in addition to the saxophone. This is also the reality in American musical theater, with woodwind players assigned to play a "book" that requires doubling on several of the reed instruments.

We have come a long way with the usage of electronic instruments in contemporary music. The earliest electronic instruments (guitar and bass) were designed to amplify acoustic instruments to match the volume level of louder wind and percussion instruments. The use of electronic keyboard instruments might have been a reaction to pianists being frustrated by poor-quality or out-of-tune instruments when they traveled to different venues, or to the burden of shipping and moving pianos. Some contemporary styles need to have added electronic effects to match the intent of the composer or arranger.

There is a long history of American jazz ensembles using featured vocalists. In the early twentieth century, the paying public wanted to listen and dance to "popular" music. Early traveling jazz bands attracted huge crowds at dance halls as couples danced to the hit songs of the day. While jazz eventually became just music for listening instead of dancing to, the audiences still wanted to hear vocalists perform popular songs. The featured vocalists were often considered to be the stars of the show, such as Frank Sinatra with Harry James and His Orchestra, Doris Day with Les Brown and His Band of Renown, and Anita O' Day with the Stan Kenton Orchestra.

There are plenty of arrangements available to feature vocalists. These are often the actual arrangements performed by famous artists. Many of these selections represent the "Great American Songbook," the canon of the most important and influential American popular songs and jazz standards from the early twentieth century. These are the most popular and enduring songs from the 1920s to the 1950s, and many were created for Broadway musical theater and Hollywood musical films. Recently many easier versions of vocal selections have become available to make this music accessible to developing players.

It is important to make sure that the key of the arrangement will fit the vocal range of the singer when considering this type of selection. Some publishers are now combining two versions of a song with performance sets. This allows bands to play the arrangement in either the "male key" or "female key." It is also common for vocal arrangements to include the option of using an instrument as the featured soloist instead of a vocalist. See chapter 12 in this volume for more information specific to jazz vocalists.

## Instrumentation Variables for School Bands

A fairly recent development in the music publishing industry is that additional or substitute instrument parts are included with the set of music. Some school music programs either cannot support the standard instrumentation or choose to disregard instrumentation in favor of higher participation by opening the jazz band to "nonjazz" instruments. Directors of beginning-level through intermediate-level groups often promote the policy that "anyone is welcome to join." However, directors of more advanced groups may want to limit membership to the standard instrumentation. High-achieving and motivated students are often drawn to the "open instrumentation" situation, and experienced teachers know that once students are hooked on the activity, they may be willing to learn a "jazz instrument" to stay involved as they progress to more advanced groups.

The issue of instrumentation is a philosophical decision that each teacher needs to address. Who can argue with having more students participating in music groups? However, some teachers will be equally as passionate about playing jazz ensemble music that stays true to the defined instrumentation. Perhaps teachers can bend a little regarding instrumentation if using substitute instruments creates a better learning experience for students. Ultimately, you must still find the music that matches the students playing in the band that you are actually leading. To get closer matching the music to the band you can eventually reference the selection issues identified in the entire chapter (see ⊚ appendix 20.5, Jazz Ensemble Literature Review Worksheet). Following is a list of the common "additional" or "substitute" instrument parts that are often included in jazz ensemble charts:

- flute (doubling upper-register melody parts)
- clarinet (often doubling 1st and 2nd alto saxophone or trumpet parts)

- bass clarinet (doubling the baritone saxophone)
- French horn (usually doubling the 1st trombone part)
- baritone horn in treble clef (doubling 1st and 2nd trombone parts)
- tuba (doubling either bass trombone or string bass parts)

Not all jazz ensemble charts will have these additional or substitute parts. It is recommended that directors create their own additional parts if doing so makes the published music more appropriate for the students in the group.

# Stylistic Programming Considerations

There are various styles of jazz to consider when selecting music for the jazz ensemble. Within jazz, there are three main styles: (a) swing, (b) rock, and (c) world music. Within each of these styles there are many variations, depending on factors such as tempo, rhythm section groove, rhythmic interpretation, meter, and cultural or geographical origination (see ⊙ appendix 20.6, Descriptive Grooves in Swing, Rock, and World Music Charts). Note that the descriptions listed in the appendix are often related to tempo or an indication of the feeling or mood of the music. The names of some of the descriptions may be a reference to specific dance rhythms from various cultures. Many of these jazz style subdivisions are often found in lesson books used to study rhythm section instruments. While the list is not comprehensive, it has been included to show that teachers may need to research the full content of compositions to effectively teach the music.

Ballads are a special type of chart that fits into each of the three main styles. Ballads are songs usually performed at a relaxed or slower tempo. These songs usually feature beautiful melodies, and they can be an impressive addition to any jazz ensemble program. Ballads may be technically easier than music that is played at a fast tempo, but they offer different challenges to student musicians, such as (a) maintaining tone quality on longer phrases, (b) maintaining a steady tempo (without rushing), (c) playing with intensity, and (d) interpreting melodic and soloistic nuances.

## Theme Concerts and Guest Artists

Theme concerts can be a fun experience for the players and the audience. Concerts featuring a unifying theme have been fairly common among professional bands, US military bands, and many collegiate jazz ensembles. School jazz ensembles might not have the abundance or the depth of repertoire to present a long program; but utilizing this concept for a portion of a larger concert is certainly attainable. I can imagine some great theme programs, such as "Hits of the Swing Era," "A Latin Jazz Extravaganza," "Jazz in the 21st Century," or "The Great American Song Book." Of course, this type of performance may also add another layer of limitations for your programming selections. I caution jazz ensemble directors to ensure a well-rounded jazz education for students by teaching a variety of styles throughout the entire school year. You may want to avoid themes with extreme limitations, such as "A Modal Jazz Retrospective" or "120 Beats Per Minute: An Evening of Medium Swing."

Programming for concerts can also be enhanced by utilizing guest artists. A guest can turn a concert into a very memorable educational and artistic experience, whether it is a notable and famous artist or a local semiprofessional musician. Some guests may be happy to be a featured soloist on whatever the band knows how to play, but this type of program may also add some limitations to your programming. Consult with guests to discuss their suggestions and negotiate the program so that the selected music fits both the band and the soloist.

An obvious benefit of inviting a guest is to have your students hear a professional player. Sure, you have already been encouraging them to listen to recordings and watch video performances, but there is still nothing like being on stage performing with a professional. Students can become even more inspired to practice and to attain greater proficiency as a long-term effect of having a guest artist. Since the guest can be an outstanding model of jazz playing, students may even try to copy elements of what they witnessed.

## Student Soloists

Even though music educators agree that improvisation is an important element of jazz music, this is still an often-neglected topic in the school jazz ensemble setting. Jazz players need to have a vocabulary of jazz rhythms, an understanding of colorful notes in both melodies and harmony, and the ability to spontaneously create music in the style of the composition. It is important that directors be aware of details regarding jazz improvisation when selecting literature. Although it is certainly appropriate to address improvisation during rehearsals, it is also recommended to schedule extra sessions with student soloists to teach the finer points of this topic. See chapters 8 and 11 in this volume for specific information regarding teaching improvisation.

I suggest that jazz ensemble directors emphasize to students that improvisation *is* a very important element of jazz music. While improvisation may not be a comfortable topic for every band member, some will probably be attracted to the prospect of playing solos. It is not imperative that every player in the band improvise well, but I recommend that everyone have some instruction and be given the opportunity to try. Typically, jazz ensemble solos are delegated to certain part assignments within the band. In school charts, it is most common to find solos assigned to the following parts: alto sax 1; tenor sax 1; trumpet 2, 4, or 5; trombone 1; piano; guitar; and drums. Directors should not feel obligated to give the solo parts to only those who have them printed on their music. Yes, it is acceptable to have any of the musicians in the band play improvised solos even when an arrangement indicates a solo in a specific part. Publishers often include improvisation teaching aids with arrangements targeted to school groups.

Many jazz ensemble compositions are written as "features" for specific instruments. Instrumental features usually include the soloist playing the first statement of the melody, then also improvising within the chart. There are other pieces that feature an entire section of the band (saxes, trumpets, trombones), and there may be an option for some or all of the players in the section to improvise. Pieces like this add variety to programming and can also serve as a huge incentive for the featured student musicians.

# Budget Considerations

Teachers need to be practical when acquiring the music needed for instruction because schools often have budgetary limitations when it comes to purchasing new music. I suggest that directors first take the time to become familiar with all of the pieces already owned by the school band's library. Rather than purchasing all new music every year, you may find some great music already on the shelf waiting for you to rediscover it. Another option is to borrow music from a regional library or from the libraries of colleagues. Borrowing from colleagues could be easier to arrange if you can also make *your* music library available to loan. This option can really save your budget as long as there is an understanding regarding what to do if any music on loan is lost or damaged. Guest artists may also be able to provide the music that they will be playing with your group. Assuming that you do need to purchase new music, I suggest prioritizing the selections and having a backup plan if your wish list exceeds your budget.

This chapter is meant to be a starting reference about selecting jazz ensemble literature. Your goal should be to begin the yearly process with a clear direction. I suggest focusing on a few general ideas:

- Learn to use various references to become familiar with jazz ensemble literature that is available to teach to your students.
- Learn to evaluate the capabilities of the players and determine realistic goals for the ensemble.
- Consider appropriate difficulty, various jazz styles, instrumentation options, and soloist opportunities as you review choices for each performance.
- Be committed to reviewing new and/or unfamiliar charts each year as you build a core repertoire.

Your students may never thank you for your thoughtful choices regarding jazz ensemble literature, but it is likely that you *are* having a huge impact on them. We owe it to our students to give them the very best as they study this amazing American art form!

# Questions for Discussion

1. How do you balance "what the kids want to play" with all the other considerations in choosing literature?
2. What is a good balance between breadth and depth when choosing and rehearsing music?
3. What are your thoughts and rationale regarding leading a jazz ensemble using the defined *standard* instrumentation versus an ensemble with an *optional* instrumentation policy?

4. What are some of the characteristics that you believe are evident in the charts that you will include in your core repertoire?

5. After researching literature options, are you able to list a core repertoire for the ensemble that you direct or for a hypothetical ensemble? Share your selection ideas with others.

# 21

# Teaching Jazz Standards

Nick Weiser

## You Know What, It's a Really Nice Melody

While Emily wants to expose her students to traditional big band "classics," more than that, she wants to expose them to the stylistic concepts that make up those classics. Since the classic arrangements are often technically inaccessible to middle school musicians, she tries to choose charts that are written in a characteristic style but composed at a level that is achievable for her students. This often means finding newly composed music rather than transcriptions. Transcriptions of classics, in an attempt to make them accessible to middle school students, often lose their original characteristic style. Consequently, Emily would rather have her students play newly composed pieces that are stylistically characteristic, rather than transcriptions of classics that may have lost those musical elements:

> No one ever heard them before, but you know what, it's a really nice melody, it's got nice changes, it's great to improvise over, all the parts work well together— absolutely. Would you rather have some kid take a box of cookie mix and make cookies that come out of the box that taste really good or have some kid try to make a 7-layer German torte that takes three hours and when they're done it just doesn't work?

The issue of teaching jazz standards is fraught with questions. What are "standards?" What makes a composition a standard? Why do jazz musicians use them as vehicles for improvisation? How do you distinguish greater standards from lesser standards? How do you select particular standards to suit the needs of your students? What is a student supposed to do with a standard? How can you best communicate about standards with your students in a way that will engender a meaningful connection to and interpretation of the musical material?

One could fill several volumes discussing approaches to selecting and teaching standards to students in diverse groups and settings, but attempting to do that in a few pages would be of limited use to educators. It will be more instructive to examine a set of essential principles that are useful in working with students at any level and in any size group. They retain their importance in all settings because they depend not on the students, but on the music you would like them to be creating. These principles can be observed in the greatest players' performances and should be central to your work on standards with students. Of course, in order to apply any principles to learning and internalizing the standard repertoire, one must first define the *jazz standard*.

## What Is a Standard?

Standards, most simply, are the compositions comprising the core of a repertoire. In jazz, this repertoire encompasses music from a wide variety of sources, including popular songs from the late nineteenth century and songs from Broadway, Hollywood, and Tin Pan Alley composers such as Jerome Kern, Irving Berlin, George Gershwin, Richard Rodgers, Cole Porter, Harold Arlen, and Hoagy Carmichael, as well as originals by jazz musicians. While tunes from each of these categories often have their own recognizable musical hallmarks, they all tend to lend themselves—by virtue of melodic, harmonic, and/or formal design—to jazz interpretations. These tunes are, or once were, familiar to broad swaths of the American public. They have been recorded by numerous jazz musicians and are the tunes jazz musicians expect each other to know.

Because the jazz repertoire is vast, there are differing opinions on what constitutes its "must know" cornerstones. Ted Gioia's (2012) *The Jazz Standards: A Guide to the Repertoire* is one of the most relevant publications from recent years, with a selection of more than 250 key compositions, including pertinent background information and lists of representative recordings. Another notable resource is Alec Wilder's *American Popular Song: The Great Innovators, 1900–1950*, an in-depth survey of the published music of the great American tunesmiths (Wilder and Maher, 1972). The internet can be a good resource as well.

The first requirement for a standard should be quality. This begs the question: "How does one measure quality?" Jazz standards generally fit two criteria: *catchiness* and *development*. In contrast with this repertoire, today's popular music is often catchy, but rarely includes development; it is not so much *composed* as *produced*. When it does include development, contemporary pop still offers little to the jazz improvisor. Of course, musicians took brand new music in the 1930s, 1940s, 1950s, and 1960s and injected it into the jazz repertoire, but they didn't do it because they felt all of the other jazz music was too old. Rather, these were songs people genuinely liked and songs the musicians felt were in keeping with something about the jazz tradition. Regardless, the final criterion for those past masters must have been quality.

# Why Do We Use Standards?

Having a unified repertoire of standards is useful for performers and educators alike because it provides a musical common ground. Jazz is a social music, and standards give musicians a way to relate their musical ideas to each other using materials with which they are, ideally, well acquainted. The shared repertoire provides a foundation for personal expression and development, and the music's harmonic richness and formal regularity offer limitless possibilities for musical manipulation within a relatively structured environment: "freedom in the groove," to borrow a phrase from Joshua Redman. The social aspect of playing jazz is an integral part of the evolving musical tradition, cultivated over decades through informal study sessions ("hanging out"), apprenticeships, jam sessions, sitting in, and professional affiliations with bands (Berliner, 1994). Within this community, standards allow musicians to exchange ideas and hone their improvisational craft.[1]

Common practice or "straight-ahead" jazz improvisation fits nicely with standards because it all stems from a tradition of coming up with a catchy idea *and* having the musical understanding to take it somewhere. Jazz musicians cultivate and rely on the skill of developing musical motives using principles that have been fundamental to composing and improvising for centuries (e.g., transformations of intervals or groups of intervals). In jazz, performers tend to make greater use of expressive devices and vocal effects, which can be difficult to notate but are an essential layer of a performance in the idiom. Underlying all of it is the compositional approach that emphasizes development.

With so many standards to choose from, it is impossible to learn them all. Gioia (2012) writes about knowing lots of them, but then really learning the ones that you actually like enough to play over and over again and allowing them to evolve. The late jazz pianist Marian McPartland also addressed this, recounting how she found herself coming back time after time to the same tunes that remained at the core of her standard repertoire (Perkins, n.d.). As an educator, it is important to be able to distinguish standards of greater or lesser appeal and complexity when selecting appropriate repertoire for your group. While determining a tune's quality is a subjective endeavor influenced by personal musical tastes, complexity can be gauged by familiarizing yourself with the harmonic and formal paradigms most commonly used in this music.

# Knowing the Structures

Jazz musicians are concerned with form, and standards tend to be based on a few structures. "(P)erformers commonly refer to the melody or theme as the head, and to the [harmonic] progression as the chord changes or simply changes. It has become the convention for musicians to perform the melody and its accompaniment at the opening and closing of a piece's performance. In between, they take turns improvising solos within the piece's cyclical rhythmic form. A solo can comprise a single pass through the cycle, known as a chorus, or it can be extended to include multiple choruses" (Berliner, 1994, p. 63).[2] As varied as this music is, there are several distinct harmonic and formal building blocks used in the majority of jazz standards.

**Common harmonic devices.** The harmonic language of jazz is not unlike that of Western classical music. Jazz also builds on romantic, impressionistic, and early twentieth-century harmonic sensibilities to include extended chromatic tonality. As such, the basic tonic-function harmonic structures in jazz are major or minor 6th chords for most standard tunes, or major-minor 7th chords in the case of the blues. Many of the harmonic paradigms used in jazz music are akin to those found in classical repertoire. Following is a list of the most common harmonic patterns in jazz music.

- Dominant to tonic motion—As with most European-derived music, the basic harmonic force is tension (V7) moving toward resolution (I).
- $ii^7$-$V^7$-I Progressions in major and minor—In common-practice classical music, V is often preceded by various "dominant preparation" chords. In jazz music, the dominant chord is often prepared by $ii^7$ in major and $ii^{\o7}$ in minor.
- Secondary/applied dominants—Any chord may be preceded by its dominant, which can allow for rapid motion to other key areas as well as areas of relative stability away from the tonic. When these dominant chords resolve down by 5th to a major or minor chord, they create a feeling of resolution. When they move down by 5th to other dominants, they sustain or redirect harmonic tension to further points of resolution.
- Motion to other tonal centers—Tonicizations and transient modulations to other key areas are common devices used to generate interest within sections of standard tunes. Actual modulations to related keys are common in delineating larger formal seams.
- Turnarounds, tags, and vamps—These are devices used for the purpose of tonic expansion and are most commonly found at the ends of sections to prepare a return to the tonic. They typically take the following forms: I-vi-ii-V, iii-vi-ii-V, iii-vi-ii-iv, etc.
- Use of $IV^6$ and/or $\flat VII^7$ harmonies—These borrowed chords sometimes appear in major key contexts. Their purpose is to import pitches, specifically the lowered 6th, from the parallel minor mode to add affect to emotional moments in standard songs. The minor 6th chord, too, is an incredibly versatile structure, able to be reinterpreted with many different roots to facilitate a variety of modulatory functions. (Spitzer, 2001, pp. 27–41)

These harmonic devices account for most of the chord progressions encountered in the standard repertoire and are the foundation of many of the formal structures found therein (see ⊙ video 21.1, Common Harmonic Devices).

**Common formal designs.** Whereas many of the harmonic devices used in jazz music parallel those of the classical tradition, the formal structures used in jazz music rarely do. The core repertoire tends toward 12, 16, or 32 measure forms with 4- or 8-measure interior sections and 2- or 4-measure individual phrases. These balanced phrase lengths are akin to the periodicity found in classical music, but these shorter overall forms better lend themselves to improvisatory treatment. Some of the most common of these forms follow:

- 12-bar blues—This is one of the most venerable vehicles in the jazz tradition. In its simplest form, the 12-bar blues contains only three chords—I, IV, and V—arranged in three 4-bar phrases, sometimes expressed AAB. The tonality of the blues, which is contingent on

FIGURE 21.1 Blues Form

FIGURE 21.2 32-Bar AABA Form

FIGURE 21.3 32-Bar ABAC Form

the use of major-minor 7th chords and "blue notes" (the lowered 3rd, lowered 5th, and lowered 7th scale degrees in the key), often extends beyond this form and into the realm of other harmonic progressions. It is one of the defining features of this music. Although less common, 8-bar and 16-bar versions can be found, particularly from the early years of the blues. (See figure 21.1.)

- 32-bar AABA form—Among the theater, film, and Tin Pan Alley standards, and even many jazz originals, this is the most common structure. It is also known as the AABA song form, the American popular song form, and the ballad form. It consists of two 8-bar harmonic progressions, the A section and the B section, the latter of which is also known as the bridge, release, channel, or inside, and which typically has a harmonic design in contrast to that of the A sections. Within this form, the most commonly used harmonic progression is that of George Gershwin's "I Got Rhythm." (See figure 21.2.)

- 32-bar ABAC form—This is less prominent in the repertoire, but provides opportunities for further harmonic and melodic development in the final 8-bar phrase. Depending on content, this form is sometimes expressed as ABAB'. Notable examples include "All of Me," "On Green Dolphin Street," and "There Will Never Be Another You." (See figure 21.3.)

Some lesser used forms are the quaternary AAA'A (see "So What") and ABCD (see "Stella by Starlight"), and the ternary forms AAB (see "Night and Day") and ABA (see "I'll Remember April"). Composers may take liberties with these forms, omitting or adding bars to suit the demands of particular phrases, but these are the points of departure for most standards. When working with students, it is important to be aware of these formal types and to expose the students to the various possibilities.

# Knowing the Sources

Two principles to consider with any tune are understanding the context in which it was written and respecting its integrity. In learning the standard repertoire, many jazz musicians rely on "fake books" or "real books" (often illegally distributed) containing collections of lead sheets—written melodies of tunes with shorthand harmonic notation. These books are highly problematic because they often perpetuate melodic and harmonic errors (sometimes unique to a single performer's interpretation on a particular recording), and they do not always include the lyrics of tunes. While they are convenient, they cannot be used for serious study. Instead, it is best to get as close as possible to the original source of the music.

**"Great American Songbook."** When studying American popular songs from Broadway, Hollywood, and Tin Pan Alley, the best source is the earliest published sheet music, easily found in the compiled song folios of individual tunesmiths, which are often published under the names of individual composers (*The Hoagy Carmichael Songbook*, for example) or as part of broader compilations (such as *The Singer's Musical Theatre Anthology*). While the published sheet music may not contain all of the harmonic complexity found in jazz recordings (artists often add to or even change the harmonies of songs for artistic reasons), it preserves the basic elements of the song and presents it as the composer intended. The original sheets allow us to explore the correct melodies (of often misrepresented tunes such as "All of Me" or "All the Things You Are") and the original harmonic content, which can sometimes be more compelling and musically satisfying than the mainstream interpretation. Often the originals will illuminate interesting contrapuntal relationships between the written melodies and the bass lines that tend not to find their way into the lead sheets. Other significant features of the originals are the lyrics, which are indispensable in developing a comprehensive picture of a composition, and the verses, which are almost always absent from lead sheet versions and jazz recordings, but can have fascinating relationships to the refrains jazz players more commonly know.

**Jazz tunes.** Regarding learning original compositions by jazz musicians, the earliest and seminal recordings are the primary sources. Since these compositions were often written for recording sessions, in contrast to the Tin Pan Alley–era standards, which were intended to be published and sold, finding the tunes as the composer penned them is often very difficult. In these cases, try to locate the most significant recordings, which typically first appear on albums with the composer as leader or supporting musician. In the case of some jazz standards, more prominent figures will adopt the tunes and record and release them on subsequent albums with ensembles that do not always include the composer. Sometimes these later recordings become much better known than the earlier versions and can influence the way later generations perform certain tunes. Whenever approaching these tunes, it is important to identify and listen to as many representative recordings by major artists as possible, to better understand each tune's evolution. Gioia's (2012) book is a great resource for this purpose, as is the website jazzdisco.org, which provides an extensive chronological discography for most major jazz artists.

Jazz standards have their own unique "lives," and the more you know about each tune, the more you can appreciate its place in the repertoire. When learning a standard, be able to answer the following questions:

1.  Who wrote it?
2.  When was it written?
3.  Is it from musical theater or film? If so, what show or movie does it come from?
4.  Was it written to showcase a particular performer?
5.  When was it first recorded?
6.  Who first recorded it?
7.  What are the lyrics?
8.  If it doesn't have lyrics, what are the defining characteristics of the composition theoretically, affectively, and aesthetically?
9.  What is it about this tune that makes it special and unique?
10. What made people care about it?

Contextualizing a piece enables you to transcend academic concerns such as chord-scale relationships and melodies that reflect passing harmonies. To express deeper meaning from a piece than potentially cliché chord progressions, you can evince other values that help you establish your own conceptual framework.

**Listening.** The value of listening cannot be overstated. Listening must be at the core of the study of jazz. Students need to develop a discerning ear in order to interpret the music and communicate it to others. In the case of original compositions by jazz musicians, this is the only way to develop nuance in playing a particular piece of music, although the same is generally true of older adopted standards. Ask students to listen for specific musical elements in repeated hearings of a tune, so they can better emulate the style and unique character of jazz. This is just as true of learning to phrase a melody as it is of improvising. For example, to sound like Charlie Parker, listen to recordings of Charlie Parker and learn to play what he played, exactly as he played it.

One of the great things about working with standards is that they have long recorded histories. Each arrangement and treatment reflects what the individuals in each recording felt was important or most in keeping with the spirit of the composition or the jazz tradition. The more you listen, and the more you encourage your students to listen, the more you can develop a taste for what you enjoy and an appreciation for the more effective recordings of individual tunes. As varied as these arrangements can be, there are certain inescapable features of standards that, when you internalize them, must be addressed.

# Internalizing Standards

When it comes to really learning a standard with integrity, the place to begin is the melody. We learn standards with the eventual aim of crafting our own new melodies using the underlying harmonic progression. To do this, you must first be able to render the original themes with attention to style, phrasing, articulation, and nuance. Only then can you begin to embellish the original and start crafting your personal musical thoughts. The melody is a great springboard for students with little improvisational experience, but also pushes more advanced improvisors to reframe their thoughts about improvising, organically.

The best way to ensure students are internalizing melodies is through *singing*. Singing is an honest way of assessing what you and your students are actually imagining or "hearing." As alto saxophonist Lee Konitz puts it: "Hearing in your inner ear is the first step. Something is popping around inside, and you start humming or singing. Chet Baker sang, or played, what he could hear, and so he sounds like himself in both cases. Singing is the main instrument, there's nowhere to hide" (Hamilton and Konitz, 2007, p. 108).[3] When introducing a standard, start by singing the melody either on a neutral syllable or, if applicable, with the lyrics. This ensures an awareness of the tune's overall aesthetic, tone, and mood. The next step is to sing the melody using solfège syllables to illuminate melodic motion relative to the key of the piece or the key of the moment. This allows you to draw attention to melodic signposts—such as the solfège syllables at the beginnings of formal seams—that help keep students from losing their place within the tune. Singing this way also makes the practice of learning standards in all keys more immediately approachable.

**Melodic phrasing.** Once the melody is internalized, it is time to address phrasing. Understanding how jazz musicians interpret and phrase melodies is a prerequisite to crafting convincing, stylistically appropriate statements. This is particularly important when studying standards with the original sheet music as the main source. While the sheet music is a helpful starting point, it presents the melodies of tunes in their simplest rhythmic form, simpler even than you'll hear on the earliest recordings. For this reason, turn again to the other important jazz recordings to develop a sense of effective phrasing. The most obvious techniques are slight rhythmic alteration and varied articulation. For an inexperienced player, this might already feel foreign, but embellishment is an important step toward improvising on a tune. Even for students with some jazz experience, there is much to gather from examining different statements of the same theme by three or four representative jazz artists. Even in the playing of seasoned improvisors, you can hear cursory thematic statements as if the melody is something to get past so as to reach the improvising. But embellishing the tune *is* improvising!

Lee Konitz addresses the topic of embellishment as it becomes improvisation:

> Getting a good melody to swing loosely with a beautiful sound is no easy thing to do. [ ... ] The novice should be trying, in some way, to create original melodies; but they have to ease into this discipline, of playing a theme and variations in the traditional way, and play on a level in which they can get all the moving parts into sync. [ ... ] The first improvising step as I understand it is stretching the rhythm, and the expression of the melody notes. So, before adding anything, I play the song. If I can't play that melody as if I just made it up, I need to work on it until I can. Change the key, or the tempo, and make it sound like real music, and not just some way to get into the variations too soon. Unless the basic groundwork—melody—is strong, the variations certainly will not be convincing. (Hamilton and Konitz, 2007, pp. 115–116)

Konitz elaborates further in a 1985 *Down Beat* magazine article, illustrating the use of common melodic decorations—trills, passing tones, neighbor tones, appoggiaturas, etc.—to bridge one melody note to another without having to generate completely new melodic material (Kastin, 1985, pp. 12–14). I find that presenting improvising to students on a spectrum from 1 to 10, in which 1 is the melody exactly as it is written and 10 is an act of pure inspiration (in a way, complementary to the original melody), can be an incredibly effective tool in working with a new tune. As students move from one level to the next along the spectrum, they must always relate what they are playing to the melody (even, or perhaps especially, at the point of greatest abstraction), which helps less-experienced improvisors maintain the form (see ⏵ video 21.2, Melodic Embellishment).

One way of working on and evaluating this is to record students singing the melody of a tune. Listen to their interpretation together: Does it make sense? If not, suggest improvements: Is it more effective now? You can also have them play the sung interpretation back on their instruments to deepen the connection between what they are singing—what is truly internalized—and the technique of executing that on their instruments. This is also a valuable tool for refining improvisation. You will often find that a student's improvisation is largely effective, but some areas or notes are in need of revision to more closely adhere to the melody, phrasing, or harmony of a tune. Teaching students to edit musical content is one of the most important things we can do as educators, because it requires them to listen to and honestly assess their playing and to develop a sensibility for consciously crafting music of a higher quality.

**Harmonic/root motion.** Once students are comfortable with the melody of a tune, you can begin to explore and internalize the harmonic motion by looking at the roots of the underlying chords. Just as students learn to sing the melodies of tunes on neutral syllables (or lyrics) and solfège, they should make an effort to sing the roots of the chords of each new tune. This illuminates connections between the roots of chords and the key of the piece or the key of the moment, as well as contrapuntal relationships between the roots and the melody. Again, you should draw your students' attention to harmonic signposts at formal seams, as you did with the melody. You can take this exercise further by adding additional chord tones, as seen with the first four measures of "All of Me" in figures 21.4–21.6.

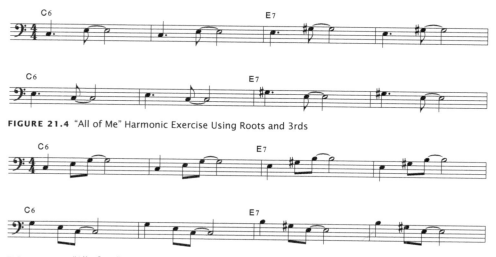

**FIGURE 21.4** "All of Me" Harmonic Exercise Using Roots and 3rds

**FIGURE 21.5** "All of Me" Harmonic Exercise Using Roots, 3rds, and 5ths

**FIGURE 21.6** "All of Me" Harmonic Exercise Using Roots, 3rds, 5ths, and 6ths or 7ths

These arpeggios gradually introduce the "guide tone lines" involving chordal 3rds and 7ths (or 3rds and 6ths in tonic major and minor chords), which can eventually frame more advanced strategies for melodic improvisation. Developing comfort with these basic chord types and their arpeggios is fundamental to understanding the underlying harmonies and how to connect them.

I encourage all nonpianists to learn to play the piano well enough to learn music on it. This can make exploring individual voices and their relationships more meaningful for students, with a clear visual representation on the keyboard. Learning the melodies, bass notes, and harmonies at the piano creates a tactile, bodily-kinesthetic experience of the "math" underlying the music. For more advanced students, you can further ingrain voice relationships by asking them to play the bass notes while singing the melody, or vice versa. You can even begin exploring other combinations of played and sung voices that incorporate guide tone lines or extensions of the basic harmonies. Always be sure to emphasize the counterpoint of outer voices, as it provides the foundation for practicing and performing the tune in other keys, as well as for other improvisational exercises you devise.

## Overcoming Fear

We all know that singing in an academic setting can make anyone feel vulnerable, but if you and your students can lose your inhibitions and sing your musical ideas for each other, you will have overcome an enormous part of the barrier most people face in trying to improvise, which is the inhibition borne from worrying that you sound like you do not know what you are doing. This can be particularly helpful for those of us who are nonsingers. We accept that our voices are not finely honed, gorgeous instruments. We have serviceable, "get-the-basic-idea" voices. This can work in our favor, because our voices are not too precious to us. If you and your students can embrace the spirit of the moment and go with your ideas on your own instruments, you will improvise at a much higher level.

Ironically, with less concern about correct technique and perfect sound, etc., you'll probably play with all of that anyway, because your years of training, cultivating muscle memory, and reinforcing good form can kick in without being hijacked by the conscious mind. If you and your students can really play your instruments, have a good imagination, and have a good enough ear to "hear" things that make sense, then all that stands between you and great jazz improvisation is the matter of execution. For some people, a lot of that barrier might be technique, but I guess that for the average person, it's probably more like 80 percent personal inhibition and self-judgment and 20 percent technical execution and ability. If you really distill the problem, a substantial portion will be *conception*, which comes from listening and deeply understanding jazz.

## Conclusion

The more standards you examine, the more their commonalities will become evident and the more their unique identities will shine through. Part of the challenge and, indeed, part of the fun in teaching standards is the need to devise your own specific exercises for a given tune. It is the task of the educator to generate material that is organically derived from each composition. Indeed, many of the greatest improvisors achieve this type of development in their solos, making them sources of inspiration for the study and furtherance of jazz music. To inspire our students, our own playing must always be improving and evolving. As we learn to learn, we learn to teach, and vice versa. It is all part of the tradition.

## Questions for Discussion

- What might you do to demonstrate the development of a catchy idea? Can you think of a way to use extramusical material to illustrate this?
- How can you use the lyrics of an American songbook standard when working with instrumental music students?
- How can you address the problem of young people being exposed to culturally impoverished music at home?

## Notes

1. See chapter 3 in this volume for more on the importance of mentoring in jazz.
2. It is worth noting that a solo may also comprise *less than* a single pass through the chorus. This is especially common in ballads, in which an improvisor may only solo over the first half of the tune.
3. See chapter 5 in this volume for further discussion of this topic.

## Bibliography

Baker, D. 1994. *A Creative Approach to Practicing Jazz: New and Exciting Strategies for Unlocking Your Creative Potential*. New Albany, IN: Jamey Aebersold Jazz.

Berkman, D. 2007. *The Musician's Guide to Creative Practicing: Notes on the Difficult, Humorous, Endless Path of Becoming a Better Improvising Musician*. Petaluma, CA: Sher Music.

Berliner, P. F. 1994. *Thinking in Jazz: The Infinite Art of Improvisation*. Chicago: University of Chicago Press.

Gioia, T. 2012. *The Jazz Standards: A Guide to the Repertoire*. New York: Oxford University Press.

Halberstadt, R. 2001. *Metaphors for the Musician: Perspectives from a Jazz Pianist*. Petaluma, CA: Sher Music.

Hamilton, A., and L. Konitz. 2007. *Lee Konitz: Conversations on the Improviser's Art*. Ann Arbor: University of Michigan Press.

Kastin, D. 1985. "Lee Konitz: Back to Basics." *Down Beat* (December): 12–14.

Perkins, T. n.d. *Jazz Standards Education – Marian McPartland*. [Online] JazzStandards.com. Available
    at: http://www.jazzstandards.com/Jazz%20Education%20-%20Marian%20McPartland.htm.
Rawlins, R., N. E. Bahha, and B. Tagliarino. 2005. *Jazzology: The Encyclopedia of Jazz Theory for All Musicians*.
    Milwaukee, WI: Hal Leonard.
Schuller, G. 1986. *Early Jazz: Its Roots and Musical Development*. New York: Oxford University Press.
Spitzer, P. 2001. *Jazz Theory Handbook*. Pacific, MO: Mel Bay Publications, Inc.
Starr, L., and C. A. Waterman. 2007. *American Popular Music: From Minstrelsy to MP3*. 2nd ed.
    New York: Oxford University Press.
Wilder, A., and J. T. Maher. 1972. *American Popular Song: The Great Innovators, 1900–1950*. New York: Oxford
    University Press.

# 22

# Arranging for School Jazz Ensembles

Matthew Clauhs

**No Need to Be the Baby Ellington Band**

Emily talks about how in the 1970s there was very little (if any) music published specifically for middle school jazz ensembles. Consequently, anything that they played she would have to first transcribe. In those early days, she arranged many Earth, Wind, and Fire tunes for the abilities and instrumentation of her middle school jazz band and was happy to do it because playing these contemporary tunes heard on the radio was worth it for the students:

> They dug it. They loved it. Somebody would get on that ratty set and maybe it was me on piano and we would play a George Benson tune or we would play an Earth, Wind, and Fire tune and they would love it. So, then it becomes motivational—not necessarily educational.

Emily notes that the harder the chart is, the less musicality middle school students can put into it. Consequently, she tries to find charts that are relatively easy but have retained characteristic elements of jazz. She finds that Kendor publishes a lot of literature that fits this description. Sometimes the really characteristic jazz charts are written with ranges outside the ability of middle school students, so she rewrites the parts in a more comfortable range. While she finds many swing charts that work well for middle school jazz ensemble, it is more difficult to find Latin charts that "work" at that level. "There's not a whole lot of literature written on the Latin side that's right—either the clave is wrong or the tune just doesn't work."

> I don't feel the need to be the baby Ellington band at this age. I think that's great, but there's time for that. I'm hoping that the kids aren't going to fall off the banana boat here and never play in another jazz band. I would rather have a tune that's motivational and fun and teaches all those skills, and down the line they can play the real thing. If they're still playing jazz in three years, as a horn player, they can probably play almost any tune that's out there.

School music teachers have a unique opportunity to cultivate creativity and critical thinking in a child's mind. Yet teachers often report that the least amount of classroom time is dedicated to creative activities, including composing, improvising, and arranging music. While much of this book has dealt with ways to implement the second domain (improvisation), this chapter examines ways to make arranging a part of the culture in a school music program. Several published texts already provide guidelines, rules, and suggestions for arranging, so the goal of this chapter is to situate the practice of jazz arranging in a school setting.

Professional musicians, arrangers, educators, and students have been writing for school jazz ensembles for nearly a century, and the study of jazz arranging is now a requirement of many jazz programs in the United States. School jazz ensemble instrumentation has been standardized, and techniques for writing have been codified and improved. While arranging is standard practice among jazz performers, many benefits result from arranging for, and together with, students in a school jazz program. Jazz arranging in a school setting (a) fosters an intrinsic desire among students to create music, (b) allows for a variety of instrumentation best suited for the school, (c) accommodates nontraditional learners, (d) differentiates for the strengths and weaknesses of the ensemble, (e) allows the teacher to assess knowledge through performance-based activities, and (f) increases the school's library of repertoire without breaking the budget.

These benefits are closely aligned with educational research and best practices and may not be obtainable through the performance of published stock arrangements. Learning to arrange takes time and practice, but the benefits are far greater than the costs of such an endeavor. The result is that students feel *ownership* of the music produced in-house, by themselves, a peer, or a teacher, because they feel strongly connected to music that was created from within their own school community.

This chapter examines a variety of fundamental arranging concepts and discusses why arranging for school ensembles is of critical importance for any music educator. It explores (a) considerations before arranging, (b) writing for rhythm sections, (c) writing for winds, and (d) basic harmonization techniques. The goal of this chapter is to demystify the process of writing for a school jazz ensemble and provide educators and their students with the basic tools to get started on a first arrangement.

## Considerations Before Arranging

**Style.** The basic harmonization techniques presented in this chapter can be applied to a variety of contemporary styles and are not limited to jazz. Just as Emily arranged Earth, Wind, and Fire songs for her jazz band, the reader may find the following techniques useful when arranging for pop/rock, salsa, R&B, funk, etc., in addition to traditional jazz styles.

**Instrumentation.** This chapter may be useful to teachers wishing to arrange for both small jazz and contemporary ensembles (one to five horns plus a rhythm section) as well as larger jazz ensembles (five saxes plus five bones plus five trumpets plus a rhythm section). While the arranging techniques discussed here are for four to five parts, voices can be doubled and layered to account for additional instruments throughout the band.

## Writing for Rhythm Sections

Rhythm sections include keyboard instruments, guitar, vibraphone, bass, drums, and percussion. These parts may be written using standard notation, rhythmic notation, slash notation, percussion notation, or tablature, depending on the instrument and experience of the player. If players are less experienced with reading chord symbols, the arranger should include chord voicings and written bass lines. More advanced players prefer to create their own chord voicings and bass lines whenever possible, especially during solo sections.

**Standard notation.** Piano, vibraphone, guitar, and bass parts may at times be "written out" (see figures 22.1 and 22.2). This means everything you want the player to perform is notated on the staff. Drum parts should never be fully written out, but may instead convey similar information through four-part drum notation (see chapter 2 in this volume for more information).

**Four-part drum notation (cymbal, hi-hat, snare, kick).** Typically, parts of the drum that are performed with the feet (kick and hi-hat) are written with stems facing down, and the parts of the drums that are performed with hands (cymbals, snare) are drawn with the stems facing up. This results in a cleaner score that is more likely to be performed correctly. (See figure 22.3.)

**Slash notation.** Slashes can be used to indicate time in a rhythm section or soloist's part (see figure 22.4). Harmonic information may be presented through chord symbols for a bass, chordal instrument, or soloist, while written directions about style and what is happening in

**FIGURE 22.1** Standard Notation for Piano

**FIGURE 22.2** Standard Notation for Bass

FIGURE 22.3 Four-Part Drum Notation

FIGURE 22.4 Slash Notation for a Bass Part

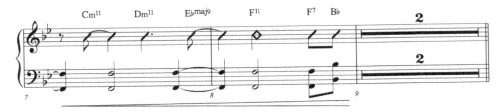

FIGURE 22.5 Rhythmic Notation for a Keyboard Instrument

FIGURE 22.6 Guitar Tablature

the piece may be more appropriate for a percussion part. This form of notation allows players the most freedom in determining how to realize the chord symbols and style.

**Rhythmic notation.** This form of notation provides more information about the underlying rhythm of the music (see figure 22.5). The stems and unique noteheads indicate to the performer that certain rhythms are to be performed together, but still allow players the freedom to create their own voicings and bass lines.

**Tablature.** Tablature is one of the oldest forms of notation for string instruments and the most ubiquitous form of notation found on the internet today (see figures 22.6 and 22.7). It is easy to understand and provides information about appropriate string and finger position not available through standard notation. While tablature is rarely provided in published jazz ensemble parts, this notation may be useful to less-experienced players.

**Chordal instruments.** Chordal instruments include keyboard instruments, vibraphone, and guitar. Their job is to provide harmonic support and rhythmic feel and occasionally to perform melodies and counterpoint. These instruments may also perform solos or provide accompaniment (comping) for other soloists. Be careful to avoid having multiple

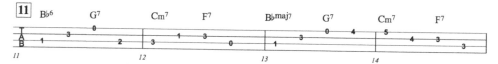

FIGURE 22.7 Bass Tablature

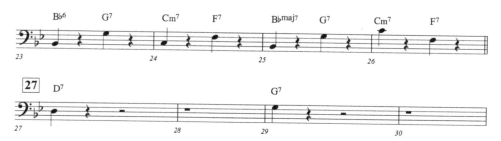

FIGURE 22.8 Scoring Chord Roots

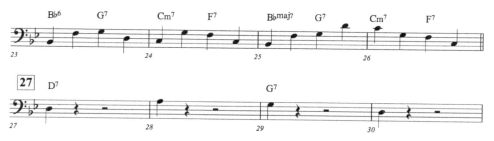

FIGURE 22.9 Scoring 5ths

chordal instruments comp at the same time, or the rhythm section will begin to sound muddy and undefined.[1]

**Bass.** The bass also provides harmonic and rhythmic support. In traditional jazz arrangements, the bass player often provides a walking bass line by outlining chord tones of the harmonic progression. Refer to chapter 18 in this volume on bass for an extended discussion of creating bass lines and realizing chord progressions. Following is a simple method for beginning to create walking bass lines in the straight-ahead swing style:

1. First, write the roots of the chords on the strong beats (typically, beats 1 and/or 3 of each measure). (See figure 22.8.)
2. Next, add the 5th of the chord on the weaker beats. (See figure 22.9.)
3. Add extended chord tones (e.g., 7ths, 9ths) and stepwise motion to fill out the part. Chromatic notes on weak beats can effectively connect chord tones. (See figure 22.10.)
4. The last note of one chord change should lead to the root of the next chord change by stepwise motion. (See figure 22.11.)

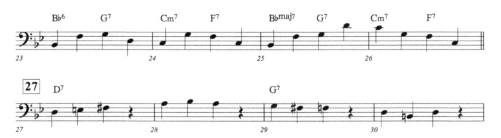

**FIGURE 22.10** Adding Chord Tones and Extensions

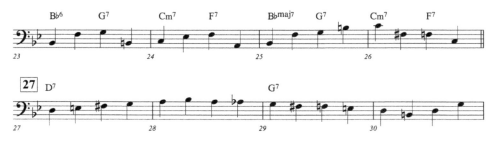

**FIGURE 22.11** Voice Leading

**Drums and percussion.** Less is more when it comes to writing for the drums, and individual parts (for cymbals, hi-hat, snare, toms, bass drum) should not be written for the entire piece but only the first few measures to demonstrate the intended style. Horn cues and figures should be written above the staff to help the drummer keep place and create complementary rhythms to set up and/or emphasize what the horns are playing. No matter what your background, work closely with the rhythm section players for whom you will be writing. No matter how experienced they are, their interpretation of your writing will teach you a great deal about how well you are communicating your ideas through rhythm section parts.

## Writing for Winds

When writing for winds it is important to understand the timbre of the instrument and the range of the player. Emily struggled to find published jazz arrangements in an appropriate range for her students and subsequently arranged parts to fit her students' abilities. Music teachers have an advantage here, because many play all of the instruments in the band at least at a rudimentary level. Following are some guidelines to consider when writing for saxophones, trumpets, and trombones.

**Saxophone.** Saxophone players have the greatest dexterity in the band, since they can change between notes and/or ranges of the instrument with the greatest ease. Young saxophone players generally have the same standard range as more experienced players, although intonation and blend can be problematic at the extreme registers of the horn. Music written in or just above the staff (when transposed) is appropriate for players of any level. Arrangements for young jazz ensembles typically do not include doubles (flute, clarinet); however, separate flute and clarinet parts can be added to (a) provide more colors and textures in an arrangement, (b) compensate for low numbers in the saxophone section, and (c) allow more students to participate in the school jazz program.

**Trumpet.** Range and fatigue are important considerations when writing for all brass instruments, including the trumpet. Typically, the 2nd trumpet player is the soloist, because improvisation requires a different set of skills than lead playing, and the lead player needs a chance to rest. Not surprisingly, the lower register of the horn creates a much darker sound than the high register. Anything higher than the G above the staff (when transposed) will really stand out in an arrangement and will be difficult for younger players. Anything written far below the staff may be difficult to project with a good sound.

**Trombone.** The trombone is heard most clearly at the very top of, and above, the staff. Experienced trombone players are accustomed to reading multiple ledger lines above the staff, and this is a very resonant range on the instrument. An F above the staff is a good limit for the lead trombone player with intermediate experience, although advanced players will have no trouble playing higher. Much like the trumpet, the trombone loses clarity in the lowest register. Certain intervals become particularly muddy below a third line F, so use caution when writing harmonies in this area.

Other brass parts can be added to allow for more participation or compensate for smaller sections. French horns and mellophones can be used to double or replace the 1st trombone part, as notes written above the bass clef are comfortable for horn players. Baritones and euphoniums can double or replace any trombone part, and the tuba can double or replace the bass part (as long as the bass player is not improvising bass lines). Be sure to involve your wind players in the arranging process and pay attention to how comfortable, or uncomfortable, parts may be for certain players and instruments. If working on a published arrangement that has brass parts that exceed the range of your students, use the voicing techniques in this chapter to revoice the arrangement to be more suitable for the players in your band.

# Harmonization

While a basic understanding of harmonization is helpful for arranging, the ultimate tool should be the ear. Some of the most interesting colors and textures come from innovative writing, or even "mistakes," that may not be easily classified into a standard arranging technique. That being said, the techniques described in this section are foolproof ways to begin a first arrangement. One does not need an extensive background in orchestration to begin writing for a school jazz ensemble. William Scism, jazz arranging professor at Berklee College of Music, puts it simply: "If you can sing a line, you can write a chart." Assuming you can already sing, here is some helpful information to begin writing your first chart!

**Basic chord types.** Most jazz chords are constructed using five fundamental qualities: major, dominant, minor, half diminished, and diminished. There are certainly other chord types as well as alterations to these chord qualities, but an understanding of these fundamental structures will help the beginning arranger get started. Demonstration of how these chord types would be spelled is found in chapter 7 in this volume (see figure 7.2, Chord Symbols).

**FIGURE 22.12** Independent Lead

**Texture.** Much jazz arranging is accomplished through four different textures: concerted harmonies (soli), independent lead plus harmony, counterpoint, and melodic subdivision. You may find it useful to change among these textures depending on what is happening in the piece or what sounds best to your ear. Concerted harmonies are similar to block chords, as the top voice is supported by harmonies that "hang" directly below. These harmonies closely follow the same rhythm as the top voice. This kind of texture is typical of soli and shout sections and can be found in nearly every classic jazz arrangement. The soli in Duke Ellington's "Cotton Tail" is one of many examples of this texture (see ⊚ Audio Example 22.1, Concerted Harmonies).

Independent line plus harmony is a homophonic texture, as a melody is supported by underlying harmonies that do not follow the same rhythm as the melody. This texture is common when featuring a soloist, in ballads, and in many other parts of a standard jazz arrangement (see figure 22.12). (See ⊚ Audio Example 22.2, Independent Lead.) In counterpoint, a melody is performed in one voice, or a group of voices, while a countermelody is performed by another individual or group. If the melody is harmonized, the countermelody should be scored in unison to avoid an overly dense harmonic texture. If the melody is in unison, the countermelody may be harmonized (see figure 22.13). (See ⊚ Audio Example 22.3, Counterpoint.) Melodic subdivision is similar to call and response, as one voice, or a group of voices, performs part of a melody, and another individual or group picks up that melody at a later point. There may be some overlap between groups of instruments to retain fluidity in the line (see figure 22.14). (See ⊚ Audio Example 22.4, Melodic Subdivision.)

**Traditional voicing techniques.** Next we explore simple voicing techniques that require just a basic understanding of 7th chords and instrument ranges. For a more nuanced explanation of the following voicing techniques, see the following resources:

- *Modern Jazz Voicings: Arranging for Small and Medium Ensembles*, by Ted Pease and Ken Pullig (Hal Leonard Corporation, 2001).
- *Arranging for Large Jazz Ensembles* (chapters 2–5), by Ken Pullig and Dick Lowell (Berklee Press, 2003).
- *The Complete Arranger* (chapter 9), by Sammy Nestico (Fenwood Music, 1993).
- *Arranging & Composing* (chapters 13–16), by David Baker
- *Jazz Arranging & Composing: A Linear Approach* (chapter 1), by Bill Dobbins (Music Exchange, 1986).
- *Inside the Score*, by Ray Wright (Kendor Music, 1982).

FIGURE 22.13 Counterpoint

FIGURE 22.14 Melodic Subdivision

***Unison and octaves.*** The arranger should not underestimate the effect of writing in unison and octaves, which produces a powerful sound with melodic clarity. This technique is particularly useful for creating contrast in a piece that is otherwise scored with dense harmonies and when writing lines with melodic subdivision and/or counterpoint passages. Unison and octave writing can be used within an instrument section to add weight to a line or across sections for a uniquely blended sound. Typical unison combinations across sections include alto sax with trumpet, tenor sax with trombone, and left-hand piano with acoustic bass (see figure 22.15). (See ⊙ Audio Example 22.5, Unison Writing Across Sections.) Octave combinations might include trumpet and trombone or flute and flugelhorn. All of these combinations create new timbres and can be very effective (see figure 22.16). (See ⊙ Audio Example 22.6, Octave Writing Across Sections.)

***Guide tone lines.*** The most defining notes of any basic jazz chord are the 3rd and 7th. These particular chord tones help identify the quality as major, minor, dominant, or diminished and are referred to as "guide tones" for this reason (see figure 22.17). Some jazz melodies, such as "All the Things You Are" and "Fly Me to the Moon," are composed using guide tone lines. Backgrounds and countermelodies may be created by having groups of instruments play 3rds and 7ths of a chord progression with smooth voice leading (see figure 22.18). (See ⊙ Audio Example 22.7, Adding Embellishments to the Line.) Following is a guide tone line procedure:

**FIGURE 22.15** Unison Writing Across Sections

**FIGURE 22.16** Octave Writing Across Sections

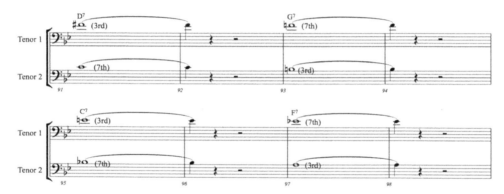

**FIGURE 22.17** Creating a Guide Tone Line

1. Considering the range and starting chord, determine which instrument(s) should start on the 3rd of the chord and which instrument(s) should begin on the 7th of the chord.
2. As the chord progression changes, the instruments continue to play whichever guide tone is nearest to allow for the smoothest transition.
3. Embellish the guide tone line with passing tones and other ornamentations to create interest.

*Close voicing technique.* In this technique, you are writing for four unique voices within the range of one octave (four-part close). It is also possible to double the lead voice exactly one octave below, to create a five-part close, double lead. (See figures 22.19 and 22.20.) This technique is widely used for saxophone soli writing, where the bari sax player is doubling the 1st alto, one octave lower. Listen to arrangements performed by Supersax for examples of this highly effective technique. Following is close voicing procedure:

**FIGURE 22.18** Adding Embellishments to the Line

**FIGURE 22.19** Placing Chord Tones Directly Below Target Notes

**FIGURE 22.20** Close Voicing, Doubled Lead

1. Identify the "target notes" in each measure. These typically occur on the strong beats, downbeats, and/or anticipations, and they should be harmonized first.
2. Place the remaining chord tones directly below each target note.

3. Harmonize the remaining notes in the melody using passing tones in between chord tones and/or approach notes (leading to a chord tone) wherever necessary. Use your ear to help you decide how to harmonize these notes. Consult the reference list of jazz arranging texts for further explanation of harmonization.
4. If writing for a saxophone section, double the alto 1 in the bari sax part, transposed down one octave.

There are some special considerations for close voicing technique:

- If the melody note is not a chord tone (1-3-5-7), but falls on a strong beat of the measure, skip the chord tone that would be immediately below the melody note and continue the voicing from that point. For example, if the melody note is an A, and the chord is $C^7$, skip the next chord tone below the A (which would be a G), use the E, then C, then B♭.
- Avoid an interval of a minor 2nd or minor 9th between the top voice and any other voice. When the melody note is "1" over a major 7th chord, don't use the 7th in the rest of the voicing, but the 6th scale degree instead.
- Avoid repeated notes in the inner voices. Playing repeated notes can be awkward and is problematic for articulation and phrasing. You may wish to cross voices by having two inner voices switch parts for a brief moment, to avoid any one player having to play repeated notes.

*Drop 2.* In this technique, follow the same procedure and special considerations for four-part close writing, except drop the 2nd voice down one octave (see figure 22.21). You may wish to voice the lowest part first, then score the inner voices with the remaining chord tones. This technique helps the lead stand out by increasing the interval between the top voice and remaining parts.

*Drop 2 + 4.* This process is the same as drop 2, except you drop both the 2nd and 4th voicing down one octave (see figure 22.22). This helps "open" the voicing by creating more space between parts. You can switch between close, drop 2, and drop 2 + 4 voicings throughout a passage. This technique allows the arranger to better navigate instrument

**FIGURE 22.21** Drop 2 Voicing Technique

FIGURE 22.22 Drop 2 and 4

FIGURE 22.23 Combining Close, Drop 2, and Drop 2 + 4 Techniques

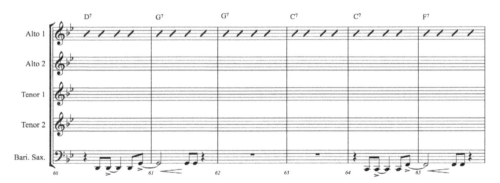

FIGURE 22.24 Chord Roots in the Bottom Voice

ranges, avoid repeated notes, and/or create more interest in a line (see figure 22.23). (See ⊙ Audio Example 22.8, Combining Close, Drop 2, and Drop 2 + 4 Techniques.)

**Spread.** The spread voicing technique creates even more space between parts, as there is typically at least an octave separating the lowest voice from the inner parts. (See figures 22.24–22.26.) The result is a much fuller and more clearly defined bottom voice, usually played by the baritone sax or bass trombone. The spread technique is especially effective for ballads, backgrounds, and passages with a slower harmonic rhythm. (See ⊙ Audio Example 22.9, Five-Part Spread Voicing Technique.) Following is spread technique procedure:

**FIGURE 22.25** Guide Tones in Inner Voices

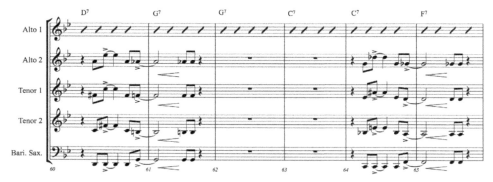

**FIGURE 22.26** Five-Part Spread Voicing Technique

1. The melody or lead line is scored in the first part (the highest voice).
2. Place the roots of the chord in the fifth or fourth part (the lowest voice).
3. Place guide tones (3rds and 7ths) in the third and fourth parts.
4. Place any remaining chord tones in the second part (5th, 9th, 13th, etc.).

   ***Voicings in 4ths.*** If you listen to voicings of some modern jazz pianists, most notably McCoy Tyner, you will hear that many of their voicings are built on quartal structures (using perfect and augmented 4ths), instead of a tertiary structure (using major and minor 3rds). This creates an open sound with more tension. Be careful when using this technique within a single brass section, because the interval between the top and bottom voice is nearly two octaves (4th + 4th + 4th + 4th) when writing four-part harmony. This technique works well within a saxophone section, combined trumpet and trombone sections, or across the band. (See figure 22.27.) Miles Davis and Wayne Shorter played in 4ths, in two-part harmony, throughout the song "Footprints." (See ⓟ Audio Example 22.10, Saxophones Voiced in 4ths.) Following is a procedure for 4ths voicing:

1. Harmonize the melody, or lead line, with notes that are 4ths apart.
2. Use the interval of a 3rd only if necessary, but avoid using two 3rds in a row.
3. Avoid the interval of a minor 9th, especially with the top voice.

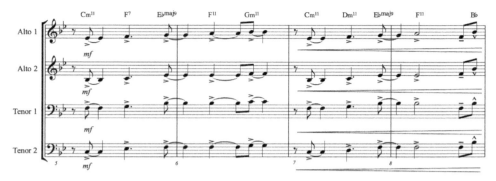

**FIGURE 22.27** Saxophones Voiced in 4ths

# Charting a Full Arrangement

Now that you have an understanding of standard voicing techniques, it is time to consider mapping out a full arrangement. It is a good idea to review some of your favorite arrangements and identify techniques the arranger is using across the form of the piece. You may be surprised at how effective simple techniques such as unison and octave writing can be! Many large arrangements begin as simple, small group arrangements that are enlarged for full big band sections. If you are new to arranging, it may be wise to listen to examples of classic jazz combos led by Art Blakey, Miles Davis, and Charles Mingus to identify arranging concepts and form on a smaller scale. Many arrangers of school jazz band music have developed their own personal template for arrangements, which allows them to produce arrangements quickly. Standard jazz band arrangements typically follow some version of this basic form:

- Intro: Set the tone of the chart by establishing tempo, style, and key.
- Melody: Feature a single instrument, section of instrument, or combination of instrument types.
- Solo section: Solos typically follow the same chord progression as the melody and often contain background figures.
- Soli section and/or shout, over a similar chord progression yet again,
- Melody: Return to the melody, usually featuring the same group of instruments that performed the melody earlier in the arrangement.
- Outro: Brings closure to the piece.

# Conclusion

Many students may be inspired to write arrangements and original compositions for jazz ensemble, and this practice should be encouraged as much as possible. You can point these students to free online notation software, such as noteflight.com or musescore.com, and encourage them to study scores that have already been published. Creating a full arrangement will be overwhelming to many students, so they should begin with just eight measures of a familiar theme, pop song, or original melody, and go from there. Even if an arrangement doesn't make it on a concert program, the act of arranging a piece, or portion of a piece, and performing it in rehearsal is an invaluable experience and lesson in creative music making that they won't forget, and you should be sure to have the band read anything and everything that your students spend time writing. By normalizing this process, you can create comfortable environments for exploring and creating music together. While these arrangements may not always be appropriate for festivals and concerts, this experience is equally as valuable for the performance of masterworks. Encourage players to identify and circle mistakes or problematic sections on their individual parts and provide feedback on the score that will help student arrangers better understand instrument ranges, texture, and other principles of arranging.

Finally, when writing arrangements by yourself or with students, ask friends and colleagues for help. If you are a horn player, be sure to ask rhythm section colleagues for advice on writing for their instruments, and vice versa. All of this feedback will further the development of a beginning arranger. This information, combined with a fundamental understanding of the arranging concepts presented in this chapter and your ear, is all that you need to get yourself and your students arranging for school jazz ensembles.

## Questions for Discussion

1. What are some reasons a director would want to arrange a piece for a school jazz ensemble?
2. What are some benefits of having students create their own arrangements?
3. What arranging opportunities can you provide students to help them appreciate this creative process?
4. How might arranging help students better understand their roles and functions in the ensemble? How might the process help them better understand the roles and functions of others in the ensemble?
5. What obstacles might you face when arranging for a school jazz ensemble? How can you overcome these challenges?

## Note

1. Refer to chapters 16 and 17 in this volume for examples of comping techniques.

# Index

Page references followed by *f* and *b* refer to figures and boxes respectively.

Printed in the USA/Agawam, MA
May 3, 2019

702510.007